Theatre Management

Theatre Management

Arts Leadership for the 21st Century

By Anthony Rhine

 palgrave

First published 2018 by
PALGRAVE

Palgrave in the UK is an imprint of Macmillan Publishers Limited, registered in England, company number 785998, of 4 Crinan Street, London N1 9XW.

Palgrave® and Macmillan® are registered trademarks in the United States, the United Kingdom, Europe and other countries.

ISBN 978–1–352–00174–7 paperback

This book is printed on paper suitable for recycling and made from fully managed and sustained forest sources. Logging, pulping and manufacturing processes are expected to conform to the environmental regulations of the country of origin.

A catalogue record for this book is available from the British Library.

A catalog record for this book is available from the Library of Congress.

Contents

List of Figures

Preface

I have had the honor of working in theatre management since I graduated high school. Over the last couple of decades the field has become incredibly professional. Academic programs geared specifically toward training the next generation of arts administrators now support the field, and its practice is rooted in sound business theory. Theatre management is vastly different from that day when my colleague and friend Allen Evenson announced he had gotten a grant to pay for computers and I congratulated him but responded, "Though I can't imagine what we will do with computers. This is theatre." Allen's vision and the dreams of his business partner Joseph Henson have always inspired me and kept me passionate about my work.

Books like this are rarely entirely the effort of a single person, and I need to acknowledge the contributions of some very important people in the development of this one. As I was getting the process going in full force, I needed assistance to ensure that the book would work the way it was intended, and that required feedback and assistance. I am grateful to Ashley Brooks, Ashley Deluke, Lauren Hermanson, Bethany Lang, Ashton Langrick, Sydney Norris, Miranda Paine, Lauren Pincus, Nicholas Richardson, Mary Beth Ritter, Aisling Ryan, Hope Tiffany, T.J. Timmons, and Maxim Yodzis for providing that feedback and help. I am also grateful to the many reviewers who provided feedback that proved ineffably helpful. It was well-received guidance.

Mary Vanko has looked over every page, fact checking and keeping the words honest and focused, and her contribution has been immeasurable. She is an incredible assistant.

Ken Faulkner, as he always does, ensured I was getting across the message that was intended. He is a consummate editor and a great friend. Ken and I met when we both started running a theatre management MFA program in the Midwest United States. The program could barely scare up an applicant, had been through half-a-dozen heads in as many years, and lacked focus. Over our eight years there, and with the support and vision of our department chair Blair V. Anderson, we were able to reinvent the program to one that focused on arts leadership. It grew in stature and became well regarded in the field for its innovative approach. We had our pick of applicants, and passed our accreditation with flying colors. Sadly, when leadership steps down there is often a gap in vision, and new vision often mandates change. During this transition Ken and I both left, and the program we loved, held dear, and committed to has become something different.

I am grateful to Cameron Jackson and the strategic management team at Florida State University, including Brad Brock, Sarah Goodson, Ombra Sandifer, Lauren Snyder, and Hilary Passo. While Ken and I worked on our program, Cameron and his team developed an almost identical approach to theatre management. My departure from the Midwest led to my eventual position in Florida where I get to work with a brilliant, inspiring, and intellectually stimulating faculty. I am privileged to interact with some of the world's leading minds in theatre studies, design and production, performance, and management. Our management program, like all the arts management programs at Florida State University, is robust, it creates amazing arts leaders, and they go on to incredible positions. These students are changing the face of arts administration. There are too many of them to name, but they have all contributed to my thinking for this book.

I want to thank Patrick, whose last name I will not mention, as I do not wish for him to be inundated on Facebook. He has shared many of his life experiences with me, and while I have used him as a focal point and amalgam of many different real situations to illustrate the concepts covered in this text, that strategy only occurred to me because I have learned so much from this fine young man about how to handle the challenges of theatre leadership.

Finally, Joel Senft deserves more credit than anyone. Because when the research seemed too daunting, the writing schedule seemed too overwhelming, or the task seemed insurmountable, he pressed me in a gentle and nurturing way to keep moving forward. Not a day went by that I was not asked what I wrote about that day. This amazing soul is the reason the book was accomplished. He is the reason for so much.

Introduction

Why a text on the topic of theatre management? If one wishes to master a subject, one must know its depths and riches. If one is to master the execution of the subject, one must think like a practitioner. This book aims to help its user think like a theatre manager. From an academic perspective, the question of "why a textbook on the topic of theatre management?" has a couple of questions hidden in it. The first wonders why a text focusing specifically on theatre management is required when a few textbooks already exist that focus on *arts* management. It is a sound question. It is the exact same question business schools asked when the first text on healthcare management was published. "Why a text on healthcare management when there are already texts on business management?" The same was asked for education management and sports management and public sector management and on and on and on. Sure, the management principles taught in business schools are the same principles upon which all of these texts are founded. But the intricacies of each field speak to the differences. These intricacies dictate how we apply the principles. Just as actors, dancers, and singers all study different specific texts about performing in their chosen fields, as opposed to all studying the same text on "performing in the arts," so must managers in the twenty-first century examine their chosen field through its specifics.

The second question concerns why the books that currently exist are not satisfactory. There are several ways to look at this question, and all of them are designed to pay the greatest of respect to the authors who have worked so diligently on those books. First, in the last century, a couple of books were published with "theatre management" in the title. Every academic who researches and teaches theatre management has an old copy or two on their office shelf. One explains "how to" make theatre, and the other provides encyclopedic information for a theatre manager. Neither serves as a strong pedagogical tool for understanding how to manage, administer, and lead an organization in one of the most challenging fields a manager could enter. This book is intended to serve faculty and students of modern theatre management, though it should prove just as useful to practitioners looking to improve their understanding of management theory and its application in theatre.

The primary goal in creating this text was to make a book that can be a true teaching and learning aid, and not just a resource of information. We have used the textbook model of teaching since the printing press emerged, but with the advent of the Internet, smartphones, and social media, society gathers information and processes that information differently, as evidenced by vast research in schools of education and business. This text is designed to be a central source for guiding a student of theatre through the learning and thinking processes that develop exceptional theatre managers, but is done so as a tool for navigating the world of theatre management rather than as a source of content and information. It can be used as a stand-alone, in part, or in conjunction with articles, current events, guest lectures, and other outside sources. Its lessons are not specific to any governmental region, but are globally applicable, though occasionally the specific terminology of one country or another may be used interchangeably. The text allows the instructor to let students explore and think critically on their own path. It is not a single-source library of theatre management information. It addresses topics, explains theories, defines challenges and resolutions, and then demands that students visualize their future to understand where theatre management and a personal career path align.

While its content is designed to be fleshed out through classroom discussion that is embedded in and guided by the text, it is not the typical collection of fifteen chapters of thirty pages of information with flashy pictures to make it palatable and then regurgitated through lecture to make sure it sticks. This text is a resource for the student interested in knowing how to manage (as opposed to simply administer) a theatre in the twenty-first century. Its cases, tools, and tasks are not ways to practice memorizing information, but are means for digging deeper into the subjects covered. The book does not purport to be, in the words of Erica McWilliam, a "sage on the stage," or a "guide on the side," but a "meddler in the middle." The person using this text is learning how to be a lifelong student in the discipline of theatre management, not just memorizing enough information to pass the class. Students completing a course utilizing this text will be well on their way to thinking like a theatre manager.

The text is designed to follow the real-life process of developing a new theatre from the ground up, and also follows the case of Patrick, a real, recent graduate entering the workplace. The brief cases are modeled after case studies in graduate business schools. They provide preliminary information, and suggest questions that classes could explore. But they are not designed to narrow in on any specific point, or to steer classes in one direction or another. They are intentionally broad to allow for real exploration. Again, they are designed to "meddle" as opposed to lecture. The discussion questions are written with the same purpose in mind. These are not questions for students to tick off a box next to "answered." Instead, they require the class to explore where the answer may lead them, and then to share their exploration in class.

Chapter 1 addresses the topics of what is theatre management, what is business administration, how are they different and why? It examines the roles and responsibilities of managers, and how they interact in both internal and external environments relative to theatre. *Chapter 2* expands on that foundation by exploring the notion of how to translate an idea for a new theatre into a working plan, and considers how to develop both short- and long-range plans and objectives. It covers the mission, vision, and values statements, and emphasizes the importance of each, as well as how they may be slightly different from similar statements in a commercial enterprise. The chapter concludes with a discussion of the importance of developing a long-term, focused strategy. Following on this path, *Chapter 3* examines the legal jungle in which theatres exist, and how the business of theatre can and does fit into society both on a macro and local scale. The chapter looks at internal issues, and is designed to expand upon the foundations and supports built in the first two chapters. It covers topics such as creativity and entrepreneurship, changes in the environment, organizational assessments, growth and adaptation, and how to plan for succession.

Chapter 4 then explores the external environments in detail, considering the business environments in which theatres exist (both their own and the commercial world) and how they relate. Business structures and the work of business professionals are considered in light of establishing or growing a theatre. *Chapter 5* begins to fill in details about processes in creating and growing a theatre. Topics include organizational design, organizational structure, and the development and management of growth, as well as how to adapt to and manage change in theatre.

Chapter 6 considers communication among stakeholders of a theatre. The chapter begins by looking at arts unions and how they represent theatre employees. It then moves into an examination of artistic management and its similarities to and differences from business management. The chapter concludes with an exploration of both internal and external communications, and how to ensure their flow is smooth, accurate, and advantageous to the theatre.

While often a dry topic, *Chapter 7* focuses on finance for the theatre manager and is designed to give the student an ability to be conversational about accounting principles, without requiring fluency. It includes topics such as the three financial statements, credit and borrowing, in-kind contributions, audits and board fiduciary duties, and how to lease property. The chapter concludes with the more interesting topic of the financial distinctions between producing and presenting. The text then, in *Chapter 8*, introduces the concept of the audience from a manager's perspective, and how customer service theories demand attention. It winds down the path the consumer follows, from first contact with the ticket office, to front-of-house operations, customer services, concessions and retail, interactions with the community, and even curtain speeches.

The text then has two chapters on marketing, with *Chapter 9* exploring modern marketing theory within the context of theatre. Topics include the history of subscription sales and how they changed theatre, the marketing plan, market research, consumer perceptions, the "four P's," creating and sustaining value, and brands and brand equity. *Chapter 10* navigates the creative side of promotion, beginning with understanding the market, how to communicate in words and images, and the promotion of theatre as an experience. It then digs deeper into how humans react to color, typefaces and imagery, responses to different social media and website design, and the traditional (but still essential) press releases and press kits.

In *Chapter 11*, the student has an opportunity to consider fund development platforms and paths for their individual theatre. The fundraising plan and pyramid is explored, along with the role of a board and executives in fundraising. The importance of stewardship is emphasized, along with the many different ways people can donate. *Chapter 12* explores leadership and leadership theory, beginning with James MacGregor Burns' theory and transactional and transformational leaders and Douglas McGregor's theory on management. Students explore their own leadership style through the context of adaptive leadership, leadership communication and relationships, informal networks, politics and the creative process, and initiative and innovation. This leads into *Chapter 13*, which is an examination of governance structures in theatre. Topics include boards of directors, volunteerism, executive staff roles and relationships, how to structure governance and lead a board, how to deal with internal political issues, and when and how to use interns.

Chapter 14 focuses on the topics of theatre advocacy and community engagement, both to serve a theatre company, and to serve the industry. The chapter follows a progression from what and how to advocate both for theatre in general and for one's own theatre, to how to engage a local community. *Chapter 15* considers theatre education in schools, where it has been and how changes in theatre education have affected management of the art form. The focus then shifts to the value of education programs in theatres, how they are best designed, and how they can best support and not detract from a theatre's mission.

For a survey course in theatre management, the text leaves nothing out, though it focuses less on philosophy and more on why and how theatres operate in the twenty-first century from both theoretical and practical perspectives. It can be used in its entirety, with each chapter representing approximately a week's worth of homework and class discussion time; or it can be used in part. I follow the entire book for my undergraduate theatre management courses, often incorporating guests or additional materials that I feel are specific to me and my location, but I also use select chapters as introductions to topics in my graduate theatre management courses. The primary objective of the text is to help develop critical thinking skills in those who use it so they can think and make decisions like a theatre manager.

CHAPTER 1

What is theatre management?

Each chapter of this book includes a case study about Patrick. Patrick is a young man who recently graduated from college with a degree in theatre management. And while Patrick is a real man, and much of this story is his, it has been augmented by the stories of other real theatre managers as well, to ensure that there are plenty of challenges to analyze, discuss, debate, and attempt to solve. Poor Patrick would be at his wits' end if every challenge presented in this text had actually befallen him, though many have. It is not unusual to see any or all of the situations Patrick found himself in at any theatre in the world. The issues Patrick has faced have proved to be challenging. And he has handled them beautifully, because he learned to think like a theatre manager. The challenges sometimes required answers that are rooted in the known, but sometimes they required philosophical analysis and assumptions based on unknown circumstances. Those are the questions that will be posed to you.

While working on his degree, Patrick spent time not only studying in depth the theories, philosophies, and lessons found in this book and books like it, but also interning as a line employee for a theatre. By the time he graduated, he was doing middle management work at his internship. And though the internship provided wonderful opportunities, Patrick often had a hard time convincing the company's executive director about an appropriate approach to issues. On several occasions, Patrick's team was developing promotional materials, based on well-understood and tested theories. His marketing materials were not only theoretically sound, but he would field test them, surveying segments of the audience as well as non-attenders to ensure that his message was being received appropriately and with the right themes, feelings, and nuance. Patrick did not like to make mistakes, and he worked diligently to ensure that every aspect of his work was perfect the first time it was submitted. He researched, analyzed, interpreted, and made solid business recommendations. But the executive director, who had no training in marketing or management, would often dismiss the work of Patrick's team, asking that it be done differently because the executive director thought his ideas were better. Patrick became quite adept at drafting business proposals that not only explained his approach and the theories behind it in detail, but they were bulletproof. Nevertheless, his work continued to be dismissed. In the three years he worked at this internship, he never figured out how to effectively communicate with the executive.

> **Chapter objectives**
>
> After reading this chapter, you should be able to explain what financial supports exist for theatres, describe the functions of theatre management, distinguish between different types of managers, and demonstrate how you execute the functions of management.

Some history of theatre management

In the early 1960s, universities worldwide began to recognize the importance of management in the arts, and academic theatre management programs began springing up with their visionary creators recognizing the need for such training well ahead of demand reaching a level of necessity.[1] Today, theatre management programs continue to improve and professionalize.

But what is theatre management? It is the coordination of resources for a theatre company or production, both human and financial, in an effective and efficient manager. So what do theatre managers do? Most people assume that management in the theatre consists of making posters for the lobby windows, selling tickets in the ticket office, and writing the checks to pay the bills. While these functions certainly fall under the auspices of "administration," they barely scratch the surface of a theatre manager's work.[2]

In the late twentieth century, law professors were often known for believing that their function was not to "teach law," but to train their students to "think like a lawyer." The axiom suggests that having students memorize tens of thousands of laws and court rulings was not the function of law school. Instead the notion was that by interacting, discussing, debating, and evaluating what had occurred in the law, students would develop a cognitive ability to affect future change.[3] Contrary to popular belief, law school is not a few years of learning how to debate before a jury. Instead, students examine laws and court rulings, arguing about why government and judicial representatives have made the decisions they have. Law school is, indeed, about learning to critically analyze what has happened in the past, so that graduates can critically analyze what is happening in the present and how it will affect the future. It is about learning to think like a lawyer. Business schools operate, more or less, in a similar fashion. Students spend countless hours discussing, debating, and analyzing case studies, looking to understand obstacles and challenges presented in the cases, as well as thinking critically about why decisions were or should have been made. Certainly, there are operational issues that students study – how things are most effectively accomplished – but even then it is often done through the use of analysis. Business schools are about learning to think like a business person.

While theatre managers, on a daily basis, have to deal with finance, ticket office sales, human resource issues, laws, fundraising and the like, they are all connected to the art. Financial decisions, such as whether to cut a budget and by how much, will have a direct bearing on what is presented on the stage. Likewise, artistic decisions such as how many costumes, or how "realistic" a set should be, can have a direct impact on finances. Unlike in the corporate world, where the product is tailored to fit the desires of the market, in theatre management the market has yet to know the worth of our core product until they have experienced it. We cannot determine if they will want a production of *A Midsummer Night's Dream* set in 1920s India until after they have experienced it. So working blind challenges a theatre manager. The decisions that a theatre manager has to make often come with far less data than corporate managers have at their disposal about how the marketplace likely will react to a product offering. The well-trained theatre manager can quickly analyze inputs, including opinions from artistic experts, marketers, fundraisers, accountants and the like, analyze that input against understood business principles, and make informed decisions for moving the company forward. Theatre managers spend a great deal of time working with, supporting, understanding, and trusting other human beings. The goal of study in theatre management is to help the student learn to think like a theatre manager.

Questions to research for class discussion:

Search the Internet and find answers for these questions before reading further. Be prepared to discuss them in class.

1.1   What national financial support exists for theatre, and why was it created?
1.2   How has that national support helped theatre?
1.3   What other resources are currently available for theatres, financial or otherwise?

In the United Kingdom, support for the arts is well over £48 per person every year. Germany spends about €19 per person on arts funding. In France, there is such an appreciation for arts and culture that reductions in arts funding have caused social unrest. The French Ministry of Culture has a budget of around €2.9 billion (about €43 per person) and the French population is about the same as the United Kingdom, about 80% the size of Germany, and less than one-fifth the size of the United States, which currently spends only about $0.33 per person annually on arts funding. In comparison, Australia spends almost $400 in Australian dollars per person annually on the arts.

But globalization is causing a regular shift away from governmental spending on the arts, and while the US government has made minimal and shrinking investments in strengthening the arts in society, it is possible that with globalization, all developed nations could follow a similar path. With shrinking governmental support, it becomes increasingly important that managers understand how to make sure that the arts are strong and influential in society. They need to be able to think like a theatre manager.

The best-known theatre managers are not those who currently run the world's largest theatre companies. Few are known by name. Even fewer are recognized in the streets. The salaries are well below those of their corporate counterparts. But even if a steady income with benefits while still working in theatre is why you have an interest in theatre management, it is important to understand that becoming vastly wealthy as a theatre manager is very unlikely to happen.[4] Few people, however, feel compelled to work in the theatre solely for money or power or celebrity. Most find that the collaborative spirit, the creative nature, and the opportunity to affect other human beings are the main draws to the theatre as a profession. For those choosing management, there is often a more significant trade-off, as managers are typically at least one step removed from the day-to-day collaborative and creative process of making the play.

That was not always the case, and even today there are many theatre managers who straddle both the commerce side of the business and the creative side. It was not that long ago when Shakespeare was writing and acting in his plays, but also directing and administering them as a form of commerce at the same time. Molière did the same in France. Centuries before them, religious leaders functioned as theatre managers, coordinating efforts to tell religious and moral stories to their flocks. But it wasn't until the twentieth century when we started to consider theatre management as a unique field of inquiry and its own, discrete profession.

Business management versus theatre management

For those who choose to pursue a career in the corporate world, the gold standard for higher education is the attainment of the Masters of Business Administration (MBA), a degree program in which students study the operations and behavior of corporate entities competing in a national and global marketplace. As higher education faces its own challenges due to shrinking revenue sources, colleges and universities have had to develop academic programs that satisfy the largest and most lucrative academic needs. Within schools of business, specialties have begun to appear to train the next generation of professionals who have unique challenges in hotel and hospitality management, educational leadership, sports management, health care administration, government leadership, law enforcement, and the like. In the arts, demand for well-trained and educated managers and leaders has not yet

Think critically

There are two ways to approach this class discussion. First, you can choose sides. Divide the class into two, by whatever means you choose, and debate the argument outlined below. Second, you can have an open discussion, each adding upon others' thoughts, and let the discussion uncover all the important details of both sides of the debate. Keep in mind that regardless of which approach you take, we want to be sure we dig deep into both sides of this important issue, in order to more effectively defend our own position. Sometimes, standing in your rival's shoes and arguing strenuously for their cause helps you understand your own position even better.

CLASS DISCUSSION: Theatre practitioners face increasing challenges to fund their work. Audiences are fractured, inundated by a vast amount of options for spending their discretionary income, and that income is being spent less frequently on theatre. Without government support, new and innovative approaches to presenting theatre will never be able to gain traction and expand our knowledge of artistic expression, emotive storytelling, and social interactions through shared artistic experiences. But only one-third of the public has any engagement with the arts. Should the entire population be required to foot the bill for supporting art that may or may not have a valuable and sustainable impact on society? We hold our government representatives accountable, and cannot expect them to give away our tax revenue without ensuring that this money is spent carefully, appropriately, and not wasted on funding frivolous or self-indulgent art. Can there be a standard by which we decide which works of theatre are funded and which are not? Should there be? Many argue that great art cannot be planned, and outlined, but that it must be nurtured and allowed to come to fruition. Without financial support, they say great art will wither and die. Others argue that art is not for the masses but for the elite, who appreciate it, and who should therefore be responsible for funding it. They argue that just as our tax revenue is not used to provide support to burgeoning sports teams, the marketplace should determine what is good and effective and allowed to rise to the top. If art is worthwhile, they say, it will also be self-sustaining. Should tax revenue be used to sustain, strengthen and support the arts? If so, how should tax revenue be allocated to the arts?

reached such heights that business schools have begun to offer specializations in the arts. This has left the educating of students of theatre management largely to theatre practitioners who have had managerial experience. Because the field of theatre management has yet to be embraced as part of the larger field of business administration, it is continuously challenged to make its voice heard. But this is not to suggest that the challenges faced by theatre managers are somehow less important, less difficult, or less unique. In fact, given our rapidly changing world, the traditions of theatre that have existed and operated with little change for centuries, and the data that suggests society as a whole is changing the way it consumes art, it is easy to see that we need well-trained, well-educated theatre managers to take the art form into the future.

It has been said that "management is management is management," but even business schools have seemed to accept that generic principles in management, though they may be applied effectively regardless of the field in which they are exercised, are not enough to compete in today's environment. This is true for theatre managers as well. In order to be effective in theatre management, one needs to understand not only what the picture is like for theatre in the world today, but also where changes are occurring in order to adapt to those changes in the future.[5] A manager trained in corporate thinking would be hard pressed to be effective running a local theatre company. It would be easy enough to select the most marketable play, hire the most marketable artists, and sell plenty of tickets, but even then, with societal preferences changing so rapidly, today's "most marketable" is yesterday's waste of time. Typically, business education is rarely focused on how to meet consumer needs and wants when we cannot reliably predict how the consumer will feel when the final curtain falls. And at the end of the day, theatre is about how it makes us feel above all else.

Theatre management: art or commerce

When we hear the term "theatre manager," we assume this to mean the people who handle the non-artistic aspects of a theatre company: administration, finance, box office, marketing, fundraising, operations, board relations, and the like. But the term can be equally applied to many working on the artistic side: stage manager, company manager, artistic director, and so on. The term "manager," as we have seen, refers to someone who is not simply providing a function, such as a bookkeeper, box office clerk, or actor, but one who coordinates the work of others, and/or who oversees financial transactions. Managers coordinate resources to ensure that the sum of all the pieces can be sold for more than the cost of those pieces.[6] Governmental policies typically lay out for employers who qualifies as a manager and who does not, though sometimes charters of professional organizations or associations set these definitions.

Questions to research for class discussion:

Search the Internet and find answers for these questions before you read any further. Be prepared to discuss them in class.

1.4   What governmental or association policies define the job classifications of "manager" and "non-manager," and what do those policies do?
1.5   How are managers paid differently from non-managers? Is this dictated by the government? What rules must be followed?
1.6   What job duties will a manager typically handle in a theatre setting that a non-manager would not?

While we know that artistic management involves technical duties that are vastly different from the technical functions of administrative management in theatre, many functions are the same; both types of theatre managers need to have an understanding of how money is earned and spent; both need to know how to cultivate and nurture groups and teams; both must have an understanding of human resource law; both evaluate performance; both must understand how the organization functions as a whole, and how it intends to grow in the future. While there are many theatres where the two different types of managers may not have a thorough understanding of the work the other types of managers do, in our current economic environment that can be quite risky.[7] And while there are no clearly defined academic programs to train artistic directors, the best artistic directors are those who demonstrate an understanding of organizational behavior, human resources, marketing, and other aspects of administration. You probably know some actors (you might even be one of them) who want to learn everything about theatre – acting, lighting, sound, costumes, stage management – but they never think about what goes into higher-level management. Theatre management is a field of study not just for administration, but also for all types of managers and directors in theatre, and that includes artistic directors,[8] because it explores how to most efficiently and effectively coordinate both human and financial resources.

Theatre today

There is no end to the arguments about the value of theatre in society today. A quick search of the Internet will tell you that theatre pumps billions annually into the economy, that thousands upon thousands of jobs exist in the field, that students exposed to theatre do better academically and financially, and that theatre enriches lives. Since you are reading this book, you likely do not need to be told about the value of theatre in the world today.

Theatre as entertainment

But notice that in the paragraph above, we did not look at theatre as a form of entertainment. In the strictest sense, theatre is most certainly entertainment. But practitioners often find this descriptor unnecessarily dismissive. Theatre provides so much more than simply entertainment. It has been said that "Theatre is art; movies are entertainment; TV is furniture," but this statement minimizes each of these three media. The clear distinction is that noncommercial theatre companies create most of the theatre produced in the world today. We will discuss the legal status of noncommercial theatre and how it works in Chapter 4, but for now, let's consider that the function of a noncommercial enterprise is to provide some public benefit. That means that a noncommercial organization is not driven primarily by the bottom line, as commercial enterprises are, but by serving the community. This is the great distinction between theatre and film and television. With the exception of commercial theatres like those on Broadway or in the West End, theatre is created to provide a benefit to society. And yet, government subsidies are small, which means that theatre makers must be extremely cognizant of the fact that they are largely on their own for financially sustaining their operations. Here is where there is some distaste. In order to create great art that comes from the soul and shares meaning and emotion with an audience, artists need some level of freedom from the constraints of commerce. A savvy theatre manager is regularly working to balance a company's financial needs with the needs of the artists to be protected from financial constraints. It is a delicate balance, and leaves no wonder why theatre companies have such a hard time sticking around for long periods of time.

However, to suggest that theatre is not entertaining is simply a manifestation of this odd dichotomy. Entertainment implies commercialism. Making plays that entertain is not wrong, but a manager demanding that a play be entertaining creates a tight link between art and commerce that challenges artists who need freedom to create their work.

Theatre as social function

Theatre as a social function is an entirely different matter. While it is rare for a manager to press an artist to create theatre that encourages greater social connectivity, that is because theatre, by its very nature, encourages social interaction. Consider applause. No one wants to be the first to applaud, but when we hear others do it, we applaud as well. The same is true for laughter. When we hear someone behind sniffling at a particularly touching moment, often that sound is all that is required to get our tears flowing. It is human nature to experience life together. These same things can be said for movies, though when someone starts applauding at the end of a movie, it is rare that the entire room joins in. We don't socialize with people in the movie lobby during intermission. When we see live people performing a story for us, there is a social connection not only to other members of the audience, but to the actors on stage as well. While any single audience might never know the difference, actors are frequently heard talking about the energy level of one performance compared to another. That energy level is associated with the social interaction that occurs between actor and audience.

Theatre as business

Theatre on a macro level is also big business, as we have already noted. But in order for theatres to operate effectively, they each must operate utilizing accepted business principles. Theatres that do not do so often find themselves in a great deal of trouble. The challenge, however, is that business principles are researched and taught in business schools, where there is scant or zero focus on theatre. This is not to suggest that those business principles cannot be applied to a theatre company. Instead, we must look at such business principles and occasionally translate them to the business of theatre, so they are understandable to the theatre manager and practitioner.

What is management?

We have already mentioned that management is the coordination of resources, both human and financial, for the purpose of achieving the goals of an organization. But what is an organization? An *organization* is a group of people brought together to achieve certain objectives. For a commercial enterprise, the primary goal is to make a profit by selling goods or services. For noncommercial organizations, the primary goal is typically to provide a quality good or service that will improve lives in the community. In an organization, tasks that are interrelated are coupled together into a *job*. Jobs are grouped together based on their relatedness. In theatre we would not expect to see the company accountant working hand in hand with actors and directors. Actors, directors, designers, and technicians, who form the core group of people creating the product, the play, are grouped into a performance department or division. Box office employees and accountants are more likely to be grouped together and coordinated by a single manager. By grouping similar jobs together, organizations are better able to produce outputs that are efficient and effective.

Efficiency, for an organization, is when an output can be created with the least amount of inputs, which maximizes results. For a commercial theatre the maximum result is the greatest profit. For a not-for-profit theatre, the maximum result would be providing the greatest amount of service. In theatre, if we can create a sell-out show for very little money, we are being efficient: The commercial production is generating maximum profit, and the not-for-profit theatre is serving the maximum number of people. *Effectiveness* has to do with the quality of outputs in relation to an organization's goals. A theatre will determine what goals it plans to meet – for example, it may choose to present the classics – and effectiveness is measured based on the quality of presentation. Unfortunately, quality in theatre is often subjectively determined, but managers can use audience polling, newspaper and online reviews, and volume of sales to make educated decisions about quality and how to improve it. Actually, *organizational performance*, for any organization, is a measure of how effectively and efficiently the company is meeting its goals of customer satisfaction. For theatre, whether it seems distasteful or not, customer satisfaction is the ultimate goal. The commercial production will generate the greatest profit when customers are fully satisfied, and the not-for-profit will be best able to serve the community if the customers are completely satisfied. Where the artistry has room to explore is in how we define what we will provide to the customer. As you can imagine, having clearly defined goals is essential for a successful organization.

The functions of management

Fortunately, our friends in the business schools have carefully studied how organizations operate, and they have created ways for us to compartmentalize work in order to understand how to improve it. The core principle behind management in all organizations is that managers perform four essential functions: *planning, organizing, leading,* and *controlling*.[9] We have already discussed some of these in general, but it is time to consider them in their specific compartments.

Planning

In a very basic sense, planning is the process whereby the manager determines what goals the organization will attempt to achieve, as well as what actions or activities will be undertaken in order to achieve them. The manager does this by considering multiple options, evaluating data to help support one option or another, and making a choice about which option will best suit the organization, achieve the goals, serve the organization's mission, and provide for the community. For a company worth billions, planning is quite a complex process, with hundreds or perhaps thousands of details that must be prepared for. Two gigantic corporations merging together, for example, may take a year or more to develop plans before they even begin to integrate.

In the theatre, one of the most important and regularly occurring plans is production planning. Managers must evaluate options for plays, costs associated with those plays, potential income based on anticipated quality and perception of the plays, and demands for personnel, supplies, and equipment required for each play, to name just some of the considerations. While marketing teams at our corporate counterparts can create test versions of potential new products, and conduct studies and focus groups to see how consumers may respond to the products, in theatre the ability to do so is very restricted. While major commercial theatre producers may conduct *out-of-town tryouts* – meaning that a show is produced in a city outside of the country's main hub of theatre, where audience and critic reaction can be gauged before the production is evaluated on a national scale – these tryouts still require the creation of a huge and potentially very expensive production. If the reaction is poor, even drastic changes may not be enough to help ensure success for the long run. And even when a production lands in a major commercial venue, producers offer *preview performances* to the public, which occur before the officially slated opening. Preview performances are designed to give the creative team an opportunity to further refine the product – their play – for the commercial theatre-going community, as well as to perfect how it plays once an audience is present. Reviewers are asked to steer clear of productions in previews, but are generally invited to attend and review the scheduled opening night performance. One notable exception occurred in 2011 with Broadway's *Spiderman: Turn Off the Dark*, which postponed its official opening for 182 preview performances. The delay lasted so long that many reviewers chose to pay for tickets and review the production prior to the official opening, as a way of serving their readers by providing an opinion on how well a consumer's money would be spent by buying a ticket. The delays were likely not because the production team did not plan well, but because the production was incredibly complex, with new ideas and technologies, and there was simply no other way to test how an audience would react until they had a chance to react to the actual production.

Organizing

The process of organizing requires that managers consider all the various tasks that will be required in order to achieve goals, group those tasks together into jobs, group the jobs together into teams, and allocate the necessary personnel and financial resources to accomplish those tasks. Organizing also includes assigning designated authority to people to use those resources and supervise personnel. For merging corporations you can see that this means looking at each like department at both companies, and determining who will do what to ensure that the two departments can become one. Both departments likely had managers, but in a merged department, only one will be needed to oversee operations. However, there will be twice as many employees doing double the work. The entire structure would need to change, as would the assignment of tasks. In the organizational process, managers make sure the resources are allocated efficiently and effectively.

For planning a theatre production or whole season of productions, the same determining of tasks, grouping of work, and allocation of resources occurs. Once a production has been planned, directors, designers, actors, and technicians are hired and given authority to manage others and to spend money to accomplish goals. The production plan is a bit like a big table onto which we put all the things we are going to do. The organizational process requires sorting all those things out in a way that groups them together so they can be accomplished most effectively and efficiently.

Leading

The process of leading requires managers to motivate employees to accomplish their assigned tasks. It also includes directing employees, guiding them, and helping them to achieve a vision for the group, department, or organization. By encouraging, developing, and nurturing employees, managers lead them toward the goals of the vision, or plan for the future.

Leaders are tasked with ensuring that the group they lead has a vision. Sometimes, leaders dictate what the vision will be, and other times they help the team develop the vision. But the word "vision" can be misleading. Leaders do not have to have a crystal ball that shows them the future. Instead, they imagine how their work group, department, or organization can be better, more productive, more efficient and effective, or improved in some other way, and the "vision" is the designation for what that group will look like when the improvements have been implemented. In the case of a corporate merger, in order to have your organizational structure effectively execute your merger plans, you have to know what you want the final product to look like.

The same thing is true in theatre. Consider the director of a play, who spends months talking to designers and considering possibilities long before the actors first show up. The director and designers are managers (though they may find the term distasteful, they do indeed coordinate both financial and human resources), while the actors and technicians are not. The managers get together, led by the director, to create plans, set up an organizational structure, and determine the vision for the play. This "vision" is actually an imagined idea of what the production should look like on opening night. Sometimes the vision changes along the way, and that is all part of the process we will look at in more detail in the next chapter.

Controlling

In the process of controlling, managers monitor the performance of employees who report to them to make sure that the work is being done both efficiently and effectively toward meeting stated goals and objectives. In the controlling process, sometimes referred to as *controlling and evaluating*, managers also take corrective action when the performance of resources is deficient. In some sense, this is why we often think of "being controlling" in a negative way. We associate the notion of controlling as demanding how things must be done. But, in fact, there is another colloquial phrase, "things being out of control," which is a better way to think about this aspect of management. A good manager is constantly watching, and making small adjustments to ensure that plans do not get out of control.

In a corporate merger, if key members are concerned about keeping their jobs once the merger is complete, they might not work efficiently to ensure its success. A good leader will be monitoring to identify any such problem and take corrective action to ensure it does not spiral out of control. Employees who fear the unknown future have valid reasons for being concerned, but without those reasons being addressed and resolved quickly, the concern could easily spread through an entire department or organization and completely jeopardize plans.

An artistic director could easily have similar problems if not exercising the control function of management. Many directors do not wish to work constrained by an organization and its mission, but part of the artistic director's function is to ensure that each play is created in line with the mission of the organization: who it serves and how it serves them. You will learn more about the mission statement and how it is the guiding principle of an organization in Chapter 2, but for now, it is important to understand that it is the mission statement that ultimately guides how managers control processes.

Questions to research for class discussion:

Search the Internet and find answers for these questions before you read any further. Be prepared to discuss them in class.

1.7   Who was Henri Fayol and what were his principles of management?

1.8   What were Fayol's five functions of management and how are they defined?

1.9   What is the management theory of Henry Mintzberg?

1.10   What are four different types of planning and how are they defined? Also, give an example of each.

Roles and skills of managers

When a manager is hired into a job, the company has expectations of that person for how they will perform and behave in the organizational setting. Those performance expectations are called the individual's *role*. As you will notice, managers, just like actors, work in a setting performing their role. And just like an actor, the work of a manager requires many different skills. In the case of a manager, the skills utilized are typically broken into three areas: *human skills, technical skills,* and *conceptual skills.*[10]

Human skills

Sometimes referred to as "people skills," human skills are the skills managers possess and develop to ensure they are able to communicate with others most effectively, and to develop and build good working relationships with others. Communication and relationships are the foundation upon which any manager's role is built. Managers have to motivate, develop and train, direct, and guide others. Interpersonal skills are the key to strong collaboration. These skills are the hallmark of working teams and groups, because they allow managers to be sensitive to the needs of others, as well as to be able to help others share and participate in the team process. Just like in a theatrical production, where the director has to ask questions of the actors, and be trusted enough to listen and nurture the responses, managers must do the same thing to help their employees excel in their roles.

Technical skills

Technical skills are those that are role or job specific, using industry standards and practices as well as tools that are specific to job tasks. Technical skills are the ones we typically think are the most important, though for managers that is not always the case. Technical skills may include knowledge of specific tasks, typical procedures for accomplishing those tasks, and best techniques for accomplishing the tasks in a specialized set of duties. A soundboard operator, for example, must have very specific technical skills. She must know how the equipment works and what each of its components does, and she must be able to identify certain sounds and use the equipment and programming to alter, amplify, distort, or make other mechanical alterations to it. These are some of her technical skills. They are specific to the type of job, because they are skills not required of actors, box office clerks, marketing directors, or even sound designers, to name a few.

Conceptual skills

Conceptual skills are a little bit different than the first two types of skills, because they have to do with how a manager interprets information. Conceptual skills are those where a manager can identify and diagnose problems, analyze situations, and reason out solutions. In order to effectively apply these cognitive techniques, managers must be able to see how their function and the function of their team fits into the whole picture of an organization, and understand how their work will affect others including fellow managers, employees, supervisors, customers, clients, competitors, and even the whole marketplace. Finely honed conceptual skills are what help us think like a theatre manager.

Questions to research for class discussion:

Conceptualize these questions and develop answers for these questions before you read any further. Be prepared to discuss them in class.

1.11 Make a list of three different managerial roles/jobs in theatre. How does each utilize the three types of skills listed above?
1.12 When considering those three jobs, which of the functions of management does each focus on the most? Which does each focus on the least? Why?
1.13 Before you started reading this chapter, how much did you think management related to creating a production? Has that perception changed? If so, why and how?

Staff, line, and functional managers

You may have heard people refer to the term "middle management," sometimes in a negative way. In fact, management is most often designed within an organization to work in hierarchy.[11] *Middle managers* are those who have managers both above them and below them. In a theatre, a marketing director, who oversees a staff, is a middle management position. This person typically reports to upper management, such as a managing director, executive director, or executive producer, and supervises managers of promotions, research, advertising, graphics and the like. But the marketing director is more than a place in the hierarchy. This job supports the work of the people creating the organization's core product, the play, so they are also considered staff management, as are all the managers within a marketing department.

Staff management

Many departments in a theatre company or commercial production have staff managers. And while they provide a support function to the managers of the play, their functions are hardly less important. In fact, in well-run organizations, production managers rely heavily on staff managers as advisors, as well as the support foundations upon which all work is created. Think about your university as an example. If its core product is education, and you are the customer, then the people on the staff are there to support the faculty who generate the core product. But without the staff both advising and supporting, the university would not be able to provide efficient and effective education. The same is true in theatre. There would be no production without someone handling the staff functions of marketing, fundraising, human resources, accounting, and legal, to name a few.

Line management

Think of an assembly line. There are numerous employees working to put together a product, each with a different piece or a different task. Someone has to have direct supervision over them to ensure that the pieces are all being put together correctly. That person is the line manager. Unlike staff managers, who have influence but rarely direct supervision over the creation of an organization's products, including plays, line managers do have that control. A master electrician, costume, scenic, sound, and lighting designer, dance captain, vocal coach, and choreographer are all line management. The production manager, technical director, and stage manager, as well as the artistic director all work directly on the production, but they are not line managers, because they are not directly supervising the people creating the play. Instead, they supervise line managers with those functions.

Functional managers

Managers who work on a specific function of an organization, but who do not directly supervise line employees or staff employees, are often referred to as functional managers. These managers are typically middle management, where they supervise large departments. But while we can see clearly how different managerial roles fall into different categories, those lines are sometimes blurred. Consider the director of a play. They do supervise actors who are directly involved in creating the core product so we might say they are line managers. But they also oversee the entire functional area of play creation, and they are middle managers because they supervise line managers as well as report to upper management.

One thing to note is that researchers have found that often line and staff managers tend to butt heads. Line managers find the advice of staff managers to be uninformed of what it takes to create great art. Line managers often find that staff get in their way and distract them from their primary work of making great theatre. Likewise, staff managers often feel kept out of the loop, ignored, or disregarded, though their functions are equally as essential for running a strong organization. As you can see, good managers are able to respect and work with all departments in a theatre, and to consider all departments as part of the collaboration. That is why human skills are so important for a theatre manager.

The environment

One of the biggest challenges any organization faces comes from a collection of unknowns or slightly-knowns that exist either inside or outside the organization. We refer to the world outside the policies and procedures of the organization as the *environment*. Organizations have to deal with both their internal environment and their external environment. The *internal environment* is much easier for a manager to control, as it is made up of all those things that occur directly under the supervision of the board or investors, and manager. While internal challenges may have to do with deficiencies in personnel or other resources (a typical scenario in noncommercial theatre) they also have to do with attitudes and characteristics of the people who work and volunteer for the organization and affect the culture within its boundaries. These things will ultimately have a bearing on what a theatre does, especially on the stage, so internal environments must be constantly scanned and interpreted.

The *external environment* is everything outside the control of the organization. It is equally important for theatre managers to regularly scan and assess external environments. There are specific environmental factors, such as local competitors, weather issues, local media, chambers of commerce, local politics, donors, and the like, whose actions may have a direct bearing on the theatre. But there is also the larger, general environment, which may affect the organization but not quite as directly or immediately, and which may include factors such as the economy, global politics, changes in national media, technological issues, international wars, and the like. Savvy theatre managers pay close attention to the news on a daily basis and regularly assess how the changing world may affect their operations. Consider that retirees make up the largest portion of theatre-going audiences, and the huge baby boomer generation is now retiring. This could greatly affect a small, local theatre, but maybe not as much if the manager plans for this general environmental change. In the same vein, advancing social media is changing how people choose to spend their entertainment time, and fixed curtain times have become less appealing. Theatre managers are now scrambling to find solutions that deal with this general environmental change.

In both internal and external environments, every theatre will have *stakeholders*.[12] These are all the people who have any vested interest in the theatre, and each one has valuable thoughts and ideas about how a theatre should establish itself, develop, grow, and change. It is easy to think of, consider, and listen to ticket buyers and donors, who are the most obvious stakeholders, just as theatre staff, managers, and board members are also very closely aligned stakeholders. But the list is actually much broader than that. Local restaurateurs have a stake in what happens at a theatre. A blockbuster performance will mean more diners, all wanting to sit at six and be out by seven-thirty for an eight o'clock performance. Chambers of Commerce have a stake in what a local theatre does. So do competitors and mayors and city councils. Local schools may have stakeholders if your theatre production brings in children, and senior homes may have stakeholders if any of their residents buy tickets. Making a decision about how to guide your production requires consideration of the decision's effect on every stakeholder.

In many cities, there is more than one production or more than one theatre company. Often, their missions and programming vary drastically, and they serve different members of the community. But sometimes, two or more theatres or productions are very similar in nature and compete for audience members. In order to stay successful and growing, each must find and emphasize their competitive advantage. The *competitive advantage* is the way in which an organization uses its unique resources more efficiently and effectively than its competitors to provide greater value to the consumer. Imagine a city with two theatres producing essentially the same type of play. But one has a huge courtyard lobby. That lobby could become a place to offer al fresco dining, pre-show or post-show entertainment, receptions, parties, or any number of other events. The courtyard lobby could be considered that theatre's competitive advantage. It can provide greater value to the consumer by providing on-site dining, which its competitor cannot. Because we serve the community, and we do that by providing the greatest value to the consumer most efficiently and effectively, the competitive advantage is very important, and it is a key principle in marketing which we will discuss in detail in Chapters 9 and 10.

Marketing is management

There is an important lesson in the fact that simply discussing the environment leads us into a discourse about marketing. Marketing is what organizations do. Do not confuse marketing with advertising. While the latter is a component of marketing, it is only a very small piece. In order to effectively manage any part of a theatre, one must have a marketing mindset that considers the consumer. Marketing may be done primarily in the marketing department, but it is really part of everyone's job in theatre, because marketing is about ensuring that you are providing what the consumer wants, the way they want it, in the most efficient and effective way possible to provide them the greatest value. Marketing is not a distasteful, commercial function, it is the main function of every organization, including every theatre. The function of most theatres is to provide for the community, and that is exactly what marketing is about: determining how to, and then providing for the community.

Summary

Before you skip past this section, know that it is not just a summation of everything covered in the chapter. Instead, it is written to point out everything you should have gotten out of the chapter, which is a lot of stuff that should not have been too exhausting or difficult, and should not have required you to take notes or memorize. This is where we look at what you should be *thinking* about now, not the facts we covered.

Theatre management is a lot more than selling tickets and making posters, and it requires a lot of critical thinking, which you are well on your way to doing. It is quite similar in many ways to many commercial enterprises, but the most important difference is that in noncommercial theatre we stay focused on serving our community rather than on making a fortune for our investors – making a return on investment for our investors is the goal of commercial theatre. In both cases theatre provides value to the community, it has an important social function, and it provides entertainment (though we don't like to say that out loud). And whether we are talking about commercial or noncommercial theatre, it is still a business that has to be run in a businesslike fashion.

The managers in theatre have line, staff, and functional responsibilities, and most importantly, they all focus on planning, organizing, leading, and controlling, though different managers have different roles with different areas of emphasis. This is why we can say that theatre management includes both artistic management and business management. Whether you want to be a managing director or an artistic director, you need to know how managers plan, organize, lead, and control in all the different environments with which they come in contact.

Build your theatre milestone 1: dreaming big

In each chapter of this text, you will find an assignment titled "Build your theatre." Think of each one as a milestone toward creating your business plan for a fully functioning theatre. With each milestone, you will be documenting not only what you are going to create and how you will do that, but also how you have minimized risk and analyzed information to make the decisions you have come to. At the end of this process, you will have a business plan that is fully executable. Remember, the first function of management is planning!

In this chapter you will find your task is relatively simple, because it mostly requires that you dream. For each question, write your essay answer as if you are a business writer, developing a proposal for a large organization's CEO. Your answer should not be flowery or filled with romantic language and metaphors. Instead, you want to be direct, clear, simple, and concise. This doesn't mean you cannot tell a story, but you do not want to use jargon or be overly dramatic. Also, be careful not to make this, or any milestone, about you. Noncommercial theatres serve the community. Anyone who reads this wants to read why your theatre will serve them and their community. They are not interested in simply supporting your personal dream (unless it is your mom and dad).

- What type of theatre do you want to be?
- What places can you think of that do not already serve the community with this type of theatre?
- What types of productions do you want to present?
- What type of space do you imagine is best for those performances?
- How could you start a theatre company right now, without using any additional money?

Case study

Each chapter of this text has a section at the end titled "Case study." While these case studies do not go into the depth that you might find in an MBA program, they present a number of challenges to think about, analyze, and discuss with your classmates. The best way to prepare to discuss a case study is to follow a progression. First, skim it. Just keep your eyes open for important issues or challenges that you believe are standing out. By the end of this first reading you want to know what the case is about and what are the two or three most basic issues; write a brief narrative of what the case is about as well as narratives about the challenges you have spotted; then read it again. This time, you are looking for information relevant to the issues you identified when you skimmed it. What are the facts you have been given? Under each issue you wrote in part one, now write a narrative explaining the facts as they appear in the case. Finally, after you have carefully considered the issues and facts, using your own knowledge and experience, develop one or more potential solutions to the challenges, and write a narrative for that.

Once you have completed writing your narratives, find some time to talk with one or more people in your class about their thoughts on the case. Are they in alignment with yours? Did they think of something you missed? Remember that there are no wrong answers here, and there is no need to rewrite what you have already written. Instead, we use the time with a classmate to help each other uncover deeper and richer ideas in our own thinking. Lastly, you will bring your thoughts to class to discuss the case in detail.

The case

Graduation necessitated Patrick's job search, and he eventually landed a good position as a functional manager in the San Francisco area, a place he had always dreamed of living. He was hired as the assistant director of marketing for a moderately sized theatre with an annual operating budget of about $3 million. It wasn't a glamorous position, but he would be doing what he was good at, developing promotional materials for plays, and he had a small staff to handle graphics design, text writing, and research. He felt well prepared for the job, and while there was much to learn about the company's way of operating, Patrick felt good about the transition. There was one odd quirk about the position. Patrick's title was to be assistant director of marketing, but the company had no actual director of marketing. Patrick wasn't going to be assisting anyone. Instead, he would report directly to upper management. His new boss, Frank, the managing director, had asked him to bring their office into the twenty-first century. Because he had the latest knowledge in the field, he was not only an excellent candidate, but also the perfect choice. Given his positive attitude, strong work ethic, ability to avoid gossip and drama, and his charming personality, he would be not only an exceptional supervisor, but also an outstanding employee. And updating processes was something he had been trying to do for three years at another theatre. He was finally given his chance to excel.

Within a few days of starting his new position, Patrick sat down with Frank to share what he was seeing.

"The team really makes some pretty images for posters and postcards, but they don't seem to have any direction in terms of advertising vehicles. Each piece is simply altered to fit in the space required, but different media need different types of messaging. Also, just because someone thinks an image is pretty or text is convincing doesn't make it true. These things need to be tested. But more than that, the office really doesn't have any goals."

"That's a great place to start," said Frank. "You need to set goals for those people."

"I'm planning on it. I just need to read the company's statement and strategic plan so I know where the goals fit in."

"Let's not get ahead of ourselves," was Frank's response. "We don't want the marketing department to be steering the ship here. You should set some nice goals for your team so they can know if they are hitting them or not."

"Yes, I agree they need goals," responded Patrick, "but without a bigger picture to look at, I'm not sure what sorts of goals we should be attempting to reach."

"What do you mean?" was the response, followed by, "they need marketing goals."

"Of course. But if we are focusing strongly on growth, we will need detailed research goals as well as sales targets. If we are focusing on quality improvement, the goals will be vastly different. And if we want to increase visibility and bring in non-attenders, they will be different again."

"Those are all good goals. Why don't you set some of each? Patrick, I sure am glad you're here."

That last comment was Patrick's cue to leave the room.

As you can imagine, Patrick was already frustrated. He explained his frustration this way:

On the very first day of studying theatre management we talked about the four functions of planning, organizing, leading, and controlling. None of that is happening. What my team does is make pictures and write blurbs. There is no plan at all. But that's because there are no goals. We don't know what this company wants us to do. It's no wonder people in my position have been fired repeatedly. They couldn't be successful because they had no idea what their role was. No one does. How can you improve the functionality of a functional area if no one has any idea what the function is? And this isn't the first time I've heard things like this. For three years I was constantly told to just put my theatre management education to work. But managers can't work in a vacuum. We all have to not only work together, but we have to trust one another. Sometimes theatres boggle my mind. Directors of plays, who know nothing about marketing, will dictate how to market, but they refuse to listen to my data, research, and analysis. Instead, they make demands based on their opinions, and often those opinions won't expand a market, build a brand, raise awareness, or sell tickets. Yet if I were to come into a rehearsal and demand how a play should be performed, I would be thrown out on my ear. I wouldn't do it. I'm smarter than that. But it seems very shortsighted to hire an expert and then tell him to behave like a novice.

To make matters worse for Patrick, his team had been around for several years, and they were very close to Frank. They would share their imagery for plays with him like they were schoolchildren looking for a spot on the refrigerator. They would proudly share their carefully crafted words. And the research was mostly regurgitated material from the ticketing system, which often seemed to go over Frank's head. Whenever Patrick tried to guide or nudge his team in one direction or another, they would share their work directly with Frank, and it would be green-lighted. Patrick couldn't even manage his own team.

Patrick began to realize that he was going to have to make some changes, and make them quickly, or he would soon be out of a job. He decided to call a daylong meeting with his team, involving members of the board, and Frank agreed to let him do so. For the meeting he invited a couple of board members to come at the start to meet the marketing team and to discuss long-term strategy for the organization. Frank was to join the board members, but Patrick asked that when they were to leave, Frank should stick around for a bit to help analyze what they had heard, and to ensure that the organization's goals were clear enough that Patrick's team could then, on its own, develop a marketing plan. As the day of the meeting rolled around, Frank called Patrick to say he was concerned about having board members attend a staff meeting, so he had told them it was cancelled. He was still available to attend, and would do so, but the board members would not be present.

Patrick was clearly in a difficult situation. He needed a plan to help right his department, he needed the support of his managing director, and he needed to know what his role was. What options do you see for Patrick? What challenges does each option present, and which would you recommend for Patrick?

Personal exploration

1) Discuss a work, school, or life situation that was either positive or negative as a direct result of the manager. Remember that this is the person who coordinates resources (and in the case of this question, you are the resource). What type of manager was this, line, staff, or functional? What made this manager effective or ineffective?

2) Discuss examples of ways you plan, organize, lead, and control your life.

Notes

1 Roche, Nancy, and Jaan Whitehead, eds., *The Art of Governance,* Theatre Communications Group, 2005.

2 Volz, Jim, *How to Run a Theatre: Creating, Leading and Managing Professional Theatre,* A&C Black, 2013.

3 Sullivan, William M., Anne Colby, Judith Welch Wegner, Lloyd Bond, and Lee S. Shulman, *Educating Lawyers: Preparation for the Profession of Law* (Vol. 2), John Wiley & Sons, 2007.

4 Volz, *How to Run a Theatre: Creating, Leading and Managing Professional Theatre,* 2013.

5 Ibid.

6 Maccoy, Peter, *Essentials of Stage Management*, A&C Black, 2014.

7 Volz, *How to Run a Theatre: Creating, Leading and Managing Professional Theatre,* 2013.

8 Maccoy, *Essentials of Stage Management,* 2014.

9 Schraeder, Mike, Dennis R. Self, Mark H. Jordan, and Ron Portis, "The functions of management as mechanisms for fostering interpersonal trust," *Advances in Business Research* 5, no. 1 (2015): 50–62.

10 Daft, Richard, and Dorothy Marcic, *Understanding Management*, Nelson Education, 2016.

11 Maccoy, *Essentials of Stage Management,* 2014.

12 Ohlandt, D., "Engaging the audience: Cultivating partners, collaborators, and stakeholders," *Theatre Topics* 25, no. 2 (2015): 139–148.

CHAPTER 2

The strategic framework of theatre

Remember Patrick? He had held two positions working in marketing in theatre, one as an internship while still studying and one in San Francisco that he landed after graduation. In both positions, he knew what he should be *doing*, because he had studied hard and educated himself about best practices for people in theatre management, but in both cases he had a supervisor who did not understand this and had not created an environment where best practices could be put in place. While there are a number of human issues involved, which we will focus on in Chapter 12, one of the biggest problems for Patrick is that there was no appropriate framework within which to work.

Chapter objectives

After reading this chapter, you should be able to apply the mission, vision, and values statements to an organization, explain what goes into a theatre's business plan, analyze the differences between organizational and artistic values, and summarize the function of a strategic plan.

What is framework?

Have you ever seen a new house being built? The first thing the contractor does is lay a foundation. Sometimes it is a solid piece of concrete, sometimes a basement, sometimes it is simply level ground into which support pillars are placed, but the very first step is to create a solid foundation. Your notion for a new theatre, what you created in your first milestone, is your foundation. It is upon this milestone that you will build your theatre. From there, you begin to plan. And in order for the plan to be effective, you start with the skeleton first. The skeleton is the framework.

Once the house has its foundation poured or placed, the contractor begins by placing pillars on the foundation. They are the biggest, strongest pieces of the house. And attached to them are studs that make up the walls, and joists that make up the floors. These pieces, when considered in total, create the framework. And just like a human skeleton, they are the structure that holds the whole thing together. They are not the walls or the floors, but they show you where the walls and floors will go. The framework has pipes placed in it so you can see where the plumbing fixtures will go. Wires run up and down the framework so you can see where outlets and lights will be. The framework shows us exactly how the whole thing will work when it is finished. That is exactly what the framework for your theatre will do as well.

You have certainly been told that when you sit down to write a paper, you should start by creating an outline. This textbook was created that exact same way. The outline tells us how the final product will work when it is finished. It is not the paper or book itself, and it does not show us if we will like the writing style or the word choice or anything about the final product – much like a theatre framework will not show us if we will like the actual plays being produced – but it gives us a sense of how everything will operate. The framework is the heart of the plan. And as you probably recall, job number one for a manager is planning!

The business plan

You have probably heard of the *business plan* before. You may have even considered what a business plan is. For not-for-profit theatre companies, the business plan is a bit more unique than plans in the commercial world, and that is because in the commercial world, the plan explains how we will accomplish the goal of making a profit. It does a whole lot more than that, as you will see, but the primary function of a commercial business plan is to demonstrate profitability. And it has to pass the laugh test. If you read it and chuckle because it sounds so impossible, it fails the laugh test. It cannot simply explain that the business will make millions by selling millions of widgets, it has to show data that supports the notion that there are buyers out there willing to pay for a million widgets, that the staff has the expertise to design, build, and sell a million widgets, that the marketing for those widgets is sound, and that the operation will run effectively. The commercial business plan is not just a detailing of the idea; it is the framework. We can see how the business will work when it is finished.

The not-for-profit theatre business plan is often a little bit different, because our plan, while it is still the framework, has the primary focus of demonstrating how the theatre can and will serve the community the way the theatre company wishes to. And before you think to yourself, "good, we don't have to be profitable," think again. You can only serve your community if you have the money on hand to fulfill that service commitment. You may not have to make a profit in the sense of an investor-controlled business, but you do have to be financially viable, and that means bringing in enough money to cover all your expenses – including salaries.[1] And if you are creating a company whose function is to develop a play for commercial distribution, you will need to be very cognizant of all the details of the business plan, including how to make a healthy profit for shareholders or investors.

A typical commercial enterprise uses the business plan to demonstrate to investors, bankers, or funders how the company will succeed, and by succeed, we mean by making money. The theatre business plan most likely will not get very far if you use it to ask a bank for a loan. Bankers learned long ago that investing in organizations that are focused on providing for the community is a risky option. And bankers have investors themselves, who are expecting to see a profit on their investment. Loaning money to a new theatre company is not likely to generate a profit for the bank, no matter how good the idea and the business plan is. Even the most well-respected commercial theatre artists cannot go to a bank for a loan to create a new commercial theatre production. It is just too risky for the bank. That does not mean, however, that theatres can therefore forego writing a business plan. It just means that theatres create their business plan a little differently.

Often businesses write *internal business plans*, which detail the launching of a new product or division. These plans, like their bigger cousin, detail how the new product or division will work when they are finished. Internal plans are typically only for internal stakeholders, so they may include detailed, sometimes confidential information about how the company will create success.[2] A theatre company launching a new education program might write an internal business plan for that purpose.[3] For the purpose of creating a new theatre, however, the company would write an external business plan.

The *external business plan* is designed for stakeholders both inside and outside the organization. You probably recall that stakeholders are the people who have a vested interest in the theatre. When starting a new theatre or production, that could be just about anyone in the community, but as you go about creating your business plan through the milestones in this text, you will want to focus on potential donors or investors – these are the people who are willing to give you some of their hard-earned money, just because your idea and your framework is so logical, well-thought-out, and detailed that they cannot see how it will not lead to a theatre or production that will serve the community for years to come.[4]

Questions to research for class discussion:

Search the Internet and find answers for these questions before you read any further. Be prepared to discuss them in class.

2.1   What are three elements that go into a typical business plan? List and describe them.

2.2 What elements of a typical business plan may not be appropriate for a non-commercial theatre business plan and why?

2.3 What additional elements seem critical to include in a noncommercial theatre business plan? What would those elements include, and why?

You have probably come to realize that in many ways the business plan is actually a large collection of other plans: marketing plan, operations plan, financial plan, and so on. In fact, you can think of the business plan as though it is the script for the play. It has all the words the actors are supposed to say, it describes what the scenery will look like, and it gives stage directions to ensure that the characters move and react as the playwright intended. Your business plan will give that level of detail to your theatre description.

We noted that the theatre plan, by its very nature, is not going to focus on how to make a profit for investors unless it is for a major commercial production. For noncommercial theatres we are interested in improving the community through theatre. But "improving the community through theatre" could mean many things. To some it may mean bringing new, unique, avant-garde productions to the neighborhood. To others it may be presenting re-creations of the biggest hit musicals. And to others still, it may mean providing a theatre school for disadvantaged youth who get a chance to perform. Really, there is no limit to what "improving the community through theatre" can mean.[5] But it is important that you consider that if your community already has a theatre that presents re-creations of the biggest hit musicals, it probably does not need a second one. If that is your passion, consider joining the company that already does what you are passionate about. If there were already a revival of *South Pacific* playing in the West End, it would not make much sense to develop a company to create another revival of *South Pacific* in the West End. But if the thing you are passionate about is unique, and not something already provided to your community, then you are a person with a mission.

The mission statement

The main ingredient in any business plan, in fact the main ingredient in any good business, is the *mission statement*. The mission statement is an explanation of what you are passionate about, and it is the core principle under which your theatre or production will operate. It is a statement that not only tells the community what you do and who you serve, but it informs your theatre's decision-making. If your mission is to bring great Shakespeare to the people of Southampton, then producing *Oklahoma!* in Brighton would be a poor decision!

There are countless experts who disagree on what makes a good mission statement. Management guru Peter Drucker once said a good mission statement should fit on a bumper sticker. The message he wanted to get across was that a good mission statement is concise. It doesn't have lots of flowery words. It is brief. You can memorize it, and so can the community. And while fitting on a bumper sticker is not a criterion for a mission, it is a good piece of advice to follow. If you can write your statement in twenty words, why not try reducing it to fifteen? You want everyone to know what it is that you do. And if your mission statement is long, once it is written it will sit on a web page somewhere, ignored by everyone.

Mission statement function

Sometimes you will see mission statements that are long, complex, cumbersome, and several paragraphs of explanations. Your university may have such a mission statement. Large corporations often have a lengthy mission statement covering the myriad of things that the organization does. Do not be fooled. While these statements may have value for the organizations that have them, a lengthy mission statement for a noncommercial theatre is an exercise in futility. It is highly unlikely that writing such a statement will do you any good. As we have seen, the mission statement needs to drive decisions. Of course, it cannot give us all the richness of detail we may need in order to make perfect decisions, but it is intended to be strong enough to help guide us.

How to draft your statement

Usually a mission statement is something worked on by a board of directors or a collection of important stakeholders for an organization. Because you are developing your own theatre, you may only have a friend or family member to help, or you may have to craft the statement all by yourself. That's okay. But once your theatre is up and running, you will probably want to revisit your mission statement every year or two. The goal then is to make sure it is still the exact mission you wish to pursue, and that it serves the exact community that you wish to serve.

Sometimes wonderful opportunities present themselves that do not fit your mission. Say a famous Hollywood director comes to your Shakespeare company and offers to direct a brand new psychodrama for free. And this famous director will bring major celebrity talent and lots of money for the production. Your mission might preclude you from accepting this offer. And the well-run theatre would really only have three options: (1) turn it down, (2) accept and go against their mission, or (3) re-write the mission. It is not unusual for a growing theatre company to need to regularly expand their mission. Even a stable company that has been around for decades should be constantly examining their mission. If the world is changing and your mission is not, you may be headed for trouble.

When you look at mission statements, you will find that many typically try to be inspiring. Inspiration is not a bad thing, but there are better ways of communicating that message to the public. The noncommercial theatre mission statement, while it may originate from those things that inspire you, should focus on two central components: who you serve and how you serve them. This means that your mission statement is going to be brief, clear, and describe how you define community, and what you provide to it. That's all. This may sound like an easy task, but many a board of directors has spent countless hours bickering about whether the word "the" is more appropriate than the word "a" in a mission statement. This is the backbone of your organization. It is the concrete foundation on which the entire framework will be built. It is important to get it right (even though you can always change it and improve upon it at any time).

Questions to research for class discussion:

Search the Internet and find answers for these questions before you read any further. Be prepared to discuss them in class.

2.4 What are two examples of excellent mission statements? What makes them good?

2.5 What are two examples of poor mission statements? What makes them poor?

2.6 What are the most common mistakes you find in mission statements?

Missions and fiscal prudence

Some mission statements also include words that note the company will operate in a fiscally prudent way. This is not wrong! While we said there were two topics that go into a mission statement – who you serve and how you serve them – like many other ways you serve your community, you must do so in a fiscally prudent manner. If not, your theatre will go bankrupt. Experts disagree on this point, as well. Most believe that there is no need to state in the mission that a company will operate in a fiscally prudent fashion, because this is simply understood. Others suggest, especially for organizations that serve the public good, that making a bold statement in the mission about operating in a fiscally prudent manner is an important constant reminder. There is no right or wrong way. But, as we will see, there are other places where making a bold public statement about operating in a financially sound manner can fit better, and that will cut a few extra words out of your mission statement. For a commercial production, a major part of the mission is returning the original investment with profits. Commercial productions serve the investors by serving the audience.

Missions that lose money

There are organizations that serve the public in such a way as to not make any money. These charitable organizations rely solely upon the gifts of others to sustain operations. Organizations dedicated to eradicating diseases are typically this type of organization. They hold fundraisers and meet with donors regularly to ensure support, which is required for their survival. Many new theatre companies see this model and think that they will also be able to secure money through donors and fundraisers in order to sustain their operations. This may or may not be true, but the challenges are uniquely different for a theatre company, because the theatre company has an avenue for earned revenues, which many charitable organizations do not. To those of us who love theatre, we see this as an extra way to generate financial resources; but the community, the donors, and the supporters often see that we already have a means for earning money (ticket sales), and they tend to be less inclined to give. This is not to say that there are not many ways to generate unearned revenue for a theatre, but the challenges are different. If a theatre company has a mission that guarantees it cannot earn money, that theatre company may have a difficult time staying afloat. Artists and art require financial assistance to continue to thrive, but a mission that requires a constant financial drain from the community is likely to be challenged at every turn. Mission statements are not just words on a page. They are well thought out, and an important thought to consider is whether the mission is one that has some chance of financial sustainability.

The vision statement

Following every good mission statement is a second statement called the *vision statement*. The vision statement is exactly what it sounds like: a vision of the future. If you consider that a theatre director has a vision for the play, this is what they are planning for at the end of their work, on opening night. They are envisioning what the entire play will look and feel like. The vision statement for an organization serves the exact same purpose; it tells us what the organization will look like at the end of the work. Think about the charitable organization raising money to end homelessness. Their vision should be pretty clear, because their work will be done when there is no homelessness;

so their vision is probably a community, a country, or a world with no home-lessness. That is a pretty grand vision, and it is highly improbable that it will be achieved for centuries, if then. But it is *possible*. This is the crux of the vision statement. It is the definition of the ultimate goal an organization works toward that is highly improbable, but nevertheless possible.

For a theatre company, the vision statement can sometimes prove chal-lenging, because we do not ever want to see a world where theatre is no longer necessary, but that does not mean we do not need a vision state-ment. Remember that the vision statement is the ultimate goal that is improbable but possible to achieve. A local theatre company might envi-sion winning a Tony Award or transferring a production to the West End. Or perhaps a company envisions providing free theatre that is enjoyed by everyone in their city. These are very lofty goals, and it seems unlikely they can be achieved, but they are not impossible. The vision statement shoots for the moon.

This is not to suggest that the vision statement is simply a useless dream. The vision statement supports the mission. While the mission reminds us on a daily basis who we serve and how we serve them, the vision tells us why. It helps us craft long-range strategy, and guides the direction in which we head in the future. The mission guides day-to-day decisions while the vision guides decisions that have long-term impact.

When you write a vision statement, you want to keep in mind some basic rules that, again, experts do not necessarily agree upon. First, be sure you keep it brief. Long statements are never remembered, and that makes it dif-ficult to be inspired by them; the vision statement should inspire people. While the end goal is something improbable or extremely lofty, it should not be totally impossible. For example, a theatre company will never be able to ensure happiness in every person on the planet. The vision also should be specific to the organization. A theatre company that envisions interstellar travel is in the wrong business.

When writing a vision statement, be sure to use words that are clear and concise, so anyone could easily understand them. Also, be sure to avoid words that are open to interpretation. A vision statement that tells us a theatre wants to bring joy to an entire community might be achievable and it might not, depending on how you interpret "bringing joy." Consider a vision statement that can actually guide long-term decision-making. With the vision you create, will you be able to see your company closer to its end goal in ten years than it is today? If you envision being the first theatre company on the moon, in ten years you will probably be no closer than you are today. Finally, those things your organization values most will drive the vision.

Questions to research for class discussion:

Search the Internet and find answers for these questions before you read any further. Be prepared to discuss them in class.

2.7   What are two examples of excellent vision statements? What makes them good?
2.8   What are two examples of poor vision statements? What makes them poor?
2.9   What are the most common mistakes you find in vision statements?

Values

There is a third statement strong organizations include in their arsenal, and it is the *value statement*. The value statement discusses those principles shared by organizational stakeholders that drive the organization and define its character. This statement guides the behavior of stakeholders in the organization. Sometimes the value statement is a sentence or two that discusses those principles the organization believes are essential to achieve the vision. Organizational values define how the company will conduct business in the course of executing both its mission and its vision. So, in a sense, the value statement is the glue that holds the statements together.

As you search the Internet for value statements, you will find that organizations often say things like, "we value diversity." Valuing diversity is an important principle for many organizations, but it is not necessarily clear. Often, organizations will have a bullet-point list of values, followed by an explanation of what each principle means to them. Here's an example:

- *Creativity: We believe that our work should demonstrate new ideas that have never been experienced by an audience, in an effort to stimulate thought and feeling in unique and exciting ways.*
- *Diversity: We believe that our productions and our company are stronger when we embrace and cherish differences, proactively including all people, treating everyone fairly and equally, and valuing all opinions.*
- *Environment: We believe in conserving resources whenever and wherever we can, and will operate in a way that will have no long-term negative impact on the environment.*
- *Financial Responsibility: We will never borrow from others or ourselves. We will maintain a savings sufficient to carry through one full production, and we will always maximize our earned and unearned income to its fullest potential.*

The value statement is the place where you may want to include something about fiscal prudence. Any theatre company that values being smart about money and puts that notion out there for the world to see is more likely to gain respect from donors.

How commercial and noncommercial values differ

Values are the main guiding principles of an organization, and in that sense, there should be no difference between types of organizations. But organizations that serve the community have a deeper list of values, because at the core of a commercial enterprise is the focus of making a profit for the owners and investors. The values under which they operate tell the world, and especially those investors, just what sort of behavior to expect from the company. But for a theatre company, there is more to a value statement than operating values.[6] Theatres also have artistic values. Sometimes you will find that a theatre refers to their value statement as "beliefs and values," or has an extra statement they call "philosophy." The words "principles" and "manifesto" are sometimes used, and likewise other organizations simply include artistic values with operating values. What does not exist is any research on the importance of one type of value statement over the other. For a theatre company, however, the idea of defining artistic values somehow is important, as we will see in the next chapter, because those artistic values drive our decision-making about what plays we intend to produce each season.

The strategic plan

One thing you will find about theatre management, and it is true of all management, is that at every level we plan. While you will find more emphasis on planning in the first few chapters of this book, you will find that all the

---

Think critically: translating corporate values to artistic ones

There are two ways to approach this class discussion. First, you can choose sides. Divide the class into four, by whatever means you choose, and debate the argument outlined below. Second, you can have an open discussion, each adding upon others' thoughts, and let the discussion uncover all the important details of all sides of the debate. Keep in mind that regardless of which approach you take, we want to be sure we dig deep into all sides of this important issue, in order to more effectively understand all positions.

CLASS DISCUSSION: There have been countless studies to support the notion that organizations can be more successful if they have a value statement.

The statement tells the world, and particular investors, what sort of behavior to expect from the company. The value statement defines the morals and ethics expected of the company and its employees, and it holds the mission and vision together. Theatre companies, however, have an additional layer of values to embrace: artistic values. The artistic values are the core principles a theatre company focuses on when creating their art. These values tell artists how to behave when working toward the organization's vision. Yet there is no clear guidance on how to devise an artistic value statement. Should the value statement be all-inclusive, covering both operating and artistic values? If so, why? Should a theatre have two statements, one an operating value statement and one an artistic value statement? If so, why? Is there another, better way to define artistic values? If so, why? Should there be no artistic value statement at all, as a statement of artistic values will only serve to stifle creativity? What other reasons might you argue against having an artistic value statement?

way through the final chapter, there are topics for which we need to plan. If the business plan is the skeleton for how we will create the organization, *the strategic plan* is the skeleton of how the organization will grow and change over time, or in the case of a commercial production, how excellence and profitability will be maintained. You will not be writing a strategic plan as one of your milestones in this text, because the strategic plan is something a board of directors or executive producers would take on in order to guide the organization or production into the future, and right now your theatre does not even have a present! But the strategic plan is an important topic for noncommercial theatres, and it is one that is often neglected.

What are strategic plans for?

As noted, strategic plans guide an organization into the future. But that is really a simple notion of a very complex document. The strategic plan details the snapshot in time of where an organization is, what strengths and assets it possesses as well as where it has deficiencies and challenges, and then details exactly how those will be used as tools to expand, change, and grow. You may think to yourself, "what if my theatre never needs to expand, change, or grow?" But like all things, change occurs. We cannot avoid it. And the organization that tries to never change will eventually become irrelevant. Theatres that plan for change through a strategic plan are much more likely to have enduring success. And they do that by documenting exactly what steps will be taken, by whom, and how, in order to successfully cause that change to occur.

But more than just planning for growth and change, strategic plans also detail what priorities an organization has set for itself. They help the organization ensure it is making the best use of its resources – both financial and human – and help make sure that all of those resources are focused on the same goals and objectives.

Devising a strategic plan

In some ways the process of devising a strategic plan is similar to the process of creating a business plan, because it requires a thorough analysis of the environment in which the business operates in order to assess the best course of action. A new commercial production would use a business plan that details how investors will be captured, how the investments will be used, and how the return on those investments will be acquired, the noncommercial enterprise uses a strategic plan to formulate changes for the future. While a company founder and their family, friends, or potential board members create the initial business plan, some or all of a company's staff and board members usually create the strategic plan with input from every stakeholder group. Strategic plans typically cover a period of as many as five years, and detail the steps required to achieve the strategic goals addressed in the plan.

Just like a mission statement, strategic plans are regularly monitored for their effectiveness, and can be altered if necessary. In fact, if theatre executives and boards do not regularly monitor these plans, they will likely be ineffective; this is the "controlling" part of management. Typically, mission statements are re-evaluated during the strategic planning process, which requires a good deal of time and thought.

Process

The process of devising a strategic plan starts with a champion: someone who is passionate about ensuring the theatre is successful going into the future. This could be the managing director, the artistic director, the chairperson of the board, or anyone else closely associated with the organization that has both an interest in seeing future success and the authority to embark on the strategic planning process. The champion gets the ball rolling and makes certain that the strategic planning process stays on track. But they do not devise the strategic plan on their own. In fact, it is crucial that there is a wide array of participants in the process, as it is meant to give a clear picture of where the organization currently is in order to develop a strategy for the future. If only the staff participate in the strategic planning process, their perspective will skew the view of where the organization is. The same is true if only the board participates. This is why it is important to include insights from every stakeholder's point of view. The assessment is not where we think we are, but where we *really* are.

Sometimes the champion is a hired expert brought in to guide the strategic planning process, though most noncommercial theatres cannot afford to expend precious resources on consultants. That's okay. But it is important that someone takes the lead. The champion will have to identify key decision-makers and stakeholders, and also determine which stakeholder groups should be represented in the strategic planning process. Those people are then brought together for an initial meeting to discuss the process.

Because the strategic plan is a detailed explanation of where the company is at, as well as a structured set of goals for the future and how to achieve them, it is not a process that can be completed in a short meeting. Large, complex organizations can take a year or more to devise a fully executable strategy. In the case of a noncommercial theatre, the appropriate process will most likely be a series of meetings set up over several weeks, allowing time in-between for participants to research required information that can inform decision-making at the next meeting. At the initial gathering of potential participants in the strategic planning process, the first order of business will be to determine how the group will meet; who will be gathering pertinent information to share at meetings; days and times of meetings; who will lead, record, document, and report the work of the group; and what time and money (if any) will be allocated to the process. This initial meeting typically begins by explaining to all participants the function of strategic planning, and ensuring that they understand the process is for them to guide and have ownership in the organization. It is not simply to assist the staff in developing a plan.

That all sounds pretty good, but it is important to remember that when you are planning for change, it means some people will be skeptical. Human beings have various levels of comfort with change, and when you bring a group of people together to discuss change, there will certainly be some who are either vocally or quietly opposed to changing anything. Others may simply be opposed to the process because they do not see how changing anything will benefit them. The first meeting is a chance to get to understand how potential participants feel about embarking on strategic planning, to allay any fears, to hear concerns, and to foster support for the process.

Contents

Believe it or not, when doing strategic planning, the first thing we do is circle right back to the mission statement. In order to plan for the future, we have to understand how we are operating. This is why mission, vision, and value statements are often revised during the strategic planning process. The first part of the strategic plan discusses who we serve and how we serve them. Because the strategic planning process will (or should) have a broad spectrum of stakeholders, sometimes the results of a discussion about who we serve can be quite illuminating, and lead to changes in the mission statement. The same can be said for the vision and value statements. Sometimes, in the course of this discussion we find that there are important stakeholders whom we have not represented in the strategic planning process. This is a chance to consider adding people to the strategic planning process, either as regular committee members or as visitors to some meetings, in order to provide additional insight.

The next part of the strategic plan is a discussion of our theatre's world. There are two distinct areas the committee will want to brainstorm and discuss: *internal issues*, which we refer to as *strengths* and *weaknesses*; and *external issues*, which are *opportunities* and *threats*. This process is known as the *SWOT analysis*, an acronym for Strengths, Weaknesses, Opportunities, and Threats.[7] We will discuss the SWOT analysis in greater detail in Chapter 3.

After the group has identified the details in the SWOT analysis, they will begin to consider *strategic issues*. Strategic issues are those requiring attention. Oftentimes, a theatre company identifies two major strategic issues immediately: audience size is falling (or not growing), and donations are insufficient. These are definitely important issues, as they affect the entire company, its mission, and all stakeholders. Other strategic issues identified may be those which do not require immediate attention, but should be noted as important to monitor, such as an aging building.

Once the strategic issues have been determined, the committee will select those most pressing issues, typically two or three, to focus on. They will then develop a strategy for each of the issues, setting a goal. In the case of dwindling audiences, the goal might be to increase audience size by 15% within two years. The strategic plan then includes a discussion and outline of exactly how this goal will be achieved: Who will be responsible? In what ways will they be expected to proceed? What resources will they be given (both financial and human)? Who will monitor progress? How far along should they be at certain benchmarks along the way? How is the course corrected if those benchmarks are not achieved?

Usually, when the two or three strategic issues have been turned into plans for action, the strategic plan is shared with a wide array of stakeholders to get feedback. This serves two purposes: first, it allows the committee to fine-tune and adjust the plan to assure it is most likely to succeed; and second, it begins the process of buy-in from a larger segment of stakeholders. Strategic plans can only be successful if stakeholders agree to work toward their success. Once the plan has been fully vetted, it is finalized, and the work begins.

Who needs a strategic plan?

There are some instances where a strategic plan may not be needed. For your start-up theatre company, the business plan you are developing through your milestones is your guide. Start-ups are, by their very nature, fairly unstable. This is the reason that commercial productions typical develop a business plan, and noncommercial companies develop a strategic plan. Without a history or track record it is difficult to predict with any certainty very far into the future, and as a result setting long-term strategy can be very challenging. Also, theatres that have had some major change or upheaval may not wish to embark on strategic planning. If the building's roof just collapsed, the theatre is not stable enough (literally and figuratively) to simultaneously work on a strategic plan. But aside from situations that make a company unstable, every theatre should have or be developing a strategic plan. Ask yourself, when it comes to business decisions, do we want to be strategic, or do we want to be random?

A note about the importance of strategy

Many theatres think they are engaging in strategic planning because they meet once a year to decide which plays to produce. This is *not* strategic planning. Nor is a quick discussion about issues you want to tackle. These are discussions, and they might be planning, but they are by no means strategic. And in an ever-changing, fast-paced, global economy, where people are connected through smartphones, and interacting at the speed of light, planning for the future *needs* to be strategic. It is a process that is separate and distinct from season selection. It is not something that occurs at a regular staff meeting or a regular board meeting. Strategic planning is the way we design our own future. It is vital, and must be given the importance it requires.

Build your theatre milestone 2: mission, vision, and values

Remember that your goal here is to explain not only what you are going to create and how you will do that, but also how you have minimized risk and analyzed information to make the decisions you have come to.

In this milestone you will be writing three statements for your theatre company. It is vitally important that you consider your well-thought-out responses to the questions in your first, as they will drive how you go about writing the statements for your company. Using the information from the text, class discussions, and your searches on the Internet, write three complete statements for your theatre: a mission statement, a vision statement, and a value statement.

Case study

After only a couple of weeks on his job as assistant marketing director, Patrick got a chance to sit in on a season selection meeting. Participants at the meeting included some regular actors, several regular directors, a few staff members, and Patrick's boss. A number of play ideas were tossed around, and eventually a shortlist was created. Everyone at the meeting was tasked with reading those plays and coming to a subsequent meeting to discuss which ones would make it into the season. Patrick spent several nights reading each of the plays, and returned to the next meeting with his notes about why each best served the organization. But the second meeting was quite different than Patrick expected. He explained it like this:

> Before there was much of a discussion at all, one of the directors started really advocating for one particular play. It is certainly a great play, and quite intellectually challenging, but it isn't one that seemed right for us. We try to serve the theatre-going community, and this relatively unheard of play, with very dark, ugly themes set in a tiny Irish town, was really more for a very niche audience, not the general theatre-going populace. But this director had directed the play before and really loved it, which I think is completely valid. At one point, my boss, Frank, looked at me and said, "Patrick, what do you think about it from a marketing perspective?" and I said I could do some research, but was fairly certain it really wasn't a good fit for our audience and would not sell particularly well. I pointed out that it was okay to not sell well, that we would ensure that a great production would have great exposure, and we could position it to expand our brand and our traditional audience, but I didn't want anyone expecting us to do miracles. The director then interrupted me and said, "Oh, the Irish-American community will come out by the thousands to see it," and with that, Frank decided to put the play into the season. There is an Irish-American community in San Francisco, but there was no way we were going to get them to come out by the thousands, even if we held their hands and promised them free food and drink. It just doesn't work like that.

This was an interesting lesson for Patrick, and one he took with him when he attended a board retreat that was focused on evaluating and rewriting the company's mission statement. At the retreat, the board members and staff spent a great deal of time discussing the importance of who the theatre was. They talked at great lengths about who they served, and finally started to narrow in on the idea that they served people who loved "popular, entertaining, and engaging theatre," and they served them by bringing them "joy."

Patrick thought back to the season selection process he had been a part of and decided to speak up.

"But when we pick plays to produce, we really cater to the desire of our directors."

"No we don't," said Frank. "We are always thinking about our audience."

"Sure," said Patrick. "But really, if a director is passionate about directing something, we go with them. That's not wrong. In fact, I think that's a very cool thing, and I kind of like that we serve our directors first. It makes us unique. But since that's who we serve first, we should say that in our mission."

The board got quite rattled, and Patrick wondered if he hadn't stirred up a hornet's nest by even bringing up the topic. But Frank wasn't upset. Instead, Frank asked Patrick to explain further, and seemed quite interested in getting at what made the theatre company unique. The board was less interested, as they were all members of the community who loved "popular, entertaining, and engaging theatre."

As Patrick explained further, he brought up the Irish play, and several board members rolled their eyes. They clearly hadn't appreciated it. But Patrick didn't want to choose sides. He simply noted that the word "joy" meant different things to different people, and might not be the right word, but he wasn't sure there was anyone who would call the Irish play joyous, and wondered if maybe they should consider that the way they serve their community was not solely by bringing "joy."

Before there could be too much complaining about the Irish play, Patrick noted that while it did not sell as well as the rest of the plays in the season, it did bring in the largest percentage of new people to the theatre, many who had already come back a second time. The Irish play had actually served the theatre in ways that no one could have predicted (except Patrick!).

What options does this group have before them? Which seem like the best options to follow? What will be the results of following those paths?

Personal exploration

1) Write for yourself a personal mission, vision, and value statement. Keep in mind that even though these statements are about you, you want to follow the same guidelines as if they were about a theatre company.

2) Discuss how you have planned (or should have planned) for some long-term goal, how you followed through, and what the results were. Then imagine what would have happened if you had followed a strategic planning process.

Notes

1 Zimmerman, Steve, and Jeanne Bell, *The Sustainability Mindset: Using the Matrix Map to Make Strategic Decisions,* John Wiley & Sons, 2014.

2 Zavattaro, Staci M., "Expanding Goffman's theater metaphor to an identity-based view of place branding," *Administrative Theory & Praxis* 35, no. 4 (2013): 510–528.

3 Bray, Ilona, *Effective Fundraising for Nonprofits: Real-World Strategies that Work,* Nolo, 2013.

4 Galaskiewicz, Joseph, *Social Organization of an Urban Grants Economy: A Study of Business Philanthropy and Nonprofit Organizations,* Elsevier, 2016.

5 Kearns, Kevin P., "Maintaining public trust," *Ethics in Public Management,* Frederickson, H. George & Ghere, Richard K. (eds.) (p. 265), Routledge, 2014.

6 Martinsuo, Miia, and Catherine P. Killen, "Value management in project portfolios: Identifying and assessing strategic value," *Project Management Journal* 45, no. 5 (2014): 56–70.

7 Greene, Mira Clare, "Theatre patronage in the post-subscription era: Evaluating nontraditional subscription models used by nonprofit theatres and alternative methods of monetization for implementation by California Repertory Company," PhD dissertation, California State University, Long Beach, 2013.

CHAPTER 3

Theatre management today

Patrick had held two positions working in marketing. And in both jobs, he was challenged by the same situation. His audiences were older and seemed to be dying out. In both theatres, his predecessors had not cultivated a younger audience, and now Patrick faced what seemed like an insurmountable challenge: to bring in younger people to replace all the senior citizens. It was an issue that required long-term thinking decades earlier, and without the smart decisions being made long ago, the challenge became very real for Patrick.

Chapter objectives

After reading this chapter, you should be able to describe the difference between management and leadership, illustrate the contents of a SWOT analysis, analyze how theatre seasons can be selected, evaluate the effects of discretionary spending habits on theatres, and generalize some future concerns for theatre managers based on present trends.

Theatre management today

Now that we have examined what the framework has to look like in order to get a theatre off the ground, we move into some of the details. Chapters 4, 5, and 6 will take you through staffing issues, organizational structure issues, and operational issues that will all have to be decided before you can start bringing in the audience. But before making those decisions, it is important to consider some of the challenges that theatre managers face in today's global economy. Once a theatre gets going, the primary functions are making theatre and selling tickets, at least on the surface. And those two functions require so much time, with never enough resources to get them done. So it is rare that the theatre manager can take time to think through and consider the ramifications of global issues that have a local impact. But there are many of them. By thinking through the issues that are causing challenges for theatres today, managers are far more likely to be prepared for the challenges that will arise tomorrow.

We often think that big-picture ideas, such as global economics, foreign policy, and productivity changes do not have much effect on our local theatres, but in fact, these big issues can have a very real impact. For example, the Charlie Hebdo terrorist attack in Paris in 2015 led to an increase in armed troops throughout the city, which contributed to stifled tourism and lower ticket sales to theatres that had already fallen flat.[1] Major catastrophic events, whether caused by nature or human beings, can have a devastating effect on the already fragile balance of finances most theatres struggle with. The events of 9/11 in the United States put many local theatre companies in jeopardy.[2] That may seem odd, until you consider that local theatre companies in the United States operate on a large percentage of donated money, and after 9/11, donors were hard-pressed to contribute to theatres when there were millions of dollars needed to attend to the victims in the aftermath of that tragic day. We cannot plan for every conceivable possibility, but we can prepare for the possibility of sales suddenly dropping off, or loss of the ability to use our facility due to an unforeseen event. There are also global economic forces that affect theatres at the local level.

Theatre managers today include both leaders and managers. The wisest of them is looking not only at how their company is doing today, but how the company will do in the short term, from year to year, and in the long term. In order to do that, there are a number of strategies leaders employ. But in all cases, they have to be thinking about the future in terms of artistry as well as business; they have to consider next season, and how to appropriately plan for it, and they have to analyze their current situation to make the best decisions for the future.

Manager versus leader

We know that a leader devises, or guides the development of, a vision for the future. This person knows where an organization should be going, and shares that knowledge in ways that inspire others to head in the right direction. Managers coordinate resources in order to achieve that vision. While many managers are also leaders, and many leaders are also managers, the functions are quite different. In most theatres, managers are also leaders. But the leader is not simply the person with the most powerful office, and the vision may not have to do with ticket sales and bank accounts.

Creativity

Artistic directors have a function that is quite often of a managerial nature. They are responsible for coordinating resources to ensure that the artistic product meets the mission and vision of the company. They use their skills, expertise, and connections to create quality art. They do so with an understanding of how their choices may shape the nature of the art that is created by the company. Some artistic directors stretch further than this. They meet the needs of the organization, but they also have a vision for the future that includes changing how an organization creates art. That may mean developing new plays or new artists, or it may mean trying unique and experimental approaches. Some of the best artistic directors keep their theatres going in the same direction they have headed for decades; however, others are constantly working to find new ways to consider and represent the art of theatre. There is no right or wrong way to approach creativity, but well-managed theatres know which direction they choose to head, both creatively and entrepreneurially.

Entrepreneurship

While it is easy to consider artistic visions, sometimes it is not so clear what a managing director might do to be visionary, largely because most growth and change in a theatre is related, somehow, to the artistic product. But the person responsible for the non-artistic administration of a theatre has plenty of opportunity to be visionary as well. Beyond seeing artistic achievements, it is just as visionary to imagine what an audience will look like in the future, or how a company will serve a community differently. Savvy managers make investments today that will pay off for their successors in the decades ahead. This was not always the case, as evidenced by the changing attendance patterns of the baby boomer generation.

Vision

While it is important not to lose sight of the large, global issues that can and will affect theatre, it is also important to stay focused on smaller, local issues as well. Changes in the local economy, crime occurring near a theatre, a new mayor, or any number of sudden differences in a community can all affect a local theatre company. It is important to be prepared for change, and also to be adaptable and flexible when external environments change. The key is to constantly assess what might happen tomorrow, based on what is occurring today.

A vision for the long term is vitally important. But it comes with the requirement that we know what signposts we expect to see along the way. If a theatre company sets its sights on producing a new play in the West End, it may expect that along the way it will have achieved a certain volume of sales locally, a production that transfers to Edinburgh and Belfast, a tour of Europe, and finally a production on the West End. Knowing what signposts to expect in the shorter term is vitally important to achieving a vision in the long term.

SWOT analysis

To plan for the future and develop that long-term vision, a theatre has to know and understand the environment in which it presently exists. As we briefly noted in the previous chapter, the term *SWOT analysis*, or just SWOT, is an acronym for strengths, weaknesses, opportunities, and threats.[3] The SWOT is a way to examine the internal and external environments that affect a project, team, person, industry, organization, or venture. It is not a complex process, but simply a listing of those items that fall under each heading of strengths and weaknesses (which look at positive and negative internal issues) and opportunities and threats (which look at positive and negative external issues).

Strengths are those internal items that give a project or organization an advantage over other projects or organizations. The Royal Shakespeare Company (RSC) may have a particularly noteworthy artistic director whose reputation is so strong that the organization can present more risky fare without losing ticket sales. The artistic director's reputation is a strength because it gives the organization an advantage from the inside.

Weaknesses are internal items that cause the organization or project to be at a disadvantage when compared to like projects or organizations. If the RSC's artistic director has a desire to present the same productions over and over, this might be a disadvantage for the company. The artistic director's choices are a weakness because they are internal and cause a disadvantage.

Note that in both those examples, the artistic director is involved. This can be confusing, as people sometimes find that one issue appears in more than one of the lists of the SWOT. But if you look closely, the two things are actually quite different. The strength is actually artistic director reputation, and the weakness is artistic choices. It is important to recognize the difference when creating a SWOT.

Opportunities are external things that the project or organization could take advantage of to improve its situation. A new play festival in Hamburg could be an opportunity for a French theatre company to expand their reach. Note that opportunities may be available to lots of other organizations, but as they are listed, it is easy to assess which opportunities may be the most effective or unique.

Threats are occurrences external to the organization that might lead to problems for the organization. A frequently cited threat to organizations is the possibility of a strike by one of the unions that represent employees in a theatre. A threat might also be the emergence of a new theatre company, or the election of a new mayor, a new entertainment tax, a series of poor reviews, and on and on. Threats can be things that have occurred, will occur, or might occur. In the SWOT, we list them all, and consider each for how likely and potentially damaging they may be.

The SWOT is an excellent tool for analyzing potential business decisions, because it allows the decision-maker to break down key data into its relevant areas. Being able to analyze multiple projects using a SWOT allows for the positives and negatives of each potential project to be compared. Similarly, the SWOT allows us to see where a project or organization has potential downfalls that can be addressed and improved upon.

Selecting a season

To effectively run a theatre, managers need to pay extremely close attention to the two internal issues in the SWOT when they are deciding what their company will produce in a year's time. While theatre managers often approach selecting what plays to produce as a chance to exercise the biggest artistic decision, it is a challenging task. If you think of the play as the product a theatre creates, you may be able to see why selecting a play or a season is challenging. In the manufacturing sector, companies have marketing professionals who study buyer behavior and test for buyer preferences. They use the data to develop ideas for new products that fit the company's mission and serve the consumer.[4] Those new products are created by designers, developed by engineers, and then tested in the market to see if they receive the response that the data indicated. Companies can spend millions just to see if a new idea is going to prove successful.

With art, such as theatre, we cannot know how the audience will react until the art is complete. Some might argue that we should not know or consider how the audience will react. But philosophical arguments aside, theatres have presented preview performances for centuries as a way to rehearse the interaction between the production and the audience. Investors in major productions now demand test audiences be brought in to gauge likely response by the marketplace. Directors and producers often find themselves at odds regarding how much a production, or even a whole theatre, should cater to the wants of the marketplace.

Every theatre has a slightly different way in which it selects a season, and it is because audiences are different, missions are different, and the players are different. But what most theatres seem to forget is that in order to be most successful with an audience, they need to be consistent. Selecting plays on a whim is perfectly acceptable, but it should be consistent with the mission of the company. If the company serves the whims of whoever is doing the selecting, and states that in its mission, consistency has been met. Some theatre companies have an artistic director who has sole discretion to select plays, and the best of those companies make it clear in their mission that they serve their community by presenting the talents and decisions of their artistic director. But artistic directors with that sort of discretion have typically attained their position because they are adept at collecting pertinent information from others, weighing all factors, and then making a determination based on the data.

Most theatre companies have some group or committee that provides the information or feedback, and many allow that group or committee to determine the season. The challenge in this format is that the strong-willed, very vocal, or manipulative tend to push their agenda at the expense of others. But this does not have to be the case. A theatre company with a core list of artistic values can easily weigh and rank potential plays against that list. Taken even further, if the company determines how much weight they give each value in terms of a percentage, the ranking process becomes even simpler. Of course, anyone doing the ranking will have a subjective option about how well a specific play meets each value, but if the company also determines how much weight each participant's opinion matters as a percentage, the entire process can become far less political.

If a company were to give the artistic director's opinion 50% of the overall consideration and each of five other staff members 10%, simple math can be used to calculate the weight of their ranking for each play on each value. Likewise, if a value such as "well known to our audience" is worth 20% of the total list of values, and a value of "pushes our creative boundaries" is worth 30%, with five other values each worth 10%, simple math can be used to calculate how each potential play ranks against a company's artistic values. While a system such as this is by no means perfect, it does help to keep a theatre focused on mission, and allows for greater consistency. This mathematical model is simply a different way of comparing plays using the internal measures in the SWOT. Rankings allow for comparison on a sliding scale with strengths on one end of the scale, perhaps at ten, and weaknesses at the other, perhaps at zero. Art is impossible to predict, and audiences prefer things that are comfortable and familiar to them but also like theatre that is new and different. One of the best ways to balance those two diametrically opposed ideas is to remain consistent in the selection of a season.

Questions to research for class discussion:

Search the Internet and find answers for these questions before you read any further. Be prepared to discuss them in class.

3.1   Research three theatres on the Internet and based on the plays they have been presenting, create a list of criteria you think they may be using for selecting plays. Explain why you think so.

3.2   Research a real example of a theatre company presenting a play that does not fit their mission.

3.3   What are some ways theatres can improve consistency in selecting a season of play titles?

Discretionary income

Big, global issues require managers to think about the external points on the SWOT, opportunities and particularly threats. We often think the competition theatres face is from other theatres. We look at their prices, the quality of their productions, and the size of their audiences, and we try to exceed where our competitors are on those metrics. Some savvy theatre managers do not see other theatres as competitors, but instead think of them as actually good for business, because any quality theatre an audience sees encourages further theatre-going. The same might be said for the arts in general. It is better to have people enjoying the arts, even if they are not in your audience today, because if they enjoy the arts, you are far more likely to see them or their children come through your doors some day.

But theatre managers are remiss if they do not consider audiences from a much larger perspective. When considering who our competitors are, we are thinking about economics, and where people are spending money that they could be spending with us. This means that we are considering *discretionary income*. This is the money that a person has after taxes and basic needs such as housing, food, and clothing are paid for. Discretionary income is what we choose to spend our money on, and that means theatres have a lot of competition. Discretionary income is part of our *disposable income*, which is the total amount of money we have after taxes are paid. When the economy is strong, and the total amount of output the country is generating is high, goods are sold at lower prices, meaning our money can stretch further, and we end up with more discretionary income. When there is inflation, and prices are high, there is less discretionary income. For any individual, the change may seem insignificant, but when you add all that together through an entire country, the loss of discretionary income can be in the billions. And theatre is one of the first expenses people may choose to cut out. Changes in spending patterns today, unfortunately, will affect our audiences of tomorrow, because if parents are not introducing their children to the theatre, and if schools are not spending time on the arts, those children are far less likely to become audience members in the future.

Theatres may be wise in not expecting to compete for our discretionary income with things like retirement savings or college funds, but they are just as wise if they consider the vast numbers of competitors out there who are trying to capitalize on our discretionary income. Consider services such as health care and insurance. Over the course of the last fifty years, these two services have consumed an increasing amount of our discretionary income. And while we are spending a little less on goods, we have added things like cellular telephones, Internet contracts, and cable television to our lives, each of which takes a rather substantial portion of our discretionary income.

There is scant research to suggest that we are attending theatre less to dine out more, but over the last fifty years, discretionary spending on dining out has increased, perhaps because the big chain restaurants have expanded exponentially, and spending on live theatre has decreased. Every community is different and provides different opportunities for discretionary spending, but it is important to always consider who is competing against us for that money.

Questions to research for class discussion:

Search the Internet and find answers for these questions before you read any further. Be prepared to discuss them in class.

3.4 How has discretionary spending changed in our country?
3.5 Besides the studies that have been done, where do you think people may be more inclined to spend their money and why?
3.6 In your local community, where do you think discretionary spending is occurring the most, and why?

Changes in productivity

Productivity is an important concept for theatre managers to consider, though there is little we can do about it. *Productivity* is a ratio that compares the amount we are able to produce to the amount it costs to produce it. If it costs half as much today to make something, then we have doubled our productivity, and are able to lower the price or increase the profit or a combination of the two. The biggest drain on productivity is labor, because when adjusted for inflation, the cost of labor is more or less consistent. But when innovation and technology provide tools to improve the amount of output labor can produce, we become more productive. In fact, globally, we can now produce about four times what we could produce in 1950 for the same cost.[5] The world is very productive. Sounds great, right? Because if it only costs one-fourth of what it used to, then prices can drop, profits go up, and we can buy more.

Technological advances have occurred in theatre as well. We now have computerized box office systems, soundboards, light boards, and the like. But in theatre, we are not making a good. In the strictest sense, what we sell to our audience member is a leasehold on a seat in our building. We add value to that lease by putting something on the stage that makes using the seat during the term of the lease attractive. The product we put on the stage, the play, still requires the same number of performers it did in 1950, and those actors still require the same amount of rehearsal as they did in 1850. Certainly, theatres have become a bit more productive on the technical end, but live theatre cannot keep pace with global productivity increases. Why does that matter? As the world increases in productivity, prices are able to remain low. But theatres cannot keep their prices low, because they cannot improve productivity. The most expensive theatre ticket in the world today costs about four times more than the most expensive ticket in 1950, when adjusted for inflation, suggesting that the increase in productivity that has affected so many other industries, has not had the same effect on theatre.

Generational shifts

"Our audiences are dying off!" "All I see is a sea of blue hair!" "We have to get more young people in here!" Theatre managers consistently utter these phrases, and you may find yourself agreeing with them, with good reason. All three of them are true. Go back and read them again. They are all absolutely true. The interesting thing about it is that they were all true ten years ago, and twenty years ago, and a hundred years ago.[6] So you may wonder why we keep seeing an audience full of aging senior citizens, the make-up of which does not ever seem to change. The answer lies in this simple fact: as senior citizens in the audience age, they are replaced by new people who are just entering their golden years. Theatregoers tend to be people who have plenty of discretionary income, as well as the time to invest in attending the arts, and those people are typically retired, or at least more mature, with children who have left the nest. A third factor affecting attendance is that theatre audiences have to have had adequate exposure to the arts in their youth to be able to appreciate the arts in their retirement. Without that early exposure, most people cannot later be convinced to try theatre in retirement. The seeds for enjoying the theatre are planted in one's youth, and often do not bear fruit for a theatre for fifty years.

Today, the baby boomer generation is retiring. These are the children of parents who lived during World War II. They came of age during the rebellious 1970s. They were raised in a time when government support and subsidies post-World War II allowed people to live with greater wealth and opportunity. In fact, about 80% of the world's wealth is in the hands of the baby boomer generation, which got its name because there was a large population growth spurt after World War II.[7] It is a big group of people.

For theatres, the retirement of the baby boomer generation, people now in their fifties and sixties, seemed like a welcome opportunity. The generation has plenty of money, seemingly plenty of exposure to the arts in their youth,

Think critically: productivity is going to change theatre

There are two ways to approach this class discussion. First, you can choose sides. Divide the class into three, by whatever means you choose, and debate the argument outlined below. Second, you can have an open discussion, each adding upon the others' thoughts, and let the discussion uncover all the important details of all sides of the debate. Keep in mind that regardless of which approach you take, we want to be sure we dig deep into all sides of this important issue, in order to more effectively understand all positions.

CLASS DISCUSSION: Since 1950 worldwide productivity has increased four-fold. But theatre, by its very nature, seems unable to improve productivity. In that same time span the price of theatre has increased fourfold when adjusted for inflation. How can theatre survive, or even keep pace? There are many possibilities, three of which come to the forefront: Do we focus on becoming elitist and only for the wealthy? Do we band together and demand more governmental support? Do we worry about our own existence today and wait, allowing market forces and societal changes to determine what society wants?

and as they retire, they will have plenty of time. But the anticipated explosion in ticket sales has not occurred. In fact, worldwide, we continue to see a decline in theatre ticket sales.[8]

So what is going on and what does it mean for theatre in the future? Those are excellent questions, and no one knows the answers. It is possible that the baby boomer generation, the first to be raised on television, simply did not have the same type of exposure to the arts that their parents had appreciated. But if that is the case, their children and their children's children may also stay away from the theatre.

Beginning in the 1970s, schools began decreasing the amount of arts education and exposure students received. Will this have some future impact on our theatres? Only time will tell. But the smart theatre manager is the one who begins today to invest in the audiences of tomorrow. Chapter 15 addresses the challenges that theatre managers deal with in the face of declining arts education.

Questions to research for:

Search the Internet and find answers for these questions before you read any further. Be prepared to discuss them in class.

3.7   What are the reasons you believe baby boomers are not filling our theatres the way past generations have? List at least three things you think have affected this generation, and find online articles that support your ideas.

3.8 What has been done to address the problems you cited in the last question? What more can be done to address the problem?

3.9 Considering your answers to the last two questions, what do you think will happen when the next generation, Generation X, begins to retire?

Change in an electronic society

Just a few years ago, theatres did not have computers. Manual sliders dimmed lights, and tickets were printed for every seat in advance and taken from huge racks where they were stored to be sold to a patron. Programs were typed up on a typewriter and given to a typesetter who would use specialized equipment to prepare them for print. Students spent long hours focusing on projection, because microphones were rare, imprecise, and not yet wireless. Ticket purchases were made by mail or in person with a check. And most theatres could not fathom what they would ever do with a computer, even if they had one.

Today, we exchange vast amounts of goods and money on the Internet. Banking is done electronically, and even credit cards are beginning to lose traction as the most convenient form of payment. But more than financial transaction, the electronic age has revolutionized communication. Newspapers and magazines are folding at an alarming rate, as there are easier, more convenient, and less expensive ways to catch up on news and information. And while the telephone long ago replaced handwritten letters as a primary source of communication, text messages have now overtaken email. The pace at which communication methods have changed is staggering. These are important considerations not only for where we are today, but also for where communication may lead. Theatre has at its core, communication. Actors communicate with one another, they communicate a message to the audience, and audience members communicate with one another. As human beings adapt to different types of communication, their wants and needs for communication change as well. When a human being encounters some new piece of information, the brain releases dopamine, which causes a "feel good" sensation. With texts, tweets, pictures, information, and every person we have ever met virtually at our fingertips all the time, we are constantly able to experience some new piece of information. Researchers find that people click through different online windows and search different pieces of information at a startling rate. And multitasking may sound good, but it actually increases stress levels.[9]

What does all this mean for theatre? Well, we are already seeing a decline in television viewership and movie attendance, two industries with billions to spend on marketing and promotion. But this pace at which we communicate, and the ability to have more and more on demand, is changing behavior.

Theatres are seeking ways to adapt to a changing society. Britain's Digital Theatre works with top companies to record and resell high-quality videos of stage productions, on demand, and at affordable prices. New Paradise Laboratories in Philadelphia incorporates social media into its stage productions, sometimes weeks before the play opens, creating blurred lines between what is real and what is not. London's Elastic Future has done theatre with actors performing simultaneously in England, Spain, and Nigeria, using electronic means.[10]

The boundaries that have limited theatre such as time and geographical location have been and continue to be altered or lifted.[11] Devised theatre and performance art have expanded the definition of theatre, and the darkened room with lots of chairs facing a stage is giving way to performance spaces that can be found anywhere in the world. This is not to suggest that theatre as we know it is about to disappear with the likes of vaudeville. Rather, theatre is expanding in an effort to keep pace with the changing digital world.

Growth and adaptation

Human society is driven by growth. In the marketplace, in order to grow, businesses have to stay ahead of changing customer needs. Theorists and researchers have developed many different ways of looking at the growth of a fledgling business, and there seems to be little agreement on the number of stages or the relevance of each. For a theatre company, we look at the phases of start-up, initial growth, maintenance, change, and next steps. Each of these terms has a synonym in various growth theories, but regardless of how they are labeled, they represent the typical process. The distinction is that we use the audience as our benchmark, where growth theories often use gross sales and company size as the key metrics.

In the *start-up* phase, a theatre is beginning to find an audience. This phase is typically marked by going from zero audience members to a point where audience members are returning. In this phase, the theatre tends to be more focused on the product with less focus on the audience. Once a significant number of audience members are returning to the theatre, the company can be said to have transitioned into *growth* phase. In the growth phase, the company is actively seeking an increase in audience size while simultaneously working to improve repeat attendance. The internal focus shifts toward business decisions to ensure that the audience size is robust and growing. Artistry is not necessarily supplanted or moved down in importance, but audience growth and development become more important to the company.

When the theatre company meets the audience metrics it has set for itself in the growth phase, the company shifts into a *maintenance* phase. In this phase, the company continues to produce artistic product of the caliber, quantity, and style that it has become known for. The audience size may grow or shrink to some degree season after season, but it is rare that there are any enormous shifts in audience size. New programs are typically developed and added during the maintenance phase, frequently through granted funding, that connect new members of the community to the theatre. The maintenance phase is most often the longest phase, and can last several decades.

The next phase theatres typically encounter is the *change* phase. The change phase is marked by a substantial alteration in the creation of artistic product, or a sudden shift in the audience, or both. Sometimes the change phase is a result of a departing artistic director, who is replaced by someone with a new and different artistic vision. Occasionally, some particular presentation causes a sudden increase or decrease in audience size, which leads to drastically different budgetary issues than anticipated. In any case, in the change phase, the first response tends to be to attempt to bring the theatre back into maintenance, but this is rarely achievable. Most often, the theatre moves into the *next steps* phase.

In the next steps phase, the theatre is forced to make strategic decisions about how to move forward. Theatres that have lost audience must examine why the loss has occurred, and mitigate the problems while simultaneously attempting to return to the growth phase. Theatres that have changed artistic focus must determine if the company can weather the change while the audience shifts from one that appreciated the past artistic direction to one that will appreciate the new one. Theatres that fail to ask and answer the difficult questions in the next steps phase often find that the next step is shutting the company down.

Succession planning

One issue mentioned in the change phase is a change in personnel. Every organization that lasts will eventually see people go, and others come in to replace them. For well-established theatre companies, with long-serving managers (executive directors, managing directors, artistic directors, and so on), it is important to plan for their eventual departure. These managers who have worked at a company for a very long time hold a great deal of knowledge about the theatre, how it works, and who it works with, and they guide decision-making in a way the audience has become accustomed to. Drastic changes in any of that, caused by suddenly bringing in a new person unfamiliar with the theatre, can spell disaster. Well-established theatres are wise to look at who on their staff might one day be able to step into those top positions. In *succession planning*, the organization looks at who might be able to take on those positions, tries to figure out what additional training they may need, and how long that training will take before they are ready for a

Build your theatre milestone 3: develop a SWOT

Develop an exhaustive set of four lists of strengths, weaknesses, opportunities, and threats that exist or may exist for your theatre company. Be sure to consider things like the talents people will bring to your company, the economic make-up of the community in which you intend to establish your company, the types of businesses that currently exist there, and how you can create great theatre without great financial resources.

higher position. Often, more than one person is being prepared for a higher position, and when the time for change comes, one is selected, and the rest typically find other jobs. This means that you have spent a great deal of time training several people who will put that training to use elsewhere. But it also ensures that your theatre will always remain consistent and strong.

Case study

Patrick had been culling through sales numbers for the past several years, and was really starting to become concerned about the trends he was seeing. Fifteen years ago, 75% of his audience had been subscribers, purchasing the entire season of plays in one purchase. Today, about 30% of his audience was made up of subscribers. The total attendance had only dropped a small amount over the years, so the company had not had too much concern over the shifting buying patterns. And though the marketing budget had been drastically increased, because it is far less expensive to sell a season once rather than to sell several individual plays, the cost of single tickets was higher, so the extra revenue was there to pay for the increased marketing. Patrick recalled that during his interview Frank had mentioned increased marketing money and how he believed it helped to build awareness of the company. On a surface level, there seemed to be no cause for alarm.

But as Patrick dug deeper, he came to realize that fifteen years ago 75% of his total audience was over the age of fifty-five, and the majority of those audience members were buying subscriptions. Most single ticket buyers were under the age of fifty-five. Today, almost 90% of the total ticket buyers were over the age of sixty, and the subscribers were mostly over sixty-five and had been subscribing for many years. If the trend continued, in a few years there would be no more subscribers. Of course this would not be of concern as long as there continued to be buyers of single tickets to offset the loss of subscribers.

The final piece of information, which truly gave Patrick pause, was that fifteen years ago, 50% of the total audience was new, or first-time ticket buyers, but today, only about 20% of the audience was coming to attend for the first time.

The company seemed to have done an excellent job of keeping patrons coming back, but had been less successful in finding new audiences. Patrick knew that the current course would likely be unsustainable, but he saw that he had a window of several years to attempt to correct the situation. He sat down and wondered what he could do to develop a plan that would consider immediate, short-term, and long-term strategies to solve the problem he saw occurring. He could divert some of his marketing money to programs designed to strengthen future sales, but that might reduce the amount of income the company was generating presently. He could ask for additional funding to focus on the long term, but Frank was already aware that the marketing budget had been steadily increasing for the past fifteen years. He knew he needed ideas that wouldn't drastically change funding patterns, but could work toward developing a future audience, be it subscribers or single ticket buyers.

Given the information Patrick had at his disposal, what are the threats and challenges you see for him in the present as well as in the short term and long term? Since no long-term strategy had yet been employed, what do you think Patrick should propose to deal with the issues he faces? How would you expect the company to react to his proposals, and how would you demonstrate the importance of your suggestions?

Personal exploration

As a student, you are developing yourself for a future. You may not know exactly what path you intend to take, but you are thinking about what you might enjoy and what might be the most fruitful for you. Conduct a SWOT analysis on yourself as a student and future working member of society.

Notes

1 Foris, Diana, "Tourism policies and strategies: Vital in the actual security constrains context," *Universal Journal of Management* 4, no. 3 (2016): 108–112.

2 Berrebi, Claude, and Hanan Yonah, "Terrorism and philanthropy: The effect of terror attacks on the scope of giving by individuals and households," *Public Choice* 169, no. 3–4 (2016): 171–194.

3 Ashley, Amanda J., "Strategic planning for arts, culture, and entertainment districts," (2016).

4 Balfour, Danny L., and Ramya Ramanath, "Forging theatre and community: Challenges and strategies for serving two missions," *Public Voices* 12, no. 1 (2016): 46–66.

5 Lucas, Robert E., "The industrial revolution: Past and future," *Lectures on Economic Growth* (2002): 109–188.

6 Ateca-Amestoy, Victoria, and Juan Prieto-Rodriguez, "Forecasting accuracy of behavioural models for participation in the arts," *European Journal of Operational Research* 229, no. 1 (2013): 124–131.

7 Chand, Masud, and Rosalie L. Tung, "The aging of the world's population and its effects on global business," *The Academy of Management Perspectives* 28, no. 4 (2014): 409–429.

8 Zieba, Marta, "Tourism flows and the demand for regional and city theatres in Austria," *Journal of Cultural Economics* 40, no. 2 (2016): 191–221.

9 Hefner, Dorothée, and Peter Vorderer, "Permanent connectedness and multitasking," *The Routledge Handbook of Media Use and Well-Being: International Perspectives on Theory and Research on Positive Media Effects* (2016): 237.

10 Pan, Joann, 'Internet-based theatre company lives between cyberspace and the stage,' *Mashable*. 24 March 2013.

11 Wyver, John, "Screening the RSC stage: The 2014 live from Stratford-upon-Avon cinema broadcasts," *Shakespeare* 11, no. 3 (2015): 286–302.

CHAPTER 4

Business environments

Patrick was working in quite an unusual world. He was assistant marketing director, but he was actually an assistant to no one. And he found this frustrating. His
pay was not very high, given his level of responsibility, so a better title would
have provided some value to him, if it were something other than "assistant." His
job was enjoyable, and he liked the people he worked with, including Frank, so he
never complained, even though he sometimes thought his title was indicative of
a company that was structured strangely. And even though he found happiness
in his work, he wondered if there was a document somewhere that indicated the
way the company was governed had gotten off track.

Chapter objectives

After reading this chapter, you should be able to describe the different types
of business structures available to theatres, explain how commercial theatre
productions are governed, define how nonprofit organizations are structured, evaluate the value of nonprofit executive salaries, and demonstrate
the construction of by-laws.

Business environments

One of the most important decisions you will have to make when you set out
to start a theatre company is what sort of business structure you will operate
under. We often think theatre is a charitable business, because so many countries recognize the advancement of art as important for the common good,
and they offer certain benefits to those of us who endeavor to contribute in
this way to society. It is certainly true that there are many charitable theatres,
but the commercial productions on Broadway, the West End, and large cities
throughout the world are built on a business structure that is registered with
the government, just as our local theatres are. Those commercial theatres
are not asking to be treated as if their primary function is to benefit society,
although most theatres in the world are setting out to make a difference in

their communities by creating an artistic product that can elevate discourse and enrich people's lives. But whether driven by commercial profit or a desire to contribute to the world, any theatre has to have a legal business structure under which it operates.

Types of business structures

Modern countries that regulate business structures all have unique ways they approach similar challenges, but at the heart of every plan for ways to structure businesses is the idea that the way the company is created rests solely upon the notion of ownership. Ownership can be thought of as being defined by two main issues: who reaps the benefits from the company, and who takes responsibility for the company's failures. We might consider this to boil down to profit and loss, but it could also be thought of in less material terms such as the joy of viewing great theatre (a benefit), or the lawsuit when a company acts negligently and causes harm (a responsibility). Governments register the business structure so they know who is gaining what benefit (which is often taxable), and who should be addressed with legal issues if that ever needs to occur. It seems simple enough, but in fact, the process can be very complex, with many potential business structures existing. An individual may solely own a business. Another business may be a joint venture between two people. Yet a third could consist of many individuals, and many companies are made of hundreds of thousands of shareholders who jointly own the business. Perhaps the public owns an organization, like a municipality or a theatre company operating for the public good, but it still has to operate under some sort of formal structure. In many cases, even individual owners or business partners do not wish to be personally liable if their company fails, so they register for a structure that places the burden of failure on the company. But by doing so, they also make the business a taxable entity. You can see that deciding the best way to register a company is tricky. Governments have devised a collection of structures that can meet virtually any desired business design, though at their heart, there are really three main, legal business structures: sole proprietor/trader, partnership, and corporation. Depending on what country you happen to be in, the names could be slightly different, but most countries have structures for each of these three types of business.

A *sole proprietor* or *sole trader* is an individual who establishes a business and operates that business as if it was a separate entity, but for legal purposes, the business and its operator are one and the same. Once registered, a sole proprietorship can conduct business, including the hiring of employees. The business can register a business name, but all the assets of the business, and all the profits (after taxes) belong to the business owner. However, any losses, including bankruptcy, are also attached to the owner, so if the business loses money, the owner is expected to make up the loss. The owner cannot simply walk away from a sole proprietorship, as she is said to have "unlimited liability." This means that if the business is sued, and loses the lawsuit, the owner is personally liable. If a person is injured at the business and wins millions in a lawsuit, the owner is personally responsible for making good on that obligation. Being the sole person to receive the profits is a wonderful reward, but it comes with obvious risk.

A *partnership* is similar in nature to the sole proprietorship, except in the case of the partnership, two or more people share in the ownership of the company, meaning they share in the benefits and the liabilities. Partnerships do not always have to be equal. Partners can determine who will contribute to the company and in what amount, including labor, skill, money, time, property, and the like, and based on how much each will contribute, a fair distribution of benefits and liabilities is agreed upon. As you can imagine, while it is not a requirement, partnerships work best when there is a very clearly written agreement detailing how the partners contribute to and benefit from the business, how they can sell their ownership stake in the business, and how they are expected to work together. While the partnership generally has unlimited liability, many governments provide different variations on the partnership structure that allows for some liability to be limited, meaning that the partners may be partially or fully protected personally from the actions of the company.

A *corporation* is a business that is legally separate from its owners in terms of both benefit and risk. Corporations sell portions of themselves to the owners through shares in a stock offering. Those owners are not responsible for legal decisions of the company, and they receive their share of the profit, which they must pay personal income tax on, after the business has paid its corporate tax. You can see that as a shareholder, you are safe from potential liabilities, but the money you are earning is actually taxed two times, first as part of a corporation, and then as part of your income. Corporations operate under a great number of legal requirements, so unless a business is quite large, the corporate structure is rarely a good option. For theatres, the corporate structure has yet to prove to be beneficial.

These three main types of legal business structures are by no means the only types of structures that exist. Different governments offer different structures, though most offer some variation of a sole trader, partnership, and corporation that also has limited liability, meaning that the owners may not be responsible for all (or any) of the company's debts. But when a company is registered with limited liability, there are often additional tax burdens that the owners will face. And in the case of a limited liability partnership, there is typically one person who is named to manage the company, meaning the rest of the owners have less control over the operation of the business.

Questions to research for class discussion:

Search the Internet and find answers for these questions before you read any further. Be prepared to discuss them in class.

4.1   What are the different types of business structures available to you and how do they differ?

4.2   Which two of those structures that you identified in the last question seem like the best choices for a theatre company, and why? How would one of those two be better than the other?

4.3   Is there a business structure that would allow the owner to have limited liability, while also retaining complete artistic control? If so, which one and why? If not, why not?

Legal structures for theatre

Some impresarios who want to be theatre producers will register as a sole trader, and they will use their own money, or proceeds from loans they are responsible for, to fund a production. They pay to secure rights; they hire the cast, crew, and design staff; they lease a facility; they pay for a box office team; and they collect the income from the ticket sales. There are also partnerships that do the same kind of thing. Often one partner is the playwright, one will direct, and one handles the finances and hiring. They make an arrangement about the value of the contribution each makes, and they also determine how to split up any profits.

While a theatre could choose to register itself in any number of ways, the most typical registration for a theatre is the limited liability company.

Corporate entities for commercial theatre

In the case of commercial productions, such as those that tour the world, a *limited liability company* is typically created with multiple owners who invest in the production with their money, time, or talent. Typically there is an *executive producer* who is the person responsible for running the company. Often, the executive producer is the person who finds a script to produce, finds investors in the company who become additional *producers*, hires all the production staff, makes all the legal arrangements, and coordinates the details of the production. The executive producer is the managing partner of the limited liability company, and the company's function is to create and sell a production. Should the production prove successful, another production may be embarked upon. If that is the case, a new limited liability legal entity is formed so that new investors, or the same ones if they so choose, can become a part of that production, each retaining their share of ownership percentage as agreed upon based on their contribution. The executive producer may never invest his or her own money, but typically takes the largest percentage of the profit based on the amount of time and effort he or she contributes to making the production happen.

The purpose of nonprofit theatres

Many theatre companies that are created for the purpose of producing a regular season of plays incorporate as a limited liability company, but ask for the special designation of *not-for-profit* (also referred to as nonprofit), which denotes that the company's main purpose is not to make a profit. While we use nonprofit and not-for-profit interchangeably, in different jurisdictions they may have slightly different legal requirements, though in either case, they refer to a business with a primary function other than profit. Notice that the designation does not mean they cannot make a profit in the sense that bringing in excess revenue is a profit. These companies are simply not motivated primarily by the goal of profit. And because their primary function is not profit, any excess revenue is returned to the company to help further its primary function, rather than being given to owners. This is not to suggest that a nonprofit exists to simply spend money and never concern itself with generating revenue. In fact, quite the reverse is usually the case. A consistent revenue stream is essential for a nonprofit that expends money, such as a theatre company, in order to be able to continue to do the good work it does. Nonprofits of this nature sometimes are said to have a *double bottom line*, which means they must operate in a financially responsible way, growing through regular profits that are reinvested into the organization, but they are also beholden to being steadfast in their mission of service. This is one of the reasons the mission statement is so important for nonprofit theatres. It is their very reason for existence, and it is by this statement that the theatre company can determine if it is doing the best it possibly can.

Nonprofits and how they work

Since these companies actually can make a profit, which is reinvested in the company, the terms "nonprofit" and "not-for-profit" can be confusing; it has been said that referring to a company as "not-for-profit" is the same as referring to a horse as "not-an-elephant." In other words, while the name is true, it explains very little. In fact, a not-for-profit is really a company that does not have any specific, individual owners, but is actually owned by the public at large because the company's primary function is to benefit society in some way. A board of directors typically governs this public ownership.

Nonprofits come in all shapes and sizes, from private foundations that serve to support one or more causes of their choosing by providing direct financial support to those causes, to organizations focused on curing specific diseases, to religious organizations, to the arts. Remember that the primary function is to provide some societal benefit. In fact, the types of organizations mentioned above are sometimes referred to as NGOs, or *non-governmental organizations*, because they are fulfilling a need for society that is not being met adequately by government. The term NGO has been around since 1945, when it was introduced in the charter for the United Nations.[1] Though the term was initially created to allow these types of organizations to have non-voting access to United Nations assemblies, it is now generally considered to refer to nonprofits worldwide. Though the terms nonprofit and NGO are sometimes used interchangeably, because they both provide service to the community, they are technically distinct based on the legal criteria under which they are created.

When a company has registered itself as a limited liability company (or other structure that the government will allow to receive the not-for-profit status) it can then request not-for-profit or charitable status. In some governments, not-for-profit status is linked with charitable status, and in others those designations are different. But in both cases, when a company registers for not-for-profit status, it is typically asking to be relieved from some or all of its tax liabilities. Governments offer this benefit as a way of encouraging organizations to take on the work of providing a benefit to society. And it means exactly what it sounds like: not-for-profit organizations are often tax-exempt.

Questions to research for class discussion:

Search the Internet and find answers for these questions before you read any further. Be prepared to discuss them in class.

4.4   Where you live, what are the benefits of being a not-for-profit versus being a for-profit?

4.5   What are the limits on salary and benefits for the executives and staffs of nonprofits? Why do those limits exist and how are they governed or policed? Also, find the highest paid nonprofit executive you can.

4.6   What are the formal requirements and necessary forms required to incorporate a nonprofit? How would you describe the complexity of the forms required?

4.7   If you were deciding to register as a charitable organization today, what would you need to know about in order to file appropriately (for example, is being a charitable organization different than filing for not-for-profit status, and why)?

Salaries, expenses, and focus

Some nonprofits executives make a lot of money – even in the millions. There are nonprofit companies that serve all sorts of functions, and some of them are very large and require very specific skills, developed by years of work as an executive. Even in nonprofit theatre, though it is rare for executives to make huge salaries, there are a few worldwide who make many times over what the average citizen does. And they probably should. Running a large company, whether it is for-profit or non-profit, requires a lot of expertise, time, and dedication.

How a nonprofit theatre chooses to spend its money is not dictated by the government, even though the government does want to see a report of what money came in and how it was spent (this is what we report for tax purposes). But the decisions about how best to spend income is left up to the individual company, and that is true whether the company is for-profit or nonprofit. If the company determines that an executive should make millions, and there is enough money in the budget to pay it, then that is how much the executive is paid. While there are often guidelines to hinder a nonprofit from distorting or taking advantage of the system, there are typically not mandates. We certainly would not expect to see a theatre company which generates one million a year paying 900,000 to its executive. Most would consider that excessive; but reasonable pay, and even high salaries, might be appropriate.

In the commercial theatre, the executive producer receives a share of the profits (sometimes in addition to drawing a regular salary), and that can easily be in the millions if a production is a huge hit. Why would people ever want to go into nonprofit theatre if there is a limit on how much they can achieve financially? Wouldn't it make more sense to pursue commercial theatre management, where the sky is the limit? The answer is, maybe.

The big difference, and this is why the nonprofit status is granted, is because the commercial theatre producer in a for-profit company has that primary goal of making money. The nonprofit theatre has a more altruistic primary goal of making art and providing some sort of experience to the community. We say that those rewards for work that come from outside, such as a large salary, are *extrinsic rewards*. Profit is a prime example of an extrinsic reward. *Intrinsic rewards* are those we gain that are not provided from outside us, but are actually things we feel on the inside as a result of a behavior. So being able to provide art to the community, while it may not pay as well, provides some level of intrinsic reward. Those who feel great about doing something worthwhile often find that this is a greater reward than a high salary or a share of the profit. It is these executives who can keep a nonprofit focused on its primary mission.

Legal obligations in forming and running a nonprofit theatre

It is not simply enough to know where the forms are and how to file them in order to become a nonprofit theatre. Along with those forms comes a certain obligation to form a company that has some plan for how it will operate.[2] In many instances, along with your forms, you have to file this plan for how you plan for the organization to operate, and who will be responsible for what. Sometimes the plan is limited to a *charter*, which is a granting of certain rights from the person drafting the charter to the persons designated in the charter to receive those rights, also referred to as *articles of incorporation* when done for certain businesses, but it may also require the submission of by-laws.

Think critically: how much is too much?

There are two ways to approach this class discussion. First, you can choose sides. Divide the class into two, by whatever means you choose, and debate the argument outlined below. Second, you can have an open discussion, each adding upon others' thoughts, and let the discussion uncover all the important details of all sides of the debate. Keep in mind that regardless of which approach you take, we want to be sure we dig deep into all sides of this important issue, in order to more effectively understand all positions.

CLASS DISCUSSION: It has been said that nonprofit executives should make only what is fair and substantially appropriate given the nature of the business a nonprofit is conducting, and its mission-driven purpose. There has been worldwide outrage at nonprofits that pay excessive salaries in the hundreds of thousands, or even millions, to their top executives. Nonprofits are further questioned when they provide performance bonuses, or incentives, to staff members, since the function of the nonprofit is supposed to be altruistic and in service to the community. Often, money is contributed to these organizations for the purpose of conducting good work such as curing disease, helping those less fortunate, or providing for the social, esoteric, and artistic health of the community. Many argue that executives and staff of these organizations should be serving with a focus on, and deriving satisfaction from, the value of the work. They should not be driven, or vastly rewarded, by large sums of money. However, others argue that in order to do the best possible work, nonprofit executive salaries have to be competitive with their for-profit counterparts. If a nonprofit is limited in how much it can compensate its employees, it will never be able to hire the best people, and consequently, it will never be able to achieve the same level of success as those for-profit companies that do not have similar restrictions. Should we govern and regulate how much nonprofits should be allowed to compensate their executives, or should we allow them to pay their executives whatever they wish in order to be successful?

By-law requirements and what makes good by-laws

By-laws are rules that govern an organization. They differ from laws in that there is a sovereign that has precedence over the organization drafting the by-laws. This means that the highest ruling power has the ability to determine within what framework the lower ruling power may operate. A federal government has ruling power over a regional government, though the regional government may pass by-laws which are limited to the region, assuming they are not in conflict with the federal government. A regional government has authority over a company doing business in that region, so the company passes by-laws that govern how the company will operate.

This suggests that by-laws for a company could be very long and complex, covering scores of possibilities. In fact, the by-laws of a company are not intended to cover every policy and procedure, but are designed to explain governance of the company. If you do an Internet search of how to draft by-laws, you will likely find dozens of sources, all of which tell you slightly different things. As a general rule, it is best to always include in by-laws what is sometimes referred to as "No Mommy, see Pa," a way to pronounce the acronym NOMOMECPAA which stands for name, objective, members, officers, meetings, executives, committees, parliamentary authority, and amendments. When writing by-laws, it is good to ensure that they include the name of the company, the objective of the company (this is its mission), who the members are and how they become members, who the officers are and how they become officers, how and when the officers and company meet, who is the executive board, what are the committees, what parliamentary process does the company follow, and how the by-laws can be amended.[3]

Lawyers, accountants, insurance, and board members

As you have probably realized, when you decide to create a business, there are a lot of legal issues that you have to deal with, the first one being how to correctly fill out and submit all the legal paperwork in order to establish your business in a way that is to everyone's best interest. If you know a good lawyer, or you can afford one, it would probably be wise to seek out their help in making certain you handle all the paperwork correctly. Some of this paperwork is very lengthy, and asks complicated questions about business structure, and if you make a mistake, it could be sent back to you for correction, wasting months of time. You will also want advice on how to make sure your business is best protected, once it is up and running. It might be wise to look for a lawyer who would be willing to provide volunteer service as a board member, and also with pro bono counsel. The same goes for an accountant. Every board should have one member who understands the intricacies of financial accounting, as it can be very complicated when trying to track the worth of a company, as well as keep tabs on how the cash is actually being spent. The accountant can also help ensure that there will always be money to prepare for the next production, and guide long-term thinking so your theatre company can continue to grow. Also, both the lawyer and the accountant will probably urge you to buy insurance that protects the company as well as its board and staff members. While the legal business entity is responsible for itself in a limited liability situation, insurance can be purchased for not too much money that serves as a guarantee that the board and staff members are protected, should someone wish to pursue a claim against them.

Questions to research for class discussion:

Search the Internet and find answers for these questions before you read any further. Be prepared to discuss them in class.

4.8   What free (or cheap) legal aid and accounting assistance exists for nonprofits or start-up arts organizations, and how do you get it?
4.9   What are the types of insurances a new business can purchase, and which do you think would be best for a theatre company, and why?
4.10 What other resources are available for free to new start-up theatre companies, and how would they be useful?

Decisions for starting a company

As you can see, deciding to start a new company is not simply a matter of having an idea. In order to move forward in an effective manner, you need to have a number of items planned out, including the type of organization you intend to operate, who will make the decisions, and how it will operate. For a theatre, you also have to know what type of theatre you intend to perform, and who will be your audience – meaning who can appreciate the work you do. It also means you have to know how you will get from your idea to the place where you will start to bring in money from ticket sales. Because to get from idea to opening night, you are going to have to pay for supplies and labor, a space to perform, and for the promotion of your play.

A note about start-up money

Given all the things that could cost you money, even if you get some of it donated or done by volunteers, getting a theatre company going is not inexpensive, and you probably will not be able to pay yourself for a while. That happens to be true with most new businesses whether they are a theatre or not, and whether they are for-profit or nonprofit. But without money coming in from ticket sales, you are probably wondering where the financial support is coming from? We know that a commercial producer would find investors, hoping to make a profit from the money they put into a production, but for a nonprofit, investors are not an option. And there probably is not a bank willing to loan you money, just because your theatre is a good idea. Banks are also in the business of making a profit. You could seek donations, though people, foundations, major donors, and government granting agencies rarely like to make contributions to organizations that have not yet proven themselves. There is simply too much risk involved. So that leaves you, your friends, and family, and everyone they can think of, including crowdfunding and other online fundraising platforms. Do not let this discourage you. Raising money is not easy at first, and you will probably have to start small to get your theatre off the ground. Just remember to plan for growth, because if you plan correctly, you can absolutely grow. But be careful. When the ticket sales from that first play come in, you are going to have to use those to pay for the next play, and so on.

Build your theatre milestone 4: write your by-laws

There are many models on the Internet from which you can work to develop by-laws for your theatre. Find one, or write your own by-laws, making sure that you have given consideration to NOMOMECPAA. Be sure to include in your by-laws the type of business structure your theatre will use, and whether it will be for-profit or nonprofit.

Case study

The case this time is not something that happened to Patrick at all, but in fact, it was something he heard shortly after he arrived at his job. Many years before Patrick arrived, well before cell phones and the Internet, two best friends founded the theatre company; one was artistically minded and one was business minded. They established a partnership and decided that they were going to share equally in the profit. For three or four years they operated in this fashion, and while they never made much profit, once in a while they each took home some money as a reward for their hard work and dedication to theatre. The two figured if they kept at it long enough, they could eventually grow into a bigger company, and there would be lots of profit for them.

During one rehearsal, one of the volunteer actors fell off a platform and hit her head on the stage during a blackout and scene change. She did not move, so the curtain was closed, the actors and technicians were asked to leave the stage to let her be looked after, and another volunteer actor who was a nurse by trade jumped up to look after the girl while medical assistance was called. Eventually, the girl was taken away by ambulance, the blood was cleaned up, and the rehearsal resumed. As the actors and technicians returned to the stage they noticed the glow tape all around the platform, and wondered why she had missed it and fallen. By the end of the rehearsal the cast was informed that the girl was awake and speaking, and while she said things were blurry, and she felt dizzy, she was going to be okay.

A few weeks later, the two partners decided to change their business structure. They asked several friends to serve as their board, they filed paperwork to become a limited liability company, and they submitted a request for nonprofit status. The speculation had always been that when the girl was hurt, the partners realized they could be in serious trouble if the girl had sued and won. Did the partners do the right thing by initially establishing a for-profit partnership? Did they do the right thing by changing the structure? Were there ways they could have protected themselves under any business structure? If so, what were they?

Personal exploration

Think about the six things that make you happiest. Consider whether they are intrinsic or extrinsic rewards, and rank them in order of importance. Then write a paragraph about the kind of lifelong pursuit that might best satisfy those needs.

Notes

1 Götz, Norbert, "Civil society and NGO: Far from unproblematic concepts," *The Ashgate Research Companion to Non-State Actors* (pp. 185–196), Ashgate Publishing, 2011.

2 Lewis, Ferdinand, and Eleanor K. Sommer, "Art and community capacity-building: A case study," In *Handbook of Research on the Facilitation of Civic Engagement through Community Art* (pp. 499–523), IGI Global, 2017.

3 Lewis, Ferdinand, and Eleanor K. Sommer, "Art and community capacity-building: A case study," In *Handbook of Research on the Facilitation of Civic Engagement through Community Art* (pp. 499–523), IGI Global, 2017.

CHAPTER 5

Theatre organization

Patrick was working in a place he thought must be different from the rest of the way the world worked. Hearing stories like the one about the girl who fell, and the sudden change of organizational status made him think that things were not always on the up and up. But when he asked his friends as well as some of his peers from school, they all recounted stories from the places where they worked that indicated many organizations do not always follow all the rules, and many companies may not even know the best practices that Patrick had learned in school. One example was the strange way his theatre was organized and the fact that he was assistant marketing director, but he was the assistant to no one.

Chapter objectives

After reading this chapter you should be able to describe ways that organizations are structured, design a simple organizational chart for a theatre company, explain parity of authority and responsibility, discuss phases of organizational growth, and describe risk assessment.

Organizational design

You may not have ever paid much attention, but in your household growing up, everyone had certain duties and responsibilities they handled. Someone earned money, someone paid the bills, someone fixed certain problems, someone emptied the trashcans, and someone else probably cooked the meals and washed the dishes. We could go on and on about all the things it takes to keep a household running smoothly and efficiently, and even though you may have never thought about it, that functioning occurred because there was a structural design. It may not have always been perfect. Sometimes tasks were left undone, or no one knew who was really doing what, but for the most part, your household worked the way you expected it to work. Organizations function in much the same manner. Everyone has specific things they do because those things are in their job description, but also sometimes simply because of the type of person they are. Often, there is a nurturer who supports fellow employees emotionally when they are having a bad day. You will not typically find that duty listed in a job description. Strong organizations monitor how everything is getting accomplished, and where they find problems, they realign the workflow to make sure everything can improve. This is the process of *organizational design*.

Organic organizational design

If you have ever been involved in production meetings in the theatre, you know that the designers, director, and stage managers have regular discussions about how to ensure that their work is all coordinated effectively so that the best possible product can be achieved by opening night. And once the production closes, these teams often hold a *post mortem*, which is Latin for *after death*, and refers to a meeting where the team analyzes what went well and what can be improved upon for the future. In some sense, this is a very good example of how a theatre company exercises organizational design. You may not have seen a human resources professional taking notes and advising on how to improve organizational design, but it is happening, it is just happening organically. This is not to suggest that the best way to go about organizational design is to let it happen on its own. As we know from Chapter 1, one of the functions of management is to plan. Organizational design that is left to happen organically is unplanned.

Organizational structures

One of the first steps in organizational design is to determine an organizational structure. The *organizational structure* is the arrangement of resources, including personnel, into groupings in order to improve efficiency.[1] This process is sometimes referred to as *departmentalization*, because we are effectively grouping resources into *departments*. In theatre, we oftentimes hear someone refer to the marketing department as one entity in the organization. And while we do not typically refer to the ticket office as a department, or the artistic office as a department, we recognize that this is exactly what they are.

Outside of theatre

In the business world, there are many different ways that organizations are departmentalized, based upon how resources are grouped. Sometimes this happens organically, but more often it occurs because certain industries have developed a most effective practice over time. Once a business has an organizational structure, it is represented in a graphic referred to as an *organizational chart*, which shows the reporting lines between the people involved in running the organization, including volunteers, staff, and executives. Organizational charts demonstrate how resources are grouped together.[2] Businesses may group resources together based on function, such as marketing, sales, fundraising, finance, and so on, or they may group resources based on processes, such as design and engineering. When an organization makes several different product lines, they may organize around product, and when they serve different markets, such as consumer, government, and international, they may divide their organization around market. Organizations may also be structured around the type of customer, or around where the work is located. Sometimes, organizational charts look particularly odd because work is organized into teams that have equal reporting responsibilities. Team members are often parts of other groupings of resources, but come together to accomplish one project, and when it is completed, they return to their original grouping.[3] This team structure is referred to as a *matrix structure*. As you can imagine, this can all be very complex, and larger companies typically use a combination of different groupings to work most effectively. And that is often the case in theatre as well.

Questions to research for class discussion:

Search the Internet and find answers for these questions before you read any further. Be prepared to discuss them in class.

5.1   What are some important reasons for examining a company's organizational design?
5.2   How does the mission statement influence organizational structure?
5.3   What can most greatly impact organizational structure?

In theatre

In theatre, it is less likely that we would organize around process, because we wouldn't want to make art in a system that works like an assembly line, where each contributor focuses only on their process as part of the overall production. But if the company is focused on new play development as one example, the process structure might make a lot of sense. The top of the organizational chart might then look like the organization that appears in Figure 5.1, which is a *process structure*.

The product-oriented structure is also somewhat unusual for a theatre, though companies that create different types of theatre, such as some for education purposes and some for entertainment, might choose to organize

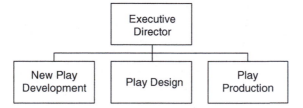

Figure 5.1 Sample process structure organizational chart

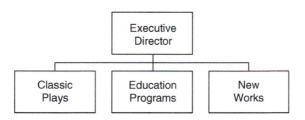

Figure 5.2 Sample product structure organizational chart

around the *product structure*. The top of that chart might look like the one that appears in Figure 5.2.

More often, theatres organize around function. Departments are set up based on the type of work they do: marketing, fundraising, sales, and so on.[4] But even though theatres tend to organize in a functional way, production teams often work more like a matrix. This is not unusual, as plays are essentially the equivalent of the modern business world's project teams. Participants come together to create a single project, and when it is completed, they return to the standard reporting structure in a functional chart. A simple *matrix* chart might look like the chart that appears in Figure 5.3.

Those project teams, and the associated matrix chart would actually fit into the *functional structure*. A typical theatre functional organization chart might look like the one in Figure 5.4.

Notice in Figure 5.4 that the lines represent a reporting structure. There are four positions that report directly to the board of directors: a lawyer, an accountant, a managing director, and an artistic director. But the lawyer and accountant are not on the same level as the managing director and artistic director. In this example, the lawyer and accountant provide consulting services to the board, and they report directly to the board, but in a fashion that is different from the managing director and the artistic director. The assistants to both the artistic director and the managing director are attached to the same reporting line as others, but they are placed on a different side of the line, suggesting a slightly different relationship. If we wanted to add

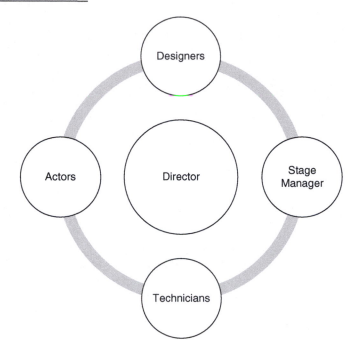

Figure 5.3 Sample matrix structure organizational chart

a matrix structure to this, the column under directors might be where we would place the radial design of the matrix chart. The organizational chart can be designed any way the organization feels best fits how its groups work together, but the vertical lines always indicate who reports to whom, and how work and authority is delegated. Note that though there are several people reporting to the managing director, and their positions are stacked vertically rather than on the same horizontal plane, none of them have reporting lines to one another. They all connect to the vertical line below the managing director in exactly the same way.

The organizational chart shows more than reporting lines. It indicates the structure for how formal authority is distributed among positions on the chart, and the shifting or delegation of authority is the core of management, because management is the coordination of resources, including personnel. So *delegation* is not only giving people work and telling them to do it, it is the transfer of authority. And with the delegation of authority, the person receiving the authority also becomes responsible for ensuring the work is done effectively and efficiently. This is *accountability*. If the employee fails to be accountable for the responsibility that has been delegated to them, the manager can always withdraw the authority.

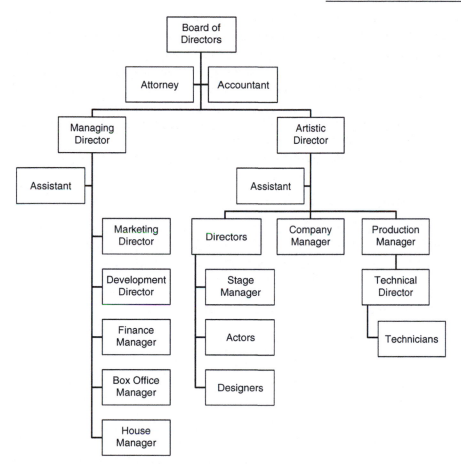

Figure 5.4 Sample functional structure organizational chart

Questions to research for class discussion:

Search the Internet and find answers for these questions before you read any further. Be prepared to discuss them in class.

5.4 What is the principle of parity of authority and responsibility? What would be two examples in theatre of a lack of this parity?

5.5 What are the dos and don'ts of delegation?

5.6 What is meant by centralization and decentralization?

As you see, there is certain risk in management, because as the organizational chart in Figure 5.4 demonstrates, the authority granted to the board of directors by the public and its government is then delegated to the managing director and artistic director. In turn, those positions delegate parts of that authority to people below them. As the authority moves further and further away from an individual the risk becomes greater that either unintentional or intentional negative consequences can occur without being caught before damage is done. As a result, it is very important that clear and specific job descriptions are written. It is also vital that supervisors are regularly providing feedback to employees on what worked, what did not work, and why. It is important to provide accurate and honest feedback through formal performance evaluations, but also through regular informal communications. We will discuss both job descriptions and performance appraisals in greater detail in Chapter 6.

Organizational growth

New businesses rarely start with the goal of being small and staying small. They plan to grow. Theatre companies are no different. And while the amount of growth anticipated by companies in their long-term plans may

---

Think critically: can we truly collaborate?

There are two ways to approach this class discussion. First, you can choose sides. Divide the class into two, by whatever means you choose, and debate the argument outlined below. Second, you can have an open discussion, each adding upon the others' thoughts, and let the discussion uncover all the important details of all sides of the debate. Keep in mind that regardless of which approach you take, we want to be sure we dig deep into all sides of this important issue, in order to more effectively understand all positions.

CLASS DISCUSSION: Companies function most effectively when work is divided into groups, and there is a clear set of assigned duties and tasks, all supervised by a person who has authority over the group. That person may be part of another group of individuals, which reports to another person of authority. Sometimes these chains of command can be very long, and there are many layers of authority between the person at the top and the worker at the bottom. By coordinating all of these people and their work, companies are best able to add value to their inputs in order to create profitable outputs. But when there is such a clear chain of command, and authority is carefully wielded, how can we truly collaborate? Won't this tight supervision stifle the collaborative process? In theatre, while we need to know who is directing whom, we also need lots of freedom to try things beyond what our job description might say in order to create art. Is it better to be freewheeling and unstructured in order to serve the art? And if we do operate that way, what is the cost? Or is it better to always strive to function, collaborate, and create art in a careful structure, ensuring that we make the best use of the precious resources we have available to create theatre?

vary, growth is typically at the forefront of strategy. In fact, if you think about it, companies are almost always either growing or contracting. It is the very rare organization that has exactly the same amount of income, expenses, and customers year after year. Whatever metrics are used, even if the company is said to be maintaining position, slight fluctuations and changes mean that the company has either grown or shrunk.

Structuring for growth

Business researchers have, for decades, looked at what it takes for organizations to grow, and they have identified a number of similarities in growth patterns. If you do a quick Internet search of business growth phases, you are likely to find many different models, with many different stages, suggesting there is a great deal of confusion about this topic. However, several models look at organizational growth in five relatively simple phases, which make it easy to understand. You may be wondering why we need to understand the different phases of growth, particularly if we know that what we want our company to do is grow. Organizations at different phases of growth require different types of leadership, and this is certainly true for theatres.[5] You have probably heard of a theatre company or two that grew and grew, became very large, and then suddenly failed and closed up shop. Or maybe you know the story of the theatre company whose founder was suddenly ousted. You may know about a theatre company that used to be a tiny little theatre with only a handful of patrons, but now an entire community shows up every opening night. Each one of these companies had a need for leadership styles that adapt through each phase. Those that successfully adapt tend to thrive. Those that do not adapt often fail. For our purposes, we will think about theatres in terms of these *five phases of the business growth cycle*: birth, survival, success, expansion, and maturity.[6] Note that these phases have many different names depending on the researcher, and sometimes there are more than five depending on who has studied them; but for our purposes we will use these five, which are adapted here for theatre.

In the birth phase, the person or people who establish the theatre are doing a lot of the work. They make the arrangements, coordinate schedules, answer phones, talk to the media, sell the tickets, cast the productions, build the sets; you name it, they are doing a lot of work. Their biggest concerns typically center on money and audience. They are often unsure if they have enough resources to put on a production that they consider to be acceptable artistically, and they feel they are in a constant struggle to find people who will appreciate the art they do create. From production to production they continue to feel overworked, underfunded, and never able to generate enough interest to make the theatre company a viable operation. Theatre companies in this phase are challenged by a leadership that focuses on getting all the work done, when the biggest part of their focus should be on bringing in additional help, usually in the form of volunteers, and making certain that the help understands what is expected of them. Leadership can then transfer authority and responsibility in parity to these people in service of the long-range plan for growth. This is also a time when the biggest risks need to be taken, but the theatre has the smallest amount of assets to put at risk.

In the survival phase, the theatre has gotten through several productions and is now less worried about how to pay for the next one. There are enough people to get the work done, and it gets done appropriately, though sometimes people still feel overworked. In the survival phase, the emphasis shifts to a need to raise enough money to grow. There is not quite enough to pay professionals at any level. The company wants to include professional actors, directors, technicians, and to hire full-time marketing and box office staffs, but growth is stymied by only a small amount of excess revenue from each production. In this phase, the founders want to and often start paying themselves, though it is typically not enough to be considered a full-time job and money is still tight. But some professionalism is starting to evolve. The challenge for leadership at this phase is to be sure that a plan has been carefully crafted about how to strategically spend the excess revenue so that it is most likely to produce greater growth, growth that is often not added to the salary of the founder. Also, for leadership, the survival phase is marked by the need to make more risky decisions with the assets the company now has. But risky decisions mean outcomes are less certain. With greater risks, however, both artistically and financially, can come greater reward. Strong leadership gathers as much information as possible in order to make the most informed decisions, but at the survival phase, any risk can be frightening.

In the success phase, the theatre has leveled off with a solid and consistent audience size. There is a core staff handling tasks, and the management of the company is smooth and consistent. The artistic product is routinely quite good, and the business is stable. In the success phase there is time to plan for long-term growth, and doing so is essential. At this phase, leadership is often replaced, because the skills to get an organization to success and the skills to move an organization to greater heights can be quite different. In the success phase, the theatre is regularly figuring out how to maintain its current level of success and avoid the pitfalls that could lead to failure. But it also needs to be planning for a strategic growth period when it can move to the next level.

In the expansion phase, the theatre company is moving from a big player in a small marketplace into a larger marketplace. This may mean that the company is expanding its reach, adding additional performances, productions, or venues, reaching new target audiences such as schools or groups, or even touring. In the expansion phase, monitoring growth becomes paramount in order to make sure the theatre is achieving each necessary benchmark to get to where it is headed. During the expansion phase, there is significantly more money coming in and going out, and it is exceptionally important that delegated authority is being monitored closely to ensure that investments are being used wisely toward the theatre's vision. Without careful monitoring in the growth phase, there is a danger that the addition of staff can slow an organization down or lead to wasting of resources. This is not to suggest that supervisors suddenly need to pay much closer attention to every detail of their employees' work (a process called *micromanagement*) but it does imply that the management style in earlier phases may be different from the management style required in expansion, when managers need to spend less time on tasks and more time on the bigger picture.

The final phase for theatres is maturity. At the maturity phase, theatres have achieved the success of their growth, and they stabilize and maintain. In this phase, leaders are often looking for ways to grow in small ways to ensure long-term stability. As society and the marketplace changes, these companies can shift and stay relevant. The resources exist to allow for small, periodic growth in new and innovative ways, without putting the company at risk.

While theatres go through all these phases, there is no clear timeline for how long each one takes. The timespan is different for every different situation. Theatres may also achieve one particular phase, only to find they fail and fall back to an earlier phase. Theatres can also repeat the cycle, consistently growing through the lifespan of the company.

Questions to research for class discussion:

Search the Internet and find answers for these questions before you read any further. Be prepared to discuss them in class.

5.7   What is the Greiner Curve and how does it compare the phases of growth we used above in talking about theatres?
5.8   What is Organizational Life Cycle and how does it compare the phases of growth we used above in talking about theatres?
5.9   Why do organizations fail?
5.10 Why do some companies fail to grow? How do those reasons translate to theatre?

Planning for growth

One of the biggest challenges a theatre company can face is how to plan for growth. Oftentimes it seems that growth has to be a secondary objective after survival. But the two actually go hand in hand. In order to survive in a marketplace that has a capitalist foundation, the company needs to have some growth trajectory. Remember, it is rare that a company remains stagnant. From year to year there is almost always either growth or contraction. To plan for growth, the wise theatre company carefully follows a strategic plan. As the fruits of the strategic plan begin to ripen, the company faces new challenges, because growth means change, and people are often averse to change.

Evaluating and managing change

To evaluate a theatre company for change, it is important to ensure the structure that exists can facilitate that change. This means that the right positions are in place to handle not only what the company is currently producing, but what it intends to produce as it grows. For example, a small theatre company might have a bookkeeper that handles the finances and pays the bills by writing checks out of a single checkbook. But as the company grows, the skills of a certified accountant may be required to handle large payrolls and hefty purchases, ensuring accurate reporting. A bookkeeper may not be equipped to handle this work, so an expansion of the skills required for the position may be required.

A theatre looking to grow also needs to consider if the processes it currently uses to produce its art are capable of handling expansion. Where do sets and costumes come from now? Can those same sources produce sets and costumes as our theatre company grows? If growth means additional productions, that may be a challenge. If growth means new, larger venues, that could be a problem. To deal with these sorts of issues, the company needs to not only consider every potential process change, but also try to anticipate changes that may not be apparent.

Finally, in order to effectively manage change, leadership needs to be very careful not to alienate people. Change for the core staff is going to be difficult, because it means they will be doing some things differently, which are still unknown. But in the theatre, change also means that the audience has to be ready to adapt to the change. Theatre leaders need to be careful to introduce change gradually, constantly gauging the reaction of all those involved to ensure that the change will be effective, without alienating people.

Risk assessment and planning

Whenever we embark on an activity or process, there is some element of risk. *Risk assessment* is how we systematically evaluate those risks. Most often we hear the term in relation to physical risks. Fire curtains in theatres can be lowered because many years ago we identified the risk of fire on the stage, and we installed the curtain to lower the risk of the fire spreading into the theatre house. But risk assessment can also be done when planning for the long term, and it is essential to do so. We call this long-term risk assessment *contingency planning*.

The challenge is that to assess long-term risk, we cannot possibly consider every potential challenge that might affect a theatre. A flood could make the theatre unusable. A bomb could collapse the building. Riots might make it unsafe to have any audiences in the neighborhood. We could write a list that goes on forever. To plan for long-term risk, it is almost impossible to consider how to handle every potential situation. Instead, we consider broader issues. Notice that in all of the above examples, the theatre building becomes unusable. In contingency planning, we consider the consequences of certain challenges, and determine how we would deal with those consequences to ensure survival of our theatre. For example, one risk might be the temporary loss of the use of a theatre. As a contingency, the company may make arrangements with another theatre that should that occur, the other facility would be available to them for a period of time. Companies sometimes make reciprocal agreements that they will, in the event of loss of their facility, be able to use the other facility, free of rent, up to a maximum amount of time. Loss of a facility is obviously a very big concern, but there are many issues requiring contingency planning, and the wise theatre manager and their team develops those plans, writes them down clearly, and updates them annually.

Build your theatre milestone 5: create an organizational chart

There are plenty of ways that you can create an organizational chart, and Microsoft Word offers one excellent example (see support.office.com and search for "Create an organization chart"). Using whatever technique you prefer, devise an organizational chart for your unique theatre company. Remember to include positions even if volunteers will staff them, at least initially. This is a chart that shows how authority is delegated, not who gets paid more.

Case study

Patrick had been doing a lot of work. In fact, reorganizing the marketing department was what he was always focused on, but as you have learned, he was also helping Frank restructure the entire theatre so it could work more effectively. Patrick's suggestions and changes were sometimes met with disagreement, but most of what he brought forth ended up being implemented in ways that helped the company grow and become more successful. But Patrick was struggling to justify that his title was assistant marketing director, and while his salary was far lower than other marketing directors of theatre companies of comparable size in comparable cities, he felt it was at least appropriate that his title reflected the work. He had lightheartedly spoken to Frank several times about the possibility of changing his title, saying things like, "yeah, it sure is a lot of work for only an assistant marketing director, maybe we should change my title," or "if you want to make me director of marketing instead of assistant, I could probably do even more." And while Frank never seemed opposed to the idea of changing Patrick's title, he also never did anything about it. Patrick suspected that Frank was concerned Patrick might also want a hefty salary increase to go along with a higher title. Realistically, even if a title change did not come with an immediate increase, it was certainly a first step toward reaching a higher salary, and that would not be inappropriate, given the work Patrick was doing. Patrick was vastly exceeding what was expected of him, and he was working at the capacity equivalent to the rest of the leadership team, which included the development director, the artistic director, the financial manager, and Frank. Though Patrick had never asked directly for a title change, he knew it was time to address the subject. He was faced with how exactly to do it. The decision to change a title and advance someone to the leadership team was a decision that would be made by the Executive Director, Megan, who reported directly to the board. Megan had essentially transferred some of her authority to Frank, who transferred it to Patrick, so in asking for a change in organizational structure, Megan would need to be the person to make the final decision. Patrick struggled with how best to handle the situation. If he asked Frank for the change in title, Frank could either turn him down directly or go to Megan and encourage her to turn the request down. Of course, Frank could also go to Megan and promote the idea, but Frank's past behavior suggested this was unlikely. Patrick could go directly to Megan to make his case, but he knew this was a bold move as he would be going over Frank's head, and Patrick recognized the importance of the reporting structure drawn onto the organizational chart. Patrick also figured if he went directly to Megan, he could make a case for both a title change and an increase in salary, but that could threaten Frank. Should Patrick even consider requesting a salary increase, or only ask for a change in status? Should he ask for the salary and not worry about the title? What are all the pros and cons of each of those options? What are the pros and cons of going to Frank? Of going to Megan? Given all those pros and cons, what do you think is Patrick's best course of action?

Personal exploration

Think about how you have planned for your own professional growth. Write about the steps you took to get you where you are, and develop a plan for where you would like to see yourself, what steps you will take to get you there, and what risks you need to be prepared to address on your path to that future.

Notes

1 Tavkhelidze, Tamar, "The role arts management in modern world," *European Scientific Journal, ESJ* 12, no. 10 (2017): 387–391.

2 Ibid.

3 Volz, Jim, *How to Run a Theatre: Creating, Leading and Managing Professional Theatre,* A&C Black, 2013.

4 Roche, Nancy, and Jaan Whitehead, eds., *The Art of Governance,* Theatre Communications Group, 2005.

5 Bridges Stecklein, Emily, "The Art of Making (It) Work: Artist-Centered Organizational Models in Small Professional Theater Companies," Master's thesis, University of Minnesota, 2016. Retrieved from the University of Minnesota Digital Conservancy: http://hdl.handle.net/11299/180413.

6 Tam, Steven, and David E. Gray, "What can we learn from the organizational life cycle theory? A conceptualization for the practice of workplace learning," *Journal of Management Research* 8, no. 2 (2016): 18–30.

CHAPTER 6

Jobs in theatre

Patrick was perfectly happy in his job, though he continued to struggle with his title. Not only did the title make no sense, since he was effectively the marketing director, not the assistant, but it represented a lessening of what he was capable of, and it would lower his résumé value if and when he ever decided to look for a new position. But he was also confused about how the title could have been developed in the first place. He knew the work he was doing was not traditionally the work of an assistant, and he could not understand why anyone in theatre would think it was. Patrick had studied how to appropriately examine jobs and classify them, and he knew that his position had clearly not ever been examined properly. And though it was not his place to do so, he was very tempted to provide the appropriate evaluation and recommendations. Maybe then he could be given an accurate title.

Chapter objectives

After reading this chapter you should be able to discuss unions associated with theatre and describe the work they do, discuss how safety is governed in theatres, debate the issues regarding ownership of communications, and demonstrate how to do a job analysis and write an associated job description.

Jobs in theatre

While we typically think of management jobs as those belonging to people who wear white shirts and handle monetary issues, you are probably now seeing that management is not a certain type of job as much as it is a skillset utilized by those who have to coordinate money and/or people. Managers have to ensure that the resources are used effectively and that includes making sure that the work of others is done efficiently and in the best interests of the company. So while you may have thought that the box office supervisor was a theatre manager of a sort, you probably did not consider that the play's director is also a theatre manager. If you aspire to work on stage in a creative capacity, you will be working with all sorts of theatre managers, such as technical directors, production managers, company managers, stage managers, directors, dance captains, and more. And if you look back at that list, you'll notice that most of those titles have either the word "manager" or "director" in them. And that list includes only managers involved in creating the production. There are plenty more managers working in the back offices, as well.

When it comes to job titles in theatre, things can get a little tricky. The title one company uses for a position may mean something entirely different at another company. Think about Patrick in our case studies. His title is "assistant marketing director," but he is doing the work that would typically be assigned to a marketing director or marketing manager, not an assistant. And the titles commonly used in one country may be unheard of in another. While the trade unions representing certain kinds of work in one country are often on friendly terms with the trade unions representing that same kind of work in another country, they may cover different specific jobs, have different classification systems, or even have different ways of assigning work.

Unions

When we talk about theatre unions, the first one that typically comes to mind is the union that represents actors. In the United Kingdom, Canada, and the United States, that union is called Actors' Equity. In the United States, the Actors' Equity Association (AEA) only represents stage actors. The Screen Actors' Guild-American Federation of Television and Radio Artists (SAG-AFTRA) represents actors when they are working in film and television. Actors who do both end up belonging to SAG-AFTRA and AEA. In Australia, Actors' Equity is part of the larger union called Media, Entertainment, and Arts Alliance, or MEAA. Though these unions called Actors' Equity (or Actors' Equity Association) share a name, and are certainly friendly to one another, they are all separate organizations. Every country has different labor laws, and Actors' Equity, as well as the actors' unions in other countries, have to work within the established laws where their employees work. Because *unions* are a group of employees who get together to have a unified voice in establishing standard practices in their workplace, it makes sense that unions would be established separately in each country. But there are certainly important work issues that impact actors equally throughout the world. To share experiences and ways to deal with those challenges, there is an organization called the International Federation of Actors (FIA) which works on behalf of actors and the issues they face in their professional environments, striving to improve working conditions as well as to impact society on the value of the creative work actors do. FIA is an international organization made up of scores of different actors' unions.

Questions to research for class discussion:

Search the FIA website and find answers for these questions before you read any further. Be prepared to discuss them in class.

6.1   What countries are represented in FIA? Who belongs to FIA, and how do they become members?

6.2   Find the FIA research archives. Summarize one of the research studies you find there.

6.3   What are the issues regarding collective bargaining that the FIA website addresses? Summarize one of those issues.

6.4   What other groups exist internationally that represent similar trade unions from many countries (such as musicians or technicians)? Who do they represent?

While actors band together in different ways in different countries, sometimes there are specialty performers who have their own unions. In the United Kingdom, variety artists are represented by Equity, but in the United States there is the American Guild of Variety Artists (AGVA). And while their members are musicians, opera performers in the United States do not belong to the musicians' union, but to the American Guild of Musical Artists (AGMA).

In theatre we are often concerned with live music, and work with members of a musicians' union such as the Canadian Federation of Musicians, the Musicians' Union of Ireland, or the Musicians' Union in the United Kingdom. Technicians typically also belong to a large union, such as the Broadcasting, Entertainment, Cinematograph and Theatre Union (BECTU) in the United Kingdom or the International Alliance of Theatrical Stage Employees (IATSE), which has local representation in both the United States and Canada.

When we talk about these unions, we are considering them on their national scale, but most unions have *local unions*, which are a group of employees in a localized region, or even at a single employer, who unify together with one voice, and have a charter with the national union. The national union will coordinate resources, such as dues, or money for health and welfare, as well as assist local unions in negotiating favorable work agreements. At the national level, there are standards the unions demand, but often the local unions are free to negotiate any way they see fit.

Negotiation can be tricky, because we tend to feel we are at odds with the other side. But in theatre, we have to remember that those people on the other side are the people we work with on a daily basis, who are also dedicated to making great plays. They are not the opposition; they are our partners. So the goal of contract negotiation is to find a solution that works best for everyone, and not to "beat" the other side.

Questions to research for class discussion:

Search the Internet and find answers for these questions before you read any further. Be prepared to discuss them in class.

6.5   How does the union organizational process work?
6.6   What are the steps/components of collective bargaining?
6.7   What are various impasse-resolution techniques?

Artistic management

In theatre, the *artistic director* is typically the manager who steers the artistic vision for the company, contracting and hiring the various artists, and overseeing their work to ensure it fits the company vision. Depending on the size of the theatre, this person may do additional work, but for the sake of our discussion here, we will address roles separately. In the case of a commercial production, the *director* of the production – the person who manages and coordinates the vision for the production – is the top artistic manager. Because the commercial production is a business established for the purpose of creating that one production, there is no need for an artistic director to ensure each production fits the company's vision. There is only one production. But in a commercial production, the director almost always answers to the executive producer, who is responsible for running the company and ensuring that the investors will make a return on their investment. Sometimes theatre companies that produce regular seasons operate the same way, with an executive director who is above the artistic director. The executive director in that scenario would oversee all functions of the company. Sometimes the artistic director is above the executive director. Sometimes there is an executive director who oversees an artistic director and a managing director. In that scenario, the *managing director* (or *general manager*) is responsible for overseeing the non-artistic functions of the theatre, such as marketing, operations, and fund development. And sometimes the artistic director oversees all functions of the company, and may have a title such as *producing artistic director*, or *artistic producer*, or simply *producer*, the latter of which is the same title often given to an investor in a commercial production. As you can see, titles in theatre can be very confusing. Of all the titles we have discussed above, they really cover only two functions in the organizational chart: the artistic side and the business side. On the artistic side, we might also find management titles such as these:

Stage Manager – This person is responsible for coordinating the entire production, and ensuring that all communication is effective. While the stage manager technically does not supervise anyone (except perhaps assistant stage managers), but instead takes direction and ensures it is followed, they are responsible for the coordination of resources, so we include them in management. This person is typically said to represent the director in the director's absence.

Company Manager – This person coordinates the basic needs of artistic personnel on behalf of the producer or artistic director. They may be responsible for housing, transportation, medical needs, ensuring paychecks are delivered, assisting with complimentary tickets, and the like. Again, the company manager often does not directly supervise anyone, but they do coordinate resources. This person, particularly in commercial productions, is often said to represent the producer.

Production Manager – This person is responsible for coordinating all the resources required to ensure a successful production from the standpoint of the designers, and does so on behalf of the producer or artistic director.

Technical Director – This is the most senior of technicians, who coordinates the work of those technicians.

Notice that we have not included set, costume, lighting, properties, or sound designers in that list. These positions are vital to a good theatre production, and they do often instruct technicians on how to execute their designs, but typically designers are independent. The function of the technical director is to translate the designs into instructions for the technicians. The function of the production manager is to coordinate all the different elements so they work together most efficiently. The function of the designers is to create great art, not to coordinate resources, so by our definition, they are not managers.

Business management

On the non-artistic side of theatre, the titles get even more confusing and diverse, and it is rare you will find two theatres with exactly the same set of titles. Part of this may have to do with the fact that when theatre companies start out, they rarely have the resources to hire lots of people, so only a handful of people take on all the work. As the company grows and the work is shared more and more, the titles must be split in ways that are most meaningful, and that depends on who wants to do what work before a new hire comes in. It is not unheard of to find strange combinations of job titles such as *marketing and education director* or *properties master and director of outreach*. Both of those combinations are from real theatres. And in both combinations, you may have noticed that there is one job that would likely fall on the artistic side of an operation (education director and properties master), and one that might fall on the business side (marketing and director of outreach). You can imagine how busy people are in either one of those companies. In addition to executive director and managing director, other titles you may typically find on the business side of a theatre include:

Marketing Director – This person, sometimes referred to as the Director of Marketing and Public Relations, or the Publicity Manager, or other similar terms, is understood to be responsible for the promotion of the company and the generation of earned revenue. This is a title that can be particularly misleading, as we will see in Chapter 9, because promotion is only one small piece of marketing.

Director of Development/Fundraising – This person is responsible for the generation of unearned revenue, through donations, contributions, grants, and the like.

Director of Education – This title can be deceiving. Sometimes a director of education is creating educational products associated with the play, such as materials to share in classrooms, and dramaturgical material. When that is the case, it would be more appropriate to be on the artistic side. When the director of education is coordinating the sales and promotion of plays to schools, they are appropriately on the business side. When they are doing all of those functions, which is often the case, they might report to either the managing director, the artistic director, or both.

Director of Facilities – This person is responsible for the operations of the building, ensuring that facilities are maintained and operating efficiently and effectively.

Business Manager (Controller) – This person, sometimes referred to as the bookkeeper or accountant or director of finance, is responsible for handling the movement of money both into and out of the company.

Box Office Manager – This person is responsible not for securing the ticket sale, which is the job of the marketing director, but for closing the sale and processing the transaction, ensuring that the customer receives the ticket to the seat they want when they want it, and collecting and reporting the revenue earned.

House Manager – This person is responsible for a smooth ushering of patrons into and out of their seats and through the lobby area during performance times. For touring productions, the house manager traditionally works for the local presenter or building owner and is the manager of the building or house.

Internal issues

When we think about theatre, the image that comes to mind is usually one of actors on stage, yet so much of what goes into making theatre happen occurs long before the audiences see that production.[1] Of course there are countless rehearsals where new elements are added every day until the play is ready to open. But there are all sorts of things going on that the audience never sees which go on behind the scenes, in the back offices.

Human resource issues

We know that managers are responsible for coordinating resources, and that includes human resources. But that does not mean that the manager gets to decide everything about how an employee works; laws to protect employees govern differently in different countries. These laws are considered a minimum standard to ensure for the health and welfare of employees. Often, unions will negotiate higher standards than the minimum required by law. For example, unions often negotiate for more mandatory holidays than required by law.

Whether a company has a dedicated manager who supervises and coordinates human resource issues or not, every manager has to be somewhat responsible. Therefore, before operating a theatre it is important to have an understanding of some of the issues related to human resource management.

Questions to research for class discussion:

Search the Internet and find answers for these questions before you read any further. Be prepared to discuss them in class.

6.8   What money are you legally allowed to deduct from employee wages? What money are you required to deduct from employee wages?

6.9   What leaves of absence are you required to offer, and how do they work?

Occupational safety and health

One of the biggest areas of concern for any business, and which therefore should always be on a manager's mind, is occupational safety and health. It is incumbent on a theatre to provide a safe and healthy work environment. While some countries may have standards and laws that allow us to operate in less than safe ways, it is unwise to do so. Even if the law does not require safety chains on lighting instruments, or fire retardant scenery, to operate without these precautions is to invite disaster. But safety goes beyond the stage house. Extension cords draped around an office can pose a fire risk or a trip hazard, or both. Boxes of papers shoved in a corner could make exiting difficult in a fire, or could themselves pose a fire hazard. If your theatre does not concern itself with the health and safety of those it interacts with, when an accident happens, you could be found liable. As the saying goes, "better safe than sorry."

Questions to research for class discussion:

Search the Internet and find answers for these questions before you read any further. Be prepared to discuss them in class.

6.10 What are the most important laws regarding health and safety, when were they established, and how do they work?
6.11 What are some important health and safety issues that theatres specifically might need to be aware of?
6.12 What does someone do if they feel they are being put at risk because of a health or safety violation? What happens after they have done it?
6.13 What are the penalties for violating health and safety laws? How would those affect a theatre?

Routine reporting and record maintenance

While we often do not think about why we maintain records, most organizations do so on a daily basis. Financial transactions must be documented and reported to various governments and tax agencies. Work hours must also be maintained and reported. We document what occurs during a rehearsal in a report. Stage managers often provide reports of production meetings. We keep personnel files that document major issues regarding each employee. We keep track of ticket buyers and donors. Theatres gather a lot of information. Sometimes it is gathered for the purpose of growing and expanding through marketing, as is the case with box office records, and sometimes it is for the purpose of protecting the company, as is the case when we document what happened when someone was injured. Documentation is designed to refresh our memories about things that have happened in the past so we can protect and ensure a better future. Regardless of the job in theatre, a manager needs to take and keep records of the work they coordinate. This not only ensures that successors can know what has happened in the past, but it allows incumbents to refresh their memory on what worked and what did not work, and why.

Computers, faxes, phones, other office equipment

Every manager in theatre is likely going to have a need to communicate with employees, supervisors, other managers, and outside sources. The vast array of ways we now communicate seems to grow almost daily. That can be good, especially when people have different preferences for how they like to communicate, but it can also be a challenge, requiring that we provide employees with many different pieces of equipment to facilitate good communication. When it comes to keeping records, computers provide many

Think critically: private versus company communication

There are two ways to approach this class discussion. First, you can choose sides. Divide the class into two, by whatever means you choose, and debate the argument outlined below. Second, you can have an open discussion, each adding upon others' thoughts, and let the discussion uncover all the important details of all sides of the debate. Keep in mind that regardless of which approach you take, we want to be sure we dig deep into all sides of this important issue, in order to more effectively understand all positions.

CLASS DISCUSSION: Keeping records of communications is important for a company in maintaining its history, being able to learn from its past, being able to plan for the future, and in protecting itself. But theatre management does not start at 9:00 and end at 17:00. Managers may find themselves troubleshooting, problem solving, or dealing with any number of management issues at all hours of the day, inside and outside of the theatre and its working hours. Managers cannot be expected to use their personal devices to communicate work issues. It is incumbent on a theatre to provide smartphones and other technology to managers so their communications can be saved and maintained. If the company cannot provide the technology, it should not expect a record of communication to be maintained. However, some theatres may choose to implement policies that forbid employees from using their personal devices for work communication unless that communication is documented and provided to the company. This allows the manager the greatest flexibility while not requiring the use of a personal device. Some maintain that this is simply a way to take advantage of managers, by requiring them to spend their own money on communication devices and then expecting them to do their job 24-7, on their own device. And anyway, some managers may not want to have a company device in addition to a personal device, which can be cumbersome and confusing, and many managers do not wish to carry out their personal business on a company device, even if that is permitted. Regardless of preference, managers should not be required to do work on their personal device, nor should they be required to document and provide to their employer communications that occur on their personal device. If a company wants a manager to handle issues that come up outside of work hours, the company should simply accept that those communications records will not be maintained and provided to the employer, regardless of who provides the communication device. Should employers have access to all business communications that occur, or does that encroach on the privacy of the employee, and this should simply be considered the cost of doing business?

advantages because they store a trail of communication which telephone calls do not. Good managers develop a plan for recording communications and storing the records, but this means that a policy must be in place to ensure employees follow the communication procedures. It is very easy to have a text message dialogue on a personal telephone with someone outside of the theatre, who is sharing information pertinent to the company, and that communication is never recorded. While the idea of paying for company smartphones for managers seems costly, the ramifications for not doing so could be worse.

External communication

Most managers in the theatre have some amount of communication with people outside of the theatre company. They may have to communicate with media firms, or potential donors. Sometimes they have to communicate with agents or licensing houses. Banks and other financial institutions such as credit card processors can be regular points of contact. Unions, suppliers, rental houses, landlords, and journalists may all be communicating with theatre managers on a regular basis. As you can imagine, how each of these managers handles those communications is a reflection on how the company presents itself publicly. Communication is an important part of the job of a manager in the theatre.

Governments and chambers of commerce

Some theatre managers, typically the executive director or managing director, may be in a position to have especially important communications. Any business, including a theatre, is part of the community in which it works, and that may require interactions and communications with government officials, chambers of commerce, or other business organizations. These communications can have a serious impact on the theatre, and the wise manager plans ahead, knowing exactly what the company requires from such communications, and exactly what approach will be likeliest to succeed.

The marketplace

When hiring employees, we start by examining what work needs to be done, how it is to be done, the skills and abilities required of the person doing the work, and how similar work is done in other places. This is called the *job analysis*. Once the analysis is complete, it can be written into a *job description*, which details the information learned in the job analysis. When hiring new employees, the theatre will use that job description as the basis for a *job announcement* or *job posting*, which is the actual promotion tactic used to find applicants.

Questions to research for class discussion:

Search the Internet and find answers for these questions before you read any further. Be prepared to discuss them in class.

6.14 What are the different ways to conduct a job analysis?
6.15 What are the most important elements in a job announcement?
6.16 Why aren't salaries always included in job postings?

Build your theatre milestone 6: job announcements

Do a brief job analysis so that you can write complete job announcements for the six top staff jobs in your theatre company. Be sure to include who they report to on your organizational chart, who reports to them, whether they are full-time, part-time, or volunteer, and how you expect them to be compensated. Don't forget to include instructions on how applicants can apply.

Case study

After Patrick had been making slow and steady improvements to his team for about eight or nine months, the company's development director met with him to say that there was a very likely possibility that a grant was available to fund additional marketing staff for two years. Patrick explained it this way:

> Sheila told me that she had been meeting with an agency that was funding grant money for nonprofit arts organizations to improve and profession-alize their marketing functions, and that the grant would essentially fund two full-time positions for two years. After those two years were up, we could reapply to extend the grant on a year-to-year basis for as long as the agency continued to fund this type of support. But in any case, if we got the initial grant, we would have to document very carefully exactly how we set about to improve our marketing efforts, what the results were, and what steps we would take moving forward to further strengthen our work. Sheila was confident that we had a very good shot at getting the initial grant, but what she needed from me was more than I thought I could handle at the time. I had a small staff of two, basically a graphics designer and an assistant. Between the three of us, we had been doing everything. The

idea of getting two new full-time people was exciting, because we could really do a lot more research, which usually took a back seat to just getting ads designed and placed. We could also do a lot of analysis of the research, of our marketing efforts, of ways to add value to our patrons, and on and on. But we would also have to be documenting all of this. And in order to explain all of that, I was going to have to take a couple weeks off from my regular work, just to do the appropriate job analysis. It didn't make sense to me to just create a bunch of fiction in order to apply for the grant. These granting agencies see right through that. And anyway, I wouldn't want two new people without having a plan. I went to Frank to ask for two weeks off, but when he realized the impact that would have on our current marketing efforts, he couldn't approve it. Then I suggested that if I had some money I could hire someone to help during those two weeks, or I could hire a firm to do the job analysis, but again Frank balked. He felt it didn't make sense to spend money chasing a grant that may or may not provide fruit. He suggested I see if Sheila had some money in her budget lines she could use, but I knew she was just as tapped out as I was. The whole thing was really frustrating. This was an opportunity to really make something of the company, but if we did not organize it appropriately, it would never pan out.

What do you think Patrick should do? Should he simply write a plan that was fanciful and hope that it would be good enough to earn the grant? Should he focus on his job and not go chasing after an opportunity that simply is not going to fit his company right now? Should he try to find other solutions? If so, what might they be? If you were Patrick, how would you likely decide to divide up the work of a staff of four if the grant were funded?

Personal exploration

Do a detailed job analysis on you and your present life. You may use any of the methods you studied in the questions in this chapter, though you may have to modify them. For example, you cannot interview yourself, but you may want to interview family and friends about what you do in your life. You cannot find other people who do your life like you, but you can probably find other people who are similar to you and do many things the same way. You could talk to them about what the similarities and differences are as you write your description.

Notes

1 Brockett, Oscar G., Robert J. Ball, John Fleming, and Andrew Carlson, *The Essential Theatre,* Cengage Learning, 2016.

CHAPTER 7

Financial management

While the need to conduct a job analysis in order to apply for a grant was real, what Patrick really faced was a financial issue. In order to accomplish the job analysis successfully, he either needed to take time off, which would require the temporary hiring of an assistant to help get his regular work done, or he would need to hire an outside firm to do the job analysis. But his budget was so small; he simply could not afford either of those options. He knew there was no money in anyone else's budget from which he could borrow (or steal). And Frank did not seem to have any additional money to support his venture. The problem, as Patrick considered it, was not the challenge of getting the job analysis done as much as it was that no one was budgeting appropriately for unforeseen circumstances. Certainly this could not have been the only time a need arose that had not been planned for.

Chapter objectives

After reading this chapter you should be able to discuss the differences between cash and accrual accounting, describe the three financial statements and what they are used for, explain how leasing a facility works, debate the pros and cons of using subscription money in advance of a production, and demonstrate how to build a theatre budget.

Financial management and bookkeeping

If money changes hands in the pursuit of theatre, then financial management is an important issue. You may think that your theatre company will not require any more than keeping a simple checking account to handle financial transactions, but even if your company is simple, it is still required to track and report its assets and liabilities. We use the term *financial management*, because it is generally accepted to mean the effective and efficient use of money within organizations. Sometimes people use the term interchangeably with finance, though *finance* typically refers to the management or study of financial transactions of larger corporations and their loans, investment strategies, banking, and financial systems. There are some theatres in the world with enough cash in the bank that they must have a financial strategy for investing wisely, but those companies are the exception, not the rule. For the rest, there is no need to do "finance," but there is a need to be fiscally prudent using wise financial management. Commercial productions are designed with hope of turning a profit, which is returned to the investors who pay for the original production. We say that they *finance* the original production, looking for a *return on investment* or *ROI*, which means that the money they pay to get the production up and running is paid back with interest.

Maybe you enjoyed an accounting class. Maybe you have never taken one. Or maybe you detest accounting. While fully understanding accounting and how it works is definitely an asset to any theatre manager, it may not be a necessity. True accountants are certified, because they are being asked to examine the financial position of an organization, and to present an honest assessment of that financial position. When an organization needs that level of expertise, it seeks someone with the appropriate qualifications, just as a theatre looks for someone with the qualifications of a theatre manager when it is looking for management. This does not mean, however, that a manager does not need to know anything about financial management.[1] Think of it like this: You travel to a foreign country where you do not speak the language. You walk into a hotel and they take your credit card and charge it "twenty-five." You gleefully sign and they hand you a key. You find the room the key opens and spend the night. You have a lovely stay and are very pleased. When you get home, you open your credit card statement to find that the exchange rate from their "twenty-five" translates into "one thousand" for you. Being fluent in their language was not necessary, but if you had known just a little piece of information, like the exchange rate and how it worked, you could have avoided being ripped off. Wise theatre managers may not need to be fluent in accounting, but they need to know enough to carry on an intelligent conversation with their accountant.

Cash versus accrual accounting

There are many ways to account for financial transactions. Small businesses typically do so on a cash basis, and larger organizations typically do so on an accrual basis. You probably have a bank account into which you put your earnings and out of which you pay all your bills. You operate your life on a cash basis. When the money is in the account, you recognize that you have it. When you actually spend it, you recognize you do not. Financial management on an accrual basis looks at the picture a little differently. On an accrual basis you would account for money coming into your account as soon as you earn it. At the end of a pay period you have earned a certain amount of money, and though the paycheck may not arrive for several days, on an accrual basis, you would count that money owed to you as an asset while on a cash basis you do not account for that money until it hits your bank. The same is true of those liabilities you have. On a cash basis you consider the money spent when you actually pay the bill. But on an accrual basis you would consider the money spent when the bill arrives in your mailbox, even though you may not pay it for several days.

Regardless of the type of accounting system a theatre uses, one of the most important things to consider is the statement of cash flows, which is one of the three basic financial statements.

The three financial statements

When accounting on an accrual basis, there are three different statements that help the manager understand the financial picture of the company.[2] The three statements are the statement of cash flows, the balance sheet, and the income statement, which is sometimes referred to as the profit-and-loss statement, or the P&L.

What does each do?

The *statement of cash flows* is the one that works most like your bank account. It looks at available cash during a specific period of time. Most businesses draft a statement of cash flows every month, quarter and/or year as their periods of time. For theatres, sometimes the best periods are centered on the production of a play. This can make for very confusing accounting, and often it is best to look at periods of time, such as each month, in addition to the period of a play. The statement of cash flows shows how changes in the business have affected cash on hand. It starts with the net cash you had when the period began, adds to it the amount of cash brought in during the period, subtracts the amount of cash spent during the period, and ends with the net amount of cash on hand. The *income statement* shows profitability over a designated period of time. Unlike the statement of cash flows, the income statement accounts for all assets and liabilities. If your theatre company owns sets, costumes, lights, land, buildings, office equipment, or anything else, those are assets. A commercial production has a great number of assets that are of value. You could sell them for a certain amount of money and increase the cash on hand. Because they are assets, they are accounted for on an income statement. Profitability does not just mean how much cash you have. A profitable company may not have cash because it has invested heavily in new equipment for growing in the future. A commercial production might have a slow week or two, cash flow is low, but if there are tickets already purchased for future weeks, the income statement would demonstrate money that is anticipated. Likewise, the income statement accounts for things that are owed, but have not yet been paid. This could mean outstanding bills, but it can also mean that your theatre owes people a production for which they have already purchased tickets but not yet seen. The *balance sheet* looks at a company as a snapshot in time rather than over a certain period. The reason it is called a balance sheet is because on it a company's assets always balance equally with its liabilities and equity. Equity is either the net income or owner profit, however you choose to think about it. Think of your bank account. Your balance sheet shows how much you have on one side; let's say that's 500. On the other side it shows how much you have spent plus the amount of money left over. Let's say you spent 350, and have 150 left over. Each side totals 500, so they balance.

How do you read them?

Reading the three statements, like learning to do anything, takes a little practice. But it really is not difficult. When reading these three statements, know that there can be all sorts of entries. For ease of explanation, we are using typical and standard entries, and have put numbers next to them as reference points.

THE STATEMENT OF CASH FLOWS

1 Beginning Cash Balance

2 Cash Receipts
3 Cash Disbursements
4 Cash from Operations

5 Fixed Assets Purchased
6 Net Borrowing
7 Income Taxes Paid
8 Sale of Stock

9 Ending Cash Value

Let's start by looking at the statement of cash flow. This statement would be constructed for a specific period of time, and in theatre, that period is often the time around a single production. Line 1, Beginning Cash Balance, is the amount of money that was on hand at the beginning of the period. For our play, that would be the cash we had before we sold a single ticket or purchased a single item to make the play. Line 2, Cash Receipts, is all the money we collected during the period. For our play that would include ticket sales, donations, revenue from program ads, concessions, and anything else that brought actual money into the company. From line 2, we subtract line 3, Cash Disbursements. These are any actual expenditures we made during the period. We would not include things we have promised to pay, or expect to pay; only the things we actually paid for. Receipts minus disbursements gives us line 4, Cash from Operations.

Line 5, Fixed Assets Purchased, is any expenditure of cash that is going toward something permanent (or long-term) that will be used to make our product, in our case, theatre. This could be the purchase of a building, new stage rigging, new seats, a table saw, a new copier for the office, or any other equipment we will use for a long time. It lowers the cash, but it is still of value. Line 6, Net Borrowing, is the amount of money we borrowed during the period, minus the amount of money we paid back during the period. We add line 6 to line 5. Then we subtract line 7, Income Taxes Paid, which is the amount of money we spent on actual tax payments during the period. To that we add line 8, Sale of Stock. This is a transaction in for-profit business where you sell a small percentage of the business in exchange for cash that is invested into the business. In commercial theatre we would see this line. In nonprofit theatre, it is less likely that line 8 would appear. But if we did sell stock, we brought in cash, and add that. Our line 9, Ending Cash Value, would reflect the amount of cash on hand at the end of the period. We do the following: Lines $1 + 4 - 5 + 6 - 7 + 8 =$ line 9.

THE BALANCE SHEET

ASSETS	LIABILITIES AND EQUITY
1 Cash	1 Payables
2 Receivables	2 Accrued Expenses
3 Inventory	3 Debt Service
4 Prepaid Expenses	4 Income Taxes Payable
5 Current Assets	5 Current Liabilities
6 Other Assets	6 Long-term Debt
7 Fixed Assets	7 Capital Stock
8 Accumulated Depreciation	8 Retained Earnings
9 Net Fixed Assets	9 Equity
10 Total Assets	10 Total Liabilities

Next, let's look at the balance sheet. Remember that this will give us a picture of the business as a snapshot in time – on the day it is written. We start with the left column, the assets. Line 1 is Cash, which we can take from our statement of cash flow if its reporting period ends today. Next are *receivables*, which are those things that we have already provided but have yet to be paid for. In theatre we often see "pledged receivables," which are typically pledged donations that have not yet been sent to us. We may also rent out a set, but not get paid until the set we rented out has been used for a production. Line 3 is *inventory*. Inventory is the materials we have on hand. It could be raw materials that will be made into something, materials in the process of being made into something, or completed goods. In theatre, because we are not manufacturing goods, inventory typically includes fabric for costumes, lumber for sets, and the like. Once the play is over, these things may be discarded, or dismantled and returned to raw materials, but they are of value, and so we include them in inventory. Line 4 is *prepaid expenses*, which are things the company has paid for, but that the company has not yet received. Paying rent in advance is a prepaid expense, as are insurance premiums, bonds posted with unions, and things like salary advances. We add the first four lines together to get our current assets at line 5.

In theatre, we do not see a lot of line 6, *other assets*, because these are nontangible assets of value to the company.[3] It would include things like intellectual property rights, patents, and trademarks of value. A theatre company might include the value of its subscriber list, but unless there is a market of people wanting to buy that list, it really has no value. For a commercial production there are intellectual property rights, and copyrights, but they are typically held and owned by the writers or designers and only temporarily licensed to the producer, so those assets do not belong to the production company.

Line 7 is *fixed assets* or *fixed assets at cost*, which is the amount paid for those items used to make whatever it is our company makes. Unlike inventory, fixed assets will be used over again. Lighting instruments, sewing machines, copiers, the building itself, the land on which the building sits, drops and sets we repaint, and costumes we reuse are all fixed assets. Line 8, *accumulated depreciation*, tells us how much value those fixed assets have lost over time. Nothing lasts forever, and accountants keep track of the drop in value from usage. Line 7 minus line 8 gives us line 9, *net fixed assets*. Adding lines 5, 6, and 9 gives us line 10, *total assets*.

Now let's look at the other side of the balance sheet. Line 1, *payables*, are those things the company has already acquired, but that it has yet to pay for. Most of our regular bills are payables. If we charge something on credit, that is a payable. Line 2, *accrued expenses,* is very similar to payables, but these are money obligations to people or businesses other than typical suppliers. Owing salaries for work already performed, or owing money to an accountant would be accrued expenses, as would owing interest on a loan. Line 3, *debt service* or current debt, is any money owed on loans within twelve months of the balance sheet. Line 6, *long-term debt,* is money owed out further than twelve months. Line 4, *income taxes payable,* is money owed to the government as a tax on income. This most often includes money held from an employee's paycheck as their tax burden to the government. To determine line 5, *current liabilities,* we add lines 1 through 4.

THE INCOME STATEMENT

1 Net Sales
2 Cost of Goods Sold
_____
3 Gross Margin

4 Sales/Marketing
5 Research/Development
6 General/Administrative
_____
7 Operating Expenses

8 Income from Operations

9 Interest Income
10 Income Taxes

11 Net Income
_____

The income statement tells us about profitability by showing how much net income occurred over a period of time. Line 1, *net sales,* are the total amount of sales a company does during the period. For a theatre, this would mean tickets sold. Line 2, *cost of goods sold,* is the amount of money the company had to spend in making the product that was sold. We might think of the fabric, lumber, and lighting gel that was in inventory as now moving out of inventory and into cost of goods sold. This would also include employee costs for designers, actors, and technicians working on a production. Subtracting line 2 from line 1 gives us line 3, *gross margin*. Lines 4, 5, and 6 add together to give us line 7, *operating expenses*, which are the expenditures for keeping the business going. We take line 3, gross margin, and subtract line 7, operating expenses, to come up with line 8, *income from operations*. Lines 9 and 10 are for income and expenses that are not related to operating the business, but are ancillary to it, such as interest earned from money in the bank, or paying interest on loans.

The income statement for a theatre is sometimes referred to as the "statement of financial activity," and is laid out a bit differently than the traditional income statement.[4] Instead of the first three lines being about the income and cost of creating a good, it is about revenue generated, which would include lines for earned (tickets) and unearned (donations) income, and lines for production expenses, fundraising expenses, and then general, administrative, and marketing expenses. Laid out this way, the statement treats fundraising almost like a second product in addition to the creation of plays.

Questions to research for class discussion:

Search the Internet and find answers for these questions before you read any further. Be prepared to discuss them in class.

7.1 What is cost accounting? Can you do it for a theatre? Should you?

7.2 What is the difference between a spending plan and a budget?

7.3 What is zero-based budgeting?

7.4 What are other ways you can develop a budget?

7.5 What do you do if income doesn't meet budgeted expectations, or expenses go over budget, or both?

The financial statements tell us how well a company is doing, but they are reporting after the fact. The document that helps us plan for our intended financial position is the annual budget, which is a listing of all the income we anticipate generating, and all the costs and expenses we anticipate. How detailed a budget gets depends on many things, including the size of the organization. Theatres often provide sufficient enough detail to track income and expenses for each individual show in a season. Here's a sample budget to look at:

PRODUCTION	PLAY 1	PLAY 2	PLAY 3	PLAY 4	TOTAL
SINGLE TICKETS	20000	25000	22500	27500	95000
GROUP SALES	4000	5000	3500	4500	17000
SUBSCRIPTIONS	95000	95000	95000	95000	380000
TOTAL TICKET SALES	**1190000**	**125000**	**121000**	**127000**	**492000**
ACTORS					
EQUITY	2000	2200	5500	6000	15700
NON-EQUITY	1500	1000	1000	1750	5250
ORCHESTRA	0	2000	0	3000	5000
MUSIC DIRECTOR	0	1000	0	1000	2000
DIRECTOR	2500	3000	2500	3000	11000
CHOREOGRAPHER	0	1250	0	2000	3250
TOTAL ARTIST	**6000**	**10450**	**9000**	**16750**	**42200**
STAGE MANAGER	2000	2000	2000	2000	8000
ASST. STAGE MANAGER	1700	1700	1700	1700	6800
WARDROBE CREW	2500	2000	2000	4000	10500
LIGHTING DESIGNER	1500	1500	1500	2000	6500
SOUND DESIGNER	0	1500	0	2000	3500
COSTUME DESIGNER	2000	1500	1500	2500	7500
PROPS SUPERVISOR	500	500	500	750	2250
SCENIC DESIGNER	0	2500	1000	0	3500
SCENIC ARTISTS		2000	2000		4000
STAGEHANDS-UNION	1000	5000	1000	5000	12000
STAGEHANDS-NON-UNION	1000	0	1000	0	2000
PAYROLL TAXES	4840	8220	6440	10690	30190
PRODUCTION SALARY EXPENSES	**17040**	**28420**	**20640**	**30640**	**96740**
WARDROBE MAINTENANCE	100	500	100	500	1200
FREIGHT	500	0	0	2500	3000
AGENT COMMISSIONS	200	220	550	600	1570
SET PURCHASES	0	3500	1200	0	4700
SET RENTALS	3000	0	0	7000	10000
PROPS PURCHASES	400	400	400	400	1600
PROPS RENTALS	0	0	0	0	0
COSTUME PURCHASES	1000	2500	1000	3500	8000
COSTUME RENTALS	250	500	250	1000	2000
SOUND PURCHASES	0	0	0	0	0
SOUND RENTALS	0	1000	0	1000	2000
AUDITION EXPENSES	500	500	500	500	2000
AUDITION PIANIST	0	400	0	400	800
PENSION AND WELFARE	426	711	516	766	2419
SCRIPTS AND SCORES	200	1250	200	1290	2940
ROYALTIES	1000	9000	1000	11000	22000
TRANSPORTATION	500	1000	500	1000	3000
LODGING	0	0	0	1250	1250
MEALS AND ENTERTAINMENT	250	250	250	250	1000
AUDITION MARKETING	300	300	300	300	1200
MISC. PRODUCTION EXPENSES	1000	1000	1000	1000	4000
TOTAL PRODUCTION EXPENSES	**9626**	**23031**	**7766**	**34256**	**74679**
TOTAL DIRECT COSTS	**32666**	**61901**	**37406**	**81646**	**213619**

(Continued)

ARTISTIC SALARIES	20000	20000	20000	20000	80000
TECHNICAL SALARIES	9000	9000	9000	9000	36000
PAYROLL TAX	2320	2320	2320	2320	9280
POSTAGE/MAILING	1000	1000	1000	1000	4000
BUILDING RENT	10000	10000	10000	10000	40000
TOTAL INDIRECT EXPENSES	**42320**	**42320**	**42320**	**42320**	**169280**
TOTAL SHOW EXPENSE	**74986**	**104221**	**79726**	**123966**	**382899**
NET SHOW REVENUE	**44014**	**20780**	**41274**	**3034**	**109102**

INDIVIDUAL DONATIONS	67000
BOARD DONATIONS	15000
FOUNDATION GRANTS	25000
GOVERNMENT GRANTS	25000
FUNDRAISING EVENT INCOME	60000
FUNDRAISING INCOME	**192000**
PROGRAM AD SALES	9000
THEATER RENTAL INCOME	10000
CONCESSIONS	4500
SET RENTAL INCOME	7000
OTHER INCOME	**30500**
TOTAL REVENUE	**714500** *THIS INCLUDES TOTAL TICKET SALES

FACILITIES

THEATRE RENT	22000
THEATRE UPKEEP AND UTILITIES	10000
TOTAL FACILITIES	**32000**

MARKETING AND SALES

PROGRAM PRINTING	22000
BOX OFFICE EXPENSES	30000
ADVERTISING	35000
TELEMARKETING	10000
TOTAL MARKETING AND SALES	**97000**

FUNDRAISING

SALARIES	45000
EVENTS	15000
EXPENSES	1250
TOTAL FUNDRAISING	**61250**

GENERAL AND ADMINISTRATIVE

ADMINISTRATION SALARIES	135000
POSTAGE AND MAILING	2000
PRINTING	1000
OFFICE SUPPLIES	1000
TOTAL G AND O	**139000**
TOTALS EXPENSES	**712149** *THIS INCLUDES SHOW EXPENSES
NET REVENUE	**2352**

The sample budget actually includes two types of theatre budgets rolled into one, and it is really more specifically geared to a not-for-profit theatre. The annual budget includes projections for all anticipated expenses and income, including both *direct income and expenses*, which are the cost and revenue associated with the primary function of the company, in this case the creation of theatre, and indirect income and expenses, which are the cost and revenue associate with ancillary activities such as marketing, administration, and fundraising. The first part of the sample budget provides the details of the production budgets. These include anticipated revenue and expenses for each individual production, and they can be included in detail in an annual budget, or simply listed with totals in the annual budget, and prepared as separate budgets for each production.

When it comes to anticipating revenue, this requires more than a guess. The smart manager knows how many seats are available, at what price they each sell for, how full the theatre typically gets for similar types of productions at similar times of the year (capacity), and calculates potential earned revenue based on this historical data. Often, the manager will include with a production budget a spreadsheet that demonstrates exactly how earned revenue is being calculated. For a commercial production this is very tricky, as there is little historical data, and it is extremely difficult to determine how demand will affect sales. Simply choosing the right sized theatre for a commercial production can be challenging, as a theatre that is too big might not ever fill up, and a theatre that is too small might cost potential sales when the theatre is sold out.

Note that a production budget for a commercial production is a little different. While the commercial production has a budget that considers all the expenses for creating the production, that is the amount it will take to invest in the production. Once that investment is made and the production is up and running, the commercial production operates on a weekly operating budget, which accounts for all the income generated each week, minus all the expenses that must be paid each week, with the balance or *profit* being paid to the investors as a return on investment. The weekly operating budget can be quite difficult to predict because while most of the operating costs associated with a commercial production remain fairly steady, such as salaries, rents, ticketing costs, cleaning costs, and so on, royalty payments can be quite tricky. Most members of the team that actually created the production, such as writers, designers, directors, and producers, often receive a royalty payment based on how much money is generated at the box office, and the arrangements can be quite convoluted, based on how well the production is doing. But in order for a commercial production to be successful, the ultimate goal is to make sure that the weekly operating budget is always showing net revenue.

Credit

The previous section mentioned how to account for money due on loans or items purchased with a credit card. You probably know how to get a credit card for yourself, but getting one for a business, and especially a theatre, is a little trickier.[5] If a person cannot pay a credit card, there are ways the courts can discharge the debt, and the discharge is noted on the person's credit report, warning future lenders that the person is a bad credit risk. If a company has debt discharged, however, the owner(s) of the company could simply close the company and start an entirely new one. So lending money to a company can be riskier.

How to get it

Financial institutions that loan money do so for the benefit of their shareholders. They loan the money expecting to get it back with interest, which is what generates their profit. Of course, there is a certain amount of risk involved in loaning people money, because you may not be able to collect on the debt, so it would be a loss. Financial institutions manage this loss by charging higher interest rates when they determine that making the loan (including opening a credit card for someone) is riskier. This is where the term *high credit risk* comes from. Businesses that have been established for a long time and show a history of strong financial acumen and profit can often secure loans and credit cards easily. Even new businesses that can show a very detailed plan for how they will conduct business and turn a profit may be eligible for loans at higher interest rates. Financial institutions, however, often view theatre as too risky a venture to loan money to. So many commercial productions fail, which would mean a huge financial loss of loaned money. And nonprofit theatres often survive by asking people to make donations, which is also a risky way to expect to see one's loaned money returned. Typically, a financial institution will only loan money to a theatre company if there is some sort of security for their loan. That might mean that they are promised the land or building if the company defaults on the loan. If the company does not own any physical assets to secure the loan, one or more of its members may have to promise to guarantee the loan, in case anything happens. But that means those members would be on the hook for repaying the debt.

How to avoid using it and why

You can probably see why a theatre company taking out a loan is not a good idea to begin with. While there are many theatres that can afford to repay a loan, typically they have been around a long time and have a very good track record. The biggest problem with taking out a loan is that the theatre must then pay for their current operating expenses, as well as pay back on the loan. It is a big financial burden, and one that has caused many theatres to collapse. But how do you avoid using credit, especially when you are just getting started? Chapter 11 looks at fundraising in greater detail, but when you are starting out, look for donations for everything. Donations never have to be repaid, and allow your theatre to be on stronger financial footing. There are plenty of businesses that are willing to provide some donated support to theatres including printers, lumber companies, fabric stores, and even people who have buildings that are not being used. It may require a little creativity, but getting a theatre started on only donations is not an impossible task.

Communicating with your accountant

Many accountants take courses in effective communication. The accounting industry recognizes that the way accountants see and describe the world is fairly different from how the rest of us do. That is especially true in theatre, where we tend to think in very creative ways. Accountants follow clearly defined rules and try to avoid being creative. If you understand the three financial statements, you are already way ahead of the curve. But when dealing with an accountant, be certain you ask lots of questions. The most important thing about talking to your accountant is that you always leave understanding what has been said. Many businesses have failed simply because the manager did not understand what the accountant was telling them. If there are numbers on a page you do not understand, or concepts being shared by the accountant you do not understand, stop and ask for an explanation until you do.

In-kind contributions

While we will discuss in-kind contributions in great detail in Chapter 11, it is important to touch upon them in a chapter on financial management. *In-kind contributions* are the donation of goods or services, other than money or monetary instruments such as stocks, bonds, or bank accounts. Theatre companies receive them on a regular basis. Sometimes it is free printing from a printer, or the free use of a city-owned building, or even some suits a widow donates from her husband's closet. For our purposes, it is fairly rare that we could turn around and sell those in-kind donations for cash, but for an accountant, they are worth every penny of their value, and are reported in the financial statements as such.[6] For a theatre company, you will often see lines that say "in-kind." These are references to donations of goods or services of value.

Think critically: borrowing or investing for the future

There are two ways to approach this class discussion. First, you can choose sides. Divide the class into two, by whatever means you choose, and debate the argument outlined below. Second, you can have an open discussion, each adding upon others' thoughts, and let the discussion uncover all the important details of all sides of the debate. Keep in mind that regardless of which approach you take, we want to be sure we dig deep into all sides of this important issue, in order to more effectively understand all positions.

CLASS DISCUSSION: Starting a new theatre company is an exciting project, but it also a challenging one. Making good theatre requires a substantial financial investment, and few people, foundations, or government agencies want to give money to a new company that has not proven it can eventually survive on its own. Investing in theatre is important to a well-rounded society, but investing in a new theatre is risky. And because of that risk, getting loans can be difficult, as well. But without an infusion of capital to get a theatre company started, there is no way to promote the company to potential audience members, who are the people who will be paying for the long-term viability of the company. Since those are going to be the recipients of the benefits of a theatre, perhaps they can make the initial investment and take the initial risk. By starting a theatre company with the promotion of a subscription, rather than by building the first play, we are essentially asking the subscribers to make that first financial investment. Their subscription money, which will buy them access to several productions over the course of the season, will be enough to get the company started. And because they pay in advance, the company will have working capital. As the first few subscriptions come in, all of that money can be invested to promote the sales of more subscriptions. Sure, there won't be enough money to make the last couple of productions of the season, but by that point the company can start selling subscriptions for the following season, and this new infusion of cash can pay for the remaining productions. Some see this as borrowing from the future, and others see it as an investment. But the problem with this model is that if there is ever the slightest downturn in subscription sales, or the budget doesn't quite get met, there's a period of time where the statement of cash flow shows no money. And if that happens when we are responsible for creating a new play, and do not yet have a future season to sell, then the company fails and all those subscribers lose their investment. And those subscribers do not even know that their money is being used in this way. Some argue this is the only way to get a theatre company up and running. Others argue there are better, more financially stable ways to operate. What do you think?

The financial audit and board responsibilities

Businesses have certain responsibilities to those they serve. A for-profit business serves its shareholders, and those shareholders often require an independent report on the activity that has gone on at the business. For this purpose, the company will hire an *independent auditor*, which is a person or people, typically accountants, who have no affiliation with the company, and who are certified to assess the company and its financial transactions. For a fee, this independent auditor studies the company and reports on what is occurring. While it may not be a requirement that nonprofit companies have annual audits, depending on the rules where you live, having an annual audit done is never a bad idea. The annual audit ensures that the financial management is being done correctly, and provides substantiation that the board and executives are doing their due diligence in protecting the assets of the company for the people who are being served.[7] An audit is often required when applying for grant money, to demonstrate to the grantor that the way you say you operate is, indeed, how you operate.

Leasing or buying a facility

We know what goes into buying a building to be turned into a theatre, or buying a theatre. We make a down payment, get money loaned to use to pay for the rest of the cost, and have monthly mortgage payments. When we buy it, it belongs to us, but is secured by a *note*, which recognizes that if we default on the mortgage loan, the lender has a right to the property. Buying your own theatre sounds like a great idea if you can afford to do it, but there are also good reasons to lease a space instead of buying it.

Pros and cons

Much of the time, theatre companies lease their facility, because the long-term mortgage requires a substantial down payment. Theatres also may choose to lease instead of buy because they do not want to be responsible for property taxes, property insurance, or maintenance costs associated with owning a building. Declining real estate values could have a serious effect on the balance sheet when a company owns a building. There may not be a suitable building available where the theatre wants to operate, or maybe the theatre wants to be mobile enough to change locations as they grow.

But leasing has some challenges as well. Unless you can find a pre-established theatre to rent, leasing a commercial building and transforming it into a theatre can be costly. Sometimes the lessor will participate in paying for changes to the building, but in return, they will expect you to commit to a longer-term lease. And because theatre, by its very nature, often requires regular alteration of the stage space, that may require regular approval of the owner. Also, the owner may not want certain types of productions in their facility. Perhaps they will stop a theatre from using profanity, from smoking, or from permitting nudity on stage, even if the script requires it. These may all be governed by local ordinance, but if they are not, the building owner has some control over their own building. Any right not clearly defined in a lease agreement remains with the owner.

And should you want to move out of a leased building, or to allow someone else to present their play there as well, unless there is a clearly defined process for subletting defined in the original lease, you will be stuck.

Questions to research for class discussion:

Search the Internet and find answers for these questions before you read any further. Be prepared to discuss them in class.

7.6 What is a common area in a commercial lease agreement?
7.7 What is a gross lease? What is a net lease? What is a triple-net lease? What is a percentage lease?
7.8 What is an escalation clause in a commercial lease?

The leasing agent

Owners of commercial buildings typically have an experienced leasing agent, who is trained to get the best lease on the most favorable terms for the owner. Trying to negotiate a lease with a leasing agent can be very challenging, because they know all the tricks of the trade, and you may not. If you are shopping for a building to lease, it is wise to find a commercial real estate broker to represent you. This broker will likely want you to agree to only use them for a certain period of time in an *exclusive agreement*. Having this broker is very wise, because they are just as knowledgeable about how to negotiate favorable terms for you, and the owner of the building typically pays them.

Producing versus presenting

While you have probably been thinking about a theatre company as being the business that creates plays and presents them to the public, there are actually two types of business going on in that scenario. In the first, there is the business of creating a play. In the second, there is the business of presenting plays to the public. Many companies do both of those things, but there are also lots of companies that do only one or the other.

Different responsibilities

The producer of plays, in the strictest sense of the term, is the person or company responsible for coordinating the resources necessary to make the play. The presenter of the play, then, is the person or company who actually promotes it and sells it to the public. In some sense this separates the marketing function out from the artistic function, though that is not entirely the case. In fact, even if a company is only concerned with producing the play, it still has a set of expenses for marketing the production to presenters, who will then pay the producer for the play. Oftentimes, the producing entity provides promotional materials, including press releases, posters, brochures, advertising, and the like to a presenter to assist in promoting the play to the public. The presenter, however, is the entity securing a facility for the performance, and doing the local promotion to potential audience members.

Questions to research for class discussion:

Search the Internet and find answers for these questions before you read any further. Be prepared to discuss them in class.

7.9 What is the International Society for the Performing Arts and what do they do?

7.10 Is there an association for performing arts presenters where you live? If so, what is it, where are they, and what do they do? If not, where are there such associations, and what do they do?

7.11 In what ways do producers of touring theatre reach out to potential presenters?

Finances

Most often, a producer, who sells the entire production to a local presenter, creates touring productions. Sometimes the agreements are fairly straightforward and involve a flat fee per performance. However, these arrangements can be very complex, include a split of the box revenue (known as a *gate split*) and have very detailed contracts spelling out exactly how much can be spent on what. Large touring production contracts often require that after the final performance, the representatives from the producer and the presenter go over every receipt and all the incomes, making the appropriate financial reports, and splitting the income per the contract. In these cases, the money split from the box office revenue is referred to as *NAGBOR*, which stands for net adjusted gross box office receipts.[8] *Gross box office receipts* refers to the total amount of money taken in from ticket sales. By adding the words *net adjusted*, we are stating that the amount of money being considered has been adjusted, and the remaining amount is the *net*. Box office income is adjusted because certain fees such as credit card processing charges, facility fees added to the price of a ticket, or postage and handling fees are not strictly ticket sales revenue, but they do come into the box office as part of the ticket sale so they are part of the gross, or total, box office receipts. When these and other agreed-to fees are removed from the gross total, we arrive at the NAGBOR.

Agencies

As you can imagine, there are hundreds of details involved in both producing and presenting a play, and in the case where the producer and presenter are different entities, the contract between them needs to spell out exactly who is responsible for what. There are books dedicated to the subject of presenting versus producing, but the most important lesson in any of them is, regardless of whether you are the producer or the presenter, you should find an expert agent to represent you and negotiate the terms of all those details on your behalf. Most touring productions have standard contracts that they offer to local presenters, but everything in that standard contract is negotiable. Many local presenters fail to recognize this fact, and accept the contract as presented, however the savvy local presenter hires an expert agent to negotiate and secure the best terms.

Build your theatre milestone 7: budget

In this milestone, you are going to create a realistic budget for your theatre company. Be sure when you set out to predict what income you may earn from ticket sales and donations that you are realistic. Ticket sales estimates can be made by considering the number of seats in your theatre that you expect to fill at each performance, and multiplying that by the average ticket price and the number of performances. Be as realistic as possible, even though this may all feel like guess work.

Case study

Patrick had been in his job for about a year, and during that time he had been collecting a lot of information about his ticket buyers. He had learned how they interacted with the world by conducting focus groups and surveys, and by asking about their buying habits and their communication methods. Patrick knew that the better he understood his consumers, the better prepared he would be to find more people like them, and he would know how best to communicate with them.

He created a plan for increasing single ticket sales by utilizing a new smartphone app that connected to Facebook. Customers would receive "push" notifications about discount pricing and special events occurring at the theatre, and they could purchase tickets through an in-app purchase; the day and time they were going to attend, as well as their seat numbers, would post on their Facebook wall with a message encouraging their friends to attend the same performance. Friends who downloaded the app through a link could be seated close together, and would get the same discount. The cost for this project was high, but Frank had agreed to an investment of more than $50,000 to get it up and running. The project would roll out in phases. In the first phase, the app was promoted through traditional means, including local newspapers, radio, cable ads, and social media. The cost to do in-app purchases was expensive, but it allowed Patrick to gather a wealth of information about buyers and their buying habits, and by having it all connect through Facebook, which was also very expensive, Patrick could get enough information to know exactly how to find more people who would be interested in his theatre. In the second phase, app users who made more than one purchase over a certain period of time would be given a free membership to the concierge-level app, which retailed at a premium price. Patrick set the price extremely high, because he did not want people to simply buy it. The goal of the concierge app was to shift these buyers to an app where the ticket purchase happened through a link to the box office, rather than as an in-app purchase. This meant that 100% of the income would go to the theatre, and by giving these new customers the luxury of a concierge connection to the box office, which came with a number of new perks, Patrick could ensure retention of his consumers. Each year that they purchased more than once, they would be rewarded with continuing codes for a free concierge app membership. As Patrick was preparing to roll out the second phase, Frank came to him with some startling news. The board had asked to see a statement of cash flow, and a year-to-date report of actual expenses against the budget, and it turned out the company was in dire trouble. Frank had continuously showed the board only an income statement, and they had no idea that the company had been borrowing against its future sales. There was very little cash left to complete the season, and Frank had to cut everything he could. So he told Patrick phase two was off. But Patrick knew this was a mistake.

It wasn't that we didn't have the money. It was that if phase two didn't work, we wouldn't have enough money to finish the season. But phase two was definitely going to work. I had all the data to show exactly how many people we were adding on a monthly basis, how much they were spending, and what that would translate into when we looked at cash flow. The problem was, the first phase was very expensive, and while we had increased single ticket revenue by about 12%, with each sale we were bringing in less than 30% of a traditional ticket sale, because the money was going to the app stores and Facebook. The board didn't understand the entire project, and they were satisfied that the extra revenue was great, but we should stop there until we had more cash. But that's a little like deciding in December that you're cold building the snowman, so you're going to go inside and warm up and come back in the spring to work on the snowman. By then, the snow is gone and there's nothing to build on, so you wait, and hope there's a new snowfall the next winter. But even then, you have to make the same commitment to building the snowman, and you have to see it through to completion. If we pulled the plug after phase one, we would start losing those ticket buyers, and there was no guarantee that there would be more if we waited another year. Social media and technology change so fast that we have to stay ahead of how it is being used. We can't be reactionary.

But this was about money, and Frank knew it. Patrick wondered how he could solve this problem. He was certain that by moving into phase two he could greatly increase the cash flow into the company, but the board was old school and probably not ready to hear about the behind-the-scenes process of social media marketing. They were concerned about their fiduciary responsibility to the company and were trying to play it safe. Frank told Patrick he could make a presentation to the board, but that could be extremely risky. The board might feel that what the company needed at this time was a traditional marketing director, and could just as easily ask that Patrick be replaced. On the other hand, if the board was convinced by Patrick to move forward with phase two and it did not yield the results he hoped for, he would certainly lose his job, and he might put the company at risk of going bankrupt. What are the potential solutions for Patrick? What are the pros and cons of each potential solution? Is Patrick just being too eager about his pet project at a time when the company cannot afford to be risky, or should he demand that the high risk would return high reward? What would you do?

Personal exploration

Take a few minutes to draft your personal budget for the next month. Remember that you are accounting for all your income and all your expenses. Do not simply write down fictitious numbers, but consider that the expenses side is your spending plan for the whole month, and you have to stick to this budget. Once you have completed your budget, draft a cash flow statement for yourself for the period of the last month.

Notes

1 Balfour, Danny L., and Ramya Ramanath, "Forging theatre and community: Challenges and strategies for serving two missions," *Public Voices* 12, no. 1 (2016): 46–66.
2 Jean-François, Emmanuel, *Financial Sustainability for Nonprofit Organizations,* Springer Publishing Company, 2014.

3 Pierce, Andrew, "Developing a sustainable business model for theatres: A case study of Kansas City's starlight theatre," PhD dissertation, University of Missouri, Columbia, 2016.

4 Ibid.

5 Schumann, Jennifer Diane, "Facing the Music: How Seven Theater Companies Respond to Economic Challenges," Master of Science in Arts Administration thesis, Drexel University, 2014.

6 Samu, Sridhar, and Walter W. Wymer Jr., *Nonprofit and Business Sector Collaboration: Social Enterprises, Cause-Related Marketing, Sponsorships, and Other Corporate-Nonprofit Dealings,* Routledge, 2013.

7 DiCarlo, Christopher, *Onprofit Transformation: 100 Keys to Breakthrough Results for Every Board and Chief Executive,* Archway Publishing, 2016.

8 Micocci, Tony, *Booking Performance Tours: Marketing and Acquiring Live Arts and Entertainment,* Skyhorse Publishing, 2013.

CHAPTER 8

Management and the audience

Every day that he came into the office, Patrick stopped by the ticket office to pick up the sales reports from the previous day. As part of his routine, he would chat with whichever ticket agents were in the office at the time, spend a few minutes discussing sales progress with the box office manager, and maybe even ask a few questions about the ticketing software. Patrick was the kind of person who was constantly inquisitive, always wanting to know how things worked. He maybe even thought there could be something in the ticket software that could be of even greater use to him than just the sales reports. His regular visits made it clear to him that the staff in the ticket office had plenty to do. Though sometimes, when sales were slow, they would be bored. He wondered if this was not the reason people were always leaving to find other work.

Chapter objectives

After reading this chapter, you should be able to evaluate the value of the ticket office labor force, explain the functions of ticketing systems, describe the work of a house management staff, recognize the skills required for providing excellent customer service, discuss theatre programs, concessions, bars, rentals, and ancillary operations, evaluate the interactions between a theatre and its community, and devise a box office ticketing plan.

Management and the audience

When a consumer interacts with a theatre company, they are obviously aware of the performers, and have a general understanding that a director manages those performers. Consumers see the actors and know their efforts have been coordinated. But there are other managers that audiences interact with as well. These are the people who manage front of house operations. *Front of house* refers to the areas in a theatre the audience has access to, such as the auditorium and foyer. In these areas, the audience has direct interactions with house management and box office management.

Ticketing office

The first thing an audience member typically sees before even entering a theatre is the ticket office or box office. It has been said that it is called the *box office* because in Elizabethan times the main public watched plays by standing in a pit in front of the stage while the nobility would purchase tickets for *box seats*, small seating areas separated from one another by walls, in the balcony. Tickets for those private box seats were sold from an office in the front of the theatre, which gave it the name box office. For centuries, the function of the box office was simply to collect admission fees. Today, however, box offices process vast amounts of data, not only tracking who is sitting where and when, but collecting marketing information about patrons, and serving as the primary, and often only, point of customer services interaction.

Ticketing systems

There are hundreds of ticketing systems available today, ranging in price and starting at free or almost free.[1] For the new theatre just getting going, a smaller system with limited capacity and little to no upfront cost might be the most effective; while a larger, established theatre may need a whole host of different functions to coordinate the data generated in the box office. The most basic function of a ticketing system is to track what seats are available and to print and sell tickets. But ticketing systems now are typically integrated with an online ticketing function, have app support, allow for the collection and management of marketing and fundraising data, and generate myriad reports. Some theatres offer subscriptions, and some do not. How those subscriptions are processed, how many plays are in the subscription, how many venues are associated with the company and the like are important considerations in selecting the right ticketing system. Likewise, if the company gives some tickets to an agency to sell, how those are tracked in the ticketing system is important. Many theatres rely on the collection of data about patrons buying tickets to make smart marketing decisions. Companies may ask how the patron heard about the play, informing them of which avenue of communication is proving most effective. They may track addresses in order to determine buying patterns from certain neighborhoods. Marketing managers may use the ticketing system for website automation or *search engine optimization* (SEO), which is a way to ensure that when a person does a web search for certain keywords, the optimized website pops up in the top of the list. Some ticketing systems integrate fundraising campaigns that help track a patron's giving history, when they have been contacted about particular fundraising campaigns, and even personal details that help the development professional ensure that they are providing the most rewarding relationship between the

Think critically: the most important face

There are two ways to approach this class discussion. First, you can choose sides. Divide the class into two, by whatever means you choose, and debate the argument outlined below. Second, you can have an open discussion, each adding upon others' thoughts, and let the discussion uncover all the important details of all sides of the debate. Keep in mind that regardless of which approach you take, we want to be sure we dig deep into all sides of this important issue, in order to more effectively understand all positions.

CLASS DISCUSSION: While audience members see actors and enjoy their work, the only people in a theatre they really interact with are the box office representatives and ushers. Whether it is through a phone call, an email, or a face-to-face interaction, the box office representative is the consumer's first point of contact with the theatre, and we all know that first impressions are very important. Yet ushers and box office representatives are some of the lowest paid employees in theatre. Just because they are not on stage does not mean their work is less significant in the theatre-going experience. Many argue just the reverse: the most important employee in a theatre is the one who can assure that the experience the audience member has is exemplary from beginning to end, and that one employee is the box office representative. In order to ensure the best customer service, which can translate into the best customer experience, we should be hiring only the best, most experienced people in the box office, and that requires an investment in their salaries. It does not matter how good the performance is if the customer is frustrated before the play even begins. And the box office representative is not simply processing a transaction. These employees also have a significant sales function. They need to be knowledgeable about each production, and have an ability to promote it effectively to close the sale. They also need a talent for upselling, or encouraging audience members to buy additional tickets or subscriptions. But others argue that to spend more money on box office staff takes away precious resources from the stage, and without that money there is no way to ensure we are creating great art. It makes no sense to sacrifice the art for the box office experience; after all, the audience is not attending the theatre for the joy of having a good experience at the box office. And upselling is pushing a product on someone who is not actually interested in that product, so it is a talent that should probably be kept out of the theatre. If we upsell someone on a production they did not wish to see, they will just be dissatisfied, and blame the production team for their dissatisfaction. Should the salaries of box office employees be closer to those of the artists, ensuring that we are considering the entire experience of the audience? Or should we continue to place the greatest amount of emphasis on the play itself, even if we lose some audience members because they are dissatisfied with the customer service?

theatre and the donor (or potential donor). Many times, these fundraising components can be used to generate letters directed at specific individuals based on the data stored in the system.

Finally, ticketing systems also generate essential reports. For the box office, being able to have a printed list of who is sitting where for every performance, known as the *seating book*, can be invaluable. Reports can quickly be generated to break down how people paid, where they made their purchase, how much was the average purchase, how many tickets are currently sold and/or available to future events, and on and on. Also, an essential function of the ticketing system is to track the money. Ticketing systems have grown in complexity over the last several years, and while their primary function is to sell tickets, they now function as the primary customer service management, or CSM, tool in many theatres.[2]

Accounting requirements

One of the functions of management is control, and in order to control the marketing and sales process, managers need to know if they are meeting their expected goals. If a manager has certain expectations for how well a play will sell, it is important for them to be able to track sales on an ongoing basis to see if changes need to be made in the marketing approach. Ticketing systems allow for an immediate reporting of sales based on any number of desired criteria. At the close of a production, the box office manager can print a report that breaks down all the revenue generated at the box office, and even tracks out the NAGBOR so that royalties or gate splits can be made without doing lengthy, detailed calculations and tabulations. The ticketing software takes care of all those details. Financial managers can use reports from the ticketing system to instantly update financial reporting, ensuring that the budget is on track, and allowing for immediate correction if the company is not on budget. Box office managers can also see which box office representatives generated the largest volume of sales, what time of day sales are the highest, and even how long representatives take to process transactions. The potential wealth of information is vast, and when used correctly, aids a theatre company in its success.

Questions to research for class discussion:

Search the Internet and find answers for these questions before you read any further. Be prepared to discuss them in class.

8.1 Compare three different box office ticketing systems. What unique features does each have that the others do not?

8.2 What sorts of compatibility issues might be important when selecting a ticketing system?

8.3 What is the cheapest way you can find to operate a ticketing system for a theatre (don't forget the cost of the actual equipment that may be required)?

Front of house

While the box office may serve as the initial point of contact between the patron and the theatre company, on the night of attendance, the house management staff typically meets the customer. This staff is responsible for ensuring that the audience has a safe, enjoyable experience while in attendance. The house manager, who oversees the facility, the ushers, and sometimes the concessions, typically coordinates the staff. The house manager is responsible for making certain that the facility is properly lit, clean, safe, and ready for an audience. If there are programs, the house manager ensures the appropriate quantities are available. The house management staff takes tickets at the door, and ushers show patrons to their seats.

While this all may seem routine, the house manager often spends the time just before curtain solving problems. If there are notices that must be posted for arriving audience members, posting them is the house manager's duty. If there is a duplication in ticketing, the house manager, often in consultation with the box office, has to resolve the problem quickly and efficiently, oftentimes using *house seats,* which are a block of excellent seats held for the use of management in just such situations. Sometimes, when a play is sold out, at the very last minute any unused house seats are released for the box office to sell.

The house manager also has to coordinate the timing of getting the entire audience seated by curtain, and getting them out and in again at intermission. The house manager is the theatre's representative, and the play typically does not begin until the house manager feels the audience is appropriately seated, at which time the house manager hands control to the stage manager. It is then incumbent on the house manager to appropriately handle the seating of latecomers, and to solve any problems audience members might have during the course of the play. In rare instances, house managers have to be prepared to deal with medical emergencies or other disasters.

Customer service

As you can imagine, working the front of house requires a very special person who is capable of handling routine interactions as well as sudden disasters. The most important part of the job is being certain to communicate effectively in every transaction. That means not only speaking, but also listening to the customer. An irate customer can usually be easily satisfied if they feel they have been heard. Yes, it is important to be knowledgeable about the theatre, the play, the company policies, and so forth, but it is just as important to be able to understand how the patron is feeling. While it may not be true that the customer is always right, it is best to proceed as if the customer should be treated like they are right. After all, the customer service goal is to make sure the customer has an excellent experience.[3] Sometimes this means knowing when a customer is irate, when a customer just wants to chat, or when a customer prefers to be left alone. It requires a great deal of intuition, experience, enormous amounts of patience, and a genuine desire to create happy customers.

Questions to research for class discussion:

Search the Internet and find answers for these questions before you read any further. Be prepared to discuss them in class.

8.4   What are five skills that every employee should have in order to provide excellent customer service?
8.5   What should you do when a customer is wrong?
8.6   How should you deal with an angry or irate customer?
8.7   What is the cost of poor customer service?

Concessions

You have probably been to a theatre that had a big queue at the bar during intermission. One piece of value that theatres often add is by providing refreshments and other concessions both before the play begins and/or at intermission.[4] There are plenty of theatres that do a robust business selling all sorts of things, and even operating gift shops to capture sales while the patrons are present. But most theatres end up offering concessions as a courtesy. Imagine, for a moment, that your primary business concern was selling candy bars and soda pop, but you only had fifteen minutes a day at which several hundred people lined up to buy your goods. It does not seem like a particularly good business model, does it?

Bar? Popcorn?

So many new theatres see the concessions stand as a potential for additional revenue. In particular, many are encouraged by the thought of being able to sell alcohol to patrons, thinking it can be quite profitable.[5] But that is not always the case. In most jurisdictions, obtaining the license to serve alcohol can be a long or costly process, or both. And with alcohol sales comes some negative side effects. Alcohol is a natural depressant that slows down the nervous system and relaxes muscles. This may not be the condition a theatre wishes to have its patrons in while watching a play. Also, with the sale of alcohol come certain risks.[6] If a patron were to cause injury to themselves or others as a result of being intoxicated, the business that served them alcohol could potentially be liable. The wise theatre manager knows that if alcohol is to be sold, the theatre should be prepared to invest heavily in insurance that protects the company.

Theatres have all sorts of policies on the sale and consumption of food and beverages. Many choose to limit consumption to the foyer area in order to protect the seating and floor of the auditorium from spills and excess garbage. Others find that limiting consumption to the foyer also reduces sales and limits the audience's experience. Theatres may offer beverages and candy, but choose not to offer popcorn because the smell permeates the facility, or because they find popcorn to be less sophisticated than other food. Some theatres sell ice cream in the aisles at intermission, while others do not. There is no standard procedure for how to offer concessions to patrons. But a concessions policy should be considered in light of the value it adds to patrons, and how that affects the entire audience experience. The mission of the theatre company is rarely about selling food and beverages to a hungry audience.

Costume and scenic rentals

One of the assets that theatres tend to accumulate is a stock of sets and more often costumes that can be rented out for additional revenue. While this can be an excellent source of small amounts of money, like the concessions stand, it requires careful planning to determine what policy best fits with the theatre's mission. In order to rent out materials, there must be some assurance (and insurance) that will guarantee those assets are protected and returned in the condition in which they were rented out. Sets and costumes will have to be inventoried and tracked to facilitate smooth rentals and returns. The labor required to handle renting out stock may be more time consuming than current staffing can handle. If these are additional duties, they may require additional compensation.

Program advertising

Many theatres sell advertising space in their programs to local businesses to generate extra revenue. Like concessions and stock rentals, selling advertising space needs to be considered in light of the company's mission. But it is also important to consider the cost of printing the advertising. Most theatres never bother to figure the cost per page of printing their program, and sometimes theatres actually lose money in the process of selling advertisements, because the cost to print the ads is greater than the price being charged for the space. This does not even begin to take into account the cost associated with having someone promote, sell, and coordinate the ads, as well as having to deal with program layout and the technical elements of printing. Program advertising does demonstrate a sense of community with the theatre company, and this has certain rewards on its own merit, but before choosing to sell advertising, the wise theatre manager determines how to do so in a way that works for everyone's best interests.[7]

Questions to research for class discussion:

Search the Internet and find answers for these questions before you read any further. Be prepared to discuss them in class.

8.8   What will you need to do in order to sell program advertising?
8.9   How much do theatre sets and costumes rent for, and where would you get them?
8.10 What are your local regulations regarding the handling and sale of food?
8.11 What are your local regulations regarding the sale of alcohol?

Community

In each of the examples of ancillary functions noted above – concessions, costume and set rentals, and program advertising – there is the implied notion of community. Just as there are costs and risks associated with each of those ancillary activities, there is also the unseen benefit of creating a sense of community associated with the theatre company through them. A company that is able to provide Halloween costumes as rentals, or promote other local businesses, is being a good neighbor and participating in the social quality of the community. In every community there is a slightly different reaction to these sorts of functions, but it is important for a theatre to consider how its functions may affect an entire community.[8]

Curtain speeches

Many theatres begin a performance (or occasionally end one) by having a staff member, board member, or actor address the audience directly. There are mixed feelings about curtain speeches and whether they should occur or not. Some find them distracting, and not an appropriate introduction to the art. Others find they are essential for promotion and fundraising. Whether you are for or against curtain speeches personally is less important than how to ensure they are done appropriately if they are to be done at all. Curtain speeches should be brief, or they will, indeed, be an inappropriate introduction. No more than two minutes should be spent, and it should be focused on its purpose and extremely well rehearsed. Playgoers come expecting to see a polished performance, and the curtain speech is not an exception. Most importantly, the curtain speech is going to establish a face for the theatre company, regardless of who is giving the speech. This person is representing the company and allowing the audience to feel associated with the company in a personal way. It is important to consider that this connection has ramifications. The wise theatre manager uses the curtain speech to strengthen the position of the theatre within the community, share pertinent information with audience members, and make clear what action is being requested, and make sure that it does so in a positive way in under two minutes. Theatre companies that are highly regarded in their community often have just such a manager giving a curtain speech at every performance.

Build your theatre milestone 8: design your box office

For this milestone you are going to research and write about the box office you plan to have set up for your theatre. What system are you going to use and how will you operate it? What are the functions you plan to have and how will you take advantage of them? Will you offer to sell tickets for other theatre companies? Or will you simply hire another company to sell tickets for you? What are the pros and cons to the choices you have made, and why have you decided they are the best decisions for your theatre company?

Case study

Patrick had been enjoying his successes at the theatre, but none gave him greater joy than seeing a full house when he was attending an opening. At one performance, however, he ended up doing some unexpected research. His typical routine was to wait just until curtain time, and then to take an unoccupied seat as close to the back of the auditorium as possible. But a couple of minutes before curtain the box office manager grabbed him, gave him a ticket for one of the unused house seats saying, "I only have a single house seat left, and we won't sell a single now, so go take this one." Patrick smiled and hurried down to the seat and sat next to a gentleman who seemed ruffled.

"Got the last good seat I see," the man said, "did they screw with you, too?"

"No, no," said Patrick. "I'm..." but the man cut Patrick off.

"This is the third time we've ended up in these seats. The first time, when the usher found someone sitting in our ticketed seats, she left us standing in the aisle like idiots. Finally someone else came down and took our tickets and the other people's tickets and left again. People were staring at us like we were ticket counterfeiters. I eventually went to the box office, and by the time they realized they had printed the same tickets twice, the play had started, so we had to crawl over people in the dark to get to these seats. And this place always starts ten minutes late anyway."

Patrick was a little surprised to hear this. But he let the man proceed.

"I mean, we have been subscribers for years, but this will be the last time we ever subscribe here. The next two times we came, including tonight, the same thing happened. At least this time I was smart enough to get here real early. But the other couple did the same thing and got to the seats before us, so we went through the whole thing again tonight, got treated like crap, and eventually got sent here. I like these seats and all, but it is not worth being treated this way."

The incident really bothered Patrick. He was responsible for marketing, and that meant not only bringing new people into the theatre, but also retaining current patrons, and repeated issues like this should not be happening. Customer service was part of the entire theatre-going experience, and Patrick knew that it was just as much his responsibility as anyone's to ensure that when problems occurred, all the staff, including ushers and box office staff, could quickly, efficiently, and effectively solve the problem to the customer's satisfaction. And with subscribers, it should be obvious to check future attendance dates in the ticketing system to guarantee the problem would not happen a second time, much less a third time. But Patrick's greatest concern was how to deal with this issue. The house manager and box office manager certainly would not appreciate Patrick suggesting they alter how they handle their departments. Frank might help intervene, but there would still be animosity. The box office staff and house management staff were all underpaid part-timers, so it might be unrealistic to hold them to exceedingly high standards, even if Patrick could insist the company attempt to do so. But how could Patrick do his job effectively if the situation were not corrected? It was also possible that this was one isolated incident and the rest of the patrons were all perfectly satisfied with the customer service. Patrick knew that the first thing he had to do was work to ensure these two couples who had duplicate seats were both satisfied, would not face the duplication any longer, and would consider returning in the future. Beyond that, Patrick was not quite sure how to proceed. There were a number of paths he could take, and each required several steps. Consider every path you can think of, and discuss the detailed steps each would require.

Personal exploration

Theatre companies may have concessions stands, costumes to rent, or program space, each of which can prove to be a marketable asset capable of generating income. What assets do you have that you might be able to turn into something that could generate a little extra revenue for you? Discuss three different assets, how you could market them, and why you haven't done so to date. When considering the amount of effort (or cost) required to market those assets, is it worth doing so for the revenue they could generate?

Notes

1 Skeen, Wayne Donald Maddock, Howard Gregg Cockrill, Toby Gabriner, and Mark Edward Koerner, "Automated, conditional event ticketing and reservation techniques implemented over a computer network," U.S. Patent 9,349,108, issued May 24, 2016.
2 Bernstein, Joanne Scheff, *Standing Room Only: Marketing Insights for Engaging Performing Arts Audiences,* Palgrave Macmillan, 2014.
3 Shaw, Colin, *Revolutionize Your Customer Experience,* Springer, 2016.
4 Song, Hanqun, "Theatrical performance in the tourism industry an importance–satisfaction analysis," *Journal of Vacation Marketing* 22, no. 2 (2016): 129–141.
5 Croom, Simon, and Enzo Baglieri, "Connecting factory to theatre: Lessons from a case study," *Managing Consumer Services: Factory or Theater?* Baglieri, Enzo and Karmarkar, Uday (eds.) (p. 45), Springer International, 2014.
6 Pahade, N., R. K. Kori, S. Yadav, and R. S. Ya-dav, "Adverse consequences of alcohol consumption: A preliminary study," *Toxicology Forensic Medicine Open Journal* 1, no. 1 (2016): 24–31.
7 Barry, John Francis, and Epes Winthrop Sargent, *Building Theatre Patronage: Management and Merchandising,* Chalmers Publishing Company, 1927.
8 Kim, Mirae, "The relationship of nonprofits' financial health to program outcomes empirical evidence from nonprofit arts organizations," *Nonprofit and Voluntary Sector Quarterly* (2016): doi: 10.1177/0899764016662914.

CHAPTER 9

Marketing a theatre

Patrick was originally hired into his position to handle and organize all the marketing functions of his theatre. But when he arrived, he found that there was a lot more to do than simply organize. The entire company seemed to be confused about what marketing is and how it works. While part of the marketing process has to do with promotion, that is actually just a piece of what marketers do. Patrick not only had to embark on a complete overhaul of his department, but to slowly attempt to educate and shift the thinking of his colleagues in other departments.

Chapter objectives

After reading this chapter, you should be able to demonstrate how to devise a marketing plan for a theatre, describe the elements of the marketing mix, define the distinctions between marketing and public relations, and explain consumer perceptions and how they relate to marketing.

Marketing a theatre

Ben Cameron, an influential arts administrator in the United States, once said of those who market the arts, "Our mission is the orchestration of a social interaction in which the performance is a piece, but only a piece, of what we're called to do." It is quite a perplexing statement to those who think that marketing and promotion are synonymous, or to those who believe the art is the only reason theatre managers come together to do their work. But Cameron is quite right. What theatre managers do is create a social interaction. And in this interaction, the staff communicates with audience members, the actors communicate with audience members, and the audience members communicate with each other. When you think about it in those terms, when we coordinate all this social interaction, the actors communicating with each other is only a piece of what is occurring. It is the core of the product, but the product is an entire experience made up of many layers and additional services the customers' value.[1]

What is marketing? What is PR?

Marketing is a whole lot more than simply promoting a play. *Marketing* is defined as the process of getting a product or service to a consumer, from concept to completion of the sale. Its goal is to get consumers to buy. Does the word *concept* have you scratching your head, thinking that, in theatre, the concept of a play comes from a director and has nothing to do with marketing? While that is true, the person who determines what the audience wants or needs, often by conducting research in the marketplace, is carrying out a function of marketing, even if that is the artistic director.[2] *Public Relations* has to do with maintaining a positive image for a company. Typically, public relations professionals use unpaid media sources or reputable and reliable experts to share positive information about a company to anyone who may have an interest in the organization. This could extend beyond the customers and potential customers that marketers want to reach. While a marketing team in a theatre company often does work on public relations – and in smaller theatres it may be the only promotional activity being carried out through the dissemination of press releases and social media posts – for our purposes, we will assume that public relations focuses on telling stakeholders about the company. The promotional aspects of marketing tend to be focused on convincing people to buy tickets. As we get further into this chapter, you may have to keep reminding yourself of Ben Cameron's quote. While the goal of marketing in theatre is to get tickets sold, the ticket does not just represent seeing a play; it represents a lease agreement for the buyer, who is allowed to lease a seat in a building for a specified period of time. The reason people are interested in making that lease agreement is because the marketer has bundled attributes around the period of time that make the lease attractive, and one of those things is the play that is occurring on the stage.

Danny Newman and the history of the subscription

The *subscription*, which is a payment made in advance for the purchase of items that will be provided on a recurring basis, has been around for centuries. In the theatre, it is typically the purchase of tickets to more than one play at the same time. Traditionally, subscribers would make a single payment for all the plays in a theatre company's season. In 1977, a Chicago publicist named Danny Newman published his book *Subscribe Now! Building Arts Audiences through Dynamic Subscription Promotion*, and theatre companies worldwide started following the advice Newman laid out in the book. By the time of his death in 2011, the book had been published in ten editions and was used in thirty-one countries. Newman was a traditional publicist, meaning that he was less invested in all the attributes of marketing. His job was to promote. And he was so good at it that a couple of big arts funders paid to have him tour around and train arts organizations on his methods and how they work. And for thirty years, subscription sales went up everywhere Danny Newman's technique took hold.

There really was no special secret in what Newman talked and wrote about. He was simply advocating for a wholehearted effort to regard the subscriber as the most important ticket buyer, above all others, and to make every concerted effort to attract subscribers. Newman's approach was to look everywhere and systematically appeal to every possible subscriber. And his primary tool for doing so was the subscription brochure. If you consider that promoting a subscription costs about the same as promoting just one play, it makes more sense to sell subscriptions. And since some plays draw more people and some plays draw fewer, the subscription ensured an equal number of ticket buyers for every production. Newman carefully laid out a plan that defeats every argument against promoting the subscription heavily, and it all made a lot of sense. He also ensured that the subscription was the best available offering by bundling all sorts of attributes of value onto the subscription. Subscribers got the best seats. Subscribers got the first chance to renew their subscription each year, and to improve their seating location if better seats came available. Subscribers got a deep discount, guaranteed seats, lost ticket insurance, exchange privileges should a scheduling conflict occur, and anything else a company could think of to make that subscription more valuable. Remember we said that theatre marketers are coordinating a social interaction that the play is only a part of? The subscription is not only a bundling of several tickets to plays; it is also a bundling of all those benefits. When Newman put them all together and described them with lovely pictures and words in a mailed brochure, he had a great deal of success. It worked.

But in recent years, things have started to change. Subscription sales worldwide are not as strong as they used to be. It is possible that theatres have simply stopped using Danny Newman's advice, but more likely, buying habits have changed. The global economy in which we now live has altered how we buy things, and it has also changed how messages are communicated. And that includes promotional messages such as the ones Danny Newman was encouraging. For example, in his book, Newman spends little time discussing *telemarketing*, which is telephone sales. But telephone sales are a primary source for new subscription generation in many countries. And in 1977, when the book was first written, there was no Internet, so it is never discussed as a promotional tool or sales portal.

The marketing plan

A *marketing plan* is exactly what it sounds like, a plan for how you intend to take your product or service to market. There are many ways to go about creating a marketing plan. Danny Newman did not promote a marketing plan, but he did offer a sample sales campaign outline. In his outline, he discusses all the tactics he can think of for generating subscription sales, from that beautiful brochure to throwing parties for the purpose of selling subscriptions. For each tactic he can think of, he makes a realistic guess about how many subscriptions can be generated. In his example, he estimates that four pairs of subscriptions can be sold at each of 50 coffee parties for a total of 400 subscriptions. That seems reasonable if you have 50 different people hosting a coffee party for friends at which you are able to talk about how great your theatre is. Though every year you will probably have to find 50 new hosts with friends who have not purchased tickets before.[3] But what Newman offered was really sales goals. A modern marketing plan is a thorough document that details all the activities your theatre will undertake to achieve those goals. Typically, it includes lots of information explaining the research carried out to ensure that estimates are close to accurate, and that anticipated sales can logically be achieved.

Questions to research for class discussion:

Search the Internet and find answers for these questions before you read any further. Be prepared to discuss them in class.

9.1 What needs to go into a marketing plan?
9.2 What is the difference between a business plan and a marketing plan?
9.3 What are the benefits of having a marketing plan?
9.4 What are the biggest marketing plan mistakes companies make?

Research

Any well-constructed marketing plan is put together after thorough research has been done. The plan will most likely include information readily available, such as how the company has been doing with ticket sales, and it will also probably include information not so readily available. In order to be able to take any product to market, it is wise to know who is in the market, what they are interested in, and what product or service the company has or can create that may be of interest to them. The wise theatre marketer may try to understand who the people are who already buy tickets to determine if there are characteristics that might make finding more people like them easier. And single ticket buyers may have characteristics that are different from subscribers. If the marketer knows that the majority of subscribers all use the same dry cleaner, that may suggest that placing promotional materials at the dry cleaner, or asking the dry cleaner for a copy of his customer list, might be excellent promotional tactics. This means that conducting research about people in the marketplace and reporting that information in the marketing plan is important.[4] A company will want to detail not only who is in the market, but as many characteristics about them as can be detailed, including their spending habits. This information informs the marketer on how best to reach those people most likely to buy. Research also means understanding exactly what type of theatre will work best for those consumers, while still remaining true to a theatre's mission, vision, and values. If you are dedicated to performing traditional Shakespeare, and all the Shakespeare-loving theatregoers in your community are only interested in Shakespearean comedies but have no interest in tragedies, you would want to know that before you started promoting *King Lear.*

Marketing research may also include information about the theatre industry in general, as well as what other theatre companies are in your area, meaning who is your competition. And, in fact, many theatre companies consider any business that takes advantage of a consumer's discretionary income as a competitor. This could include any arts organization, movies, theme parks, and even restaurants. Knowing what a company is up against and detailing that in the marketing plan helps paint a real picture of where the company is heading.[5]

Plenty of theatre companies believe they do marketing research because they ask their subscribers each year what plays they might like to see the following season. This very unscientific preference poll may provide some small bit of information to decision-makers, but it is actually not as useful to a marketer spending most of their time seeking new audience members who have never bought a ticket before. A marketer wants to know what are the features that are most likely to bring a new person in. Certainly that preference poll is important for knowing what will keep buyers coming back, but it does little to inform about why people are not buying tickets, and without that knowledge, it is difficult to make any changes that will convince them to buy.[6] This is not to suggest that changes mean altering the type of play being produced. It could simply be the addition of lights around a building, or different concessions, or different pricing. Remember that we are orchestrating a social interaction and bundling lots of attributes together. The play is only one of those attributes.

Questions to research for class discussion:

Search the Internet and find answers for these questions before you read any further. Be prepared to discuss them in class.

9.5   What is the marketing research process? Briefly describe each step.

9.6   What are the basic methods of market research? Briefly describe them.

9.7   What are the most frequent mistakes made in marketing research?

Managing consumer perceptions

A theatre may have two customers who perceive a play very differently. Never mind how they interpret the quality of the production, but one may think that the play-going experience was a friendly, social experience, full of lively entertainment, good company, and lots of laughs, while the other may find the same experience as stuffy, dark, and exceedingly intellectual. Theatres have a hard enough time selling tickets, so to have audience members perceiving the experience differently than is desired can pose many challenges.[7] And before you assume that the theatre in the above example would want the audience to perceive their experience as the first of those possibilities and not the second, if the company is producing *King Lear*, perhaps that is not the case. It is a matter of how you perceived what was written.

Competition in our global society continues to grow. And when considering that theatre expenditures come from discretionary income, it may not seem surprising that sales seem to be declining. When Danny Newman was promoting theatre, there were no cable bills, or cellular telephone bills, or broadband bills. And those things now eat up substantial amounts of discretionary income. In our global world, theatres are having a harder and harder time differentiating themselves from one another, and even from other offerings of artistry for our consumption. This means that when an audience member comes into a theatre, the best advantage that theatre company has for staying ahead of the marketing curve, is by keeping that person coming back. How the customer perceives their experience is what will affect their decision to return or not. *Consumer perception* has to do with how the customer sees the company or the product in relation to price and competition. For a first-time patron, the way the offer was communicated provided enough information for them to perceive the offer was worthwhile. However, if they are dissatisfied with what they receive, they are unlikely to return. Their perception could be changed by any number of factors involved in their visit to the theatre. This might include the play, but it might also include how the audience member feels about the whole experience.

In order to know how customers perceive a company's product or service, the marketing professional has to conduct research. Basically, the customers are asked how they feel about any number of attributes of the product or service. A theatre might ask about price, quality of the play, friendliness of the staff, cleanliness of the restrooms, offerings at the concessions stand, ease of ticket purchase, curtain time, length of intermission, proximity to good restaurants, and on and on. Each of these attributes is part of the entire play-going experience. And while some may not be as controllable as others, they all factor into how audience members perceive a company. If the company sets expectations about how it should be perceived, based upon mission, vision, and values, there is a way to verify if those expectations are being met. And if they are not being met, the data gathered can inform as to how to make changes.

The four P's

One of the first lessons of marketing has to do with the *marketing mix*, which refers to the factors a company uses to influence consumer behavior to buy their product or service.[8] One of the easiest ways to remember the marketing mix is by thinking of it as the four P's. The *four P's* are product, price, place, and promotion.

Product

Product is the bundle of attributes that create a good or service that a company provides to a specific type of customer in a transaction. We often think about this as meaning the core product, in our case the play, but it is actually more than that. Consider a tube of toothpaste. If you want toothpaste you go to the store to buy it, and it comes in a tube, which is in a box. That box is part of the product. How the toothpaste name is drawn on the box is part of the product. The tube is part of the product. The cap on the tube is part of the product. Each of these attributes, when bundled together, make the product, even though the core product, the thing you wanted, was toothpaste. But a marketer figured out that the product offering would be more attractive to you if the toothpaste were in a tube, with a cap, placed in a box with attractive lettering on it. Who wants to go to a store and just get a glob of toothpaste to take home?

The bundle of attributes

While the play may be the core of the product, even the play is a bundle of attributes such as actors, costumes, dialogue, sets, lights, sounds, and on and on. Each one of those attributes will have an effect on buying behavior, since audience members purchase tickets because they determine that there is value in what they are paying for. And the function of business is to put together inputs in a way that increases their value.[9] So we put together the elements of a play to create value. There are more attributes, however. A program or playbill is one. The concessions stand offerings are another. Since an audience must experience the play in a theatre, the theatre itself is part of the product. If a pre-show lecture or a post-show talkback, or additional educational materials or opportunities accompany a play, those are all part of the bundle of attributes making up the product. And in the case of a subscription, the product includes several plays and any additional features the marketer has bundled with that product offering.

Selecting a season, part II

Knowing what our audiences and potential audiences want to see is important, even if the theatre company wishes to bring to audiences art that is unknown to them. In order to do that, a marketer has to be careful to understand what types of feelings, emotions, and stimuli audience members and potential audience members consider of value, and what they consider to be not of value.[10] Selecting a season, for any theatre, is about knowing the audience well. Some theatres choose to set artistic goals for each play that align with their artistic values, so marketers can determine if those goals are being met. For example, if a company has an artistic value to stimulate the intellect, and sets a goal of one certain play to get audience members to consider both sides of the argument for human euthanasia, a marketer can poll audiences to see if the play actually got them to consider, rethink, or discuss that topic. This data can inform how well the company is meeting its own artistic values, and help it to improve in selecting plays that will best serve the audience. In a subscription, an entire season of plays may be the product offering, and those artistic values are attributes of that offering.

Think critically: art and marketing mixed

There are two ways to approach this class discussion. First, you can choose sides. Divide the class into two, by whatever means you choose, and debate the argument outlined below. Second, you can have an open discussion, each adding upon others' thoughts, and let the discussion uncover all the important details of all sides of the debate. Keep in mind that regardless of which approach you take, we want to be sure we dig deep into all sides of this important issue, in order to more effectively understand all positions.

CLASS DISCUSSION: Having artistic values for a company can be very important to help guide artistic decision-making. But artists cannot be held to some preset list of standards upon which they must create their art. They need to be able to experiment and explore in order to create art. While it is fine to have ideals about where that art may go, there can be no guarantee that the final product will go there. Artistic values are fine as suggestions, but not as walls that box an artist in. To suggest that plays have artistic goals, based on a company's artistic values that can be measured, is to suggest art is weighed on metrics, and its value is based entirely on commerce. That notion runs completely afoul of why art exists in the first place. On the other hand, the audience pays for the art. And while artists need not be required to meet specific criteria, they should be able to explain what it is they are attempting to accomplish. That is something which can be measured. A company should absolutely know what it values artistically, and if it does, it follows that each artistic offering should be designed with a plan in mind of how it will be in alignment with those artistic values. Measuring how well the company did in achieving that designed plan allows the company to know how well it is doing. Is one side more right than the other, or is there a middle ground?

Pricing – how to price a season

The second P in the four P's is *price*, which is the amount a consumer pays for a product offering. In the transaction, the consumer gives the company money in exchange for the product the company has created by putting together and improving a collection of inputs. Pricing for a play or a season can be quite complex, and it is a very important matter, because pricing can seriously alter the amount of money a company brings in, and if not done correctly, can cause a company to fail. Yet so many theatre marketers set pricing arbitrarily, with no real methodology to follow. For such an important part of a company's success, pricing needs to be considered very seriously. Setting prices too low leaves money on the table and puts the company at financial risk. Setting prices too high drives audiences away and also puts the company at financial risk. Finding what is the right price may be difficult, but by having the necessary information, it can be done.

Pricing methodology

We have already discussed the typical pricing methodology for many theatres, which is essentially to go with the gut based on past experience. But because we know the importance of pricing, it might be wise to consider alternative pricing methods that could assist theatres. When considering a pricing method, three factors come into play: cost, competition, and demand.[11] Different theatres have different challenges, but any business has to consider each of those factors when determining pricing. For example, a new theatre may have less demand, because it is an unknown commodity, and that will affect pricing.

In *cost-based pricing*, the company calculates all the costs associated with developing the product, and adds a profit margin onto that amount to determine the sales price. This method is the easiest to perform, because it requires little analysis. If it costs X amount to make a play, including all the labor, marketing, theatre rental, and so on, and there are 500 seats to sell (assuming they can all be sold), then the cost per seat (C) is X divided by 500. $C = X/500$. The amount of profit is the amount added to C. The problems with cost-based pricing are that it really does not consider the competition at all, nor does it consider how much the consumer demands the product and is willing to pay for it.

Demand-based pricing is a method that is used to consider how much the consumer desires the product, with the pricing based accordingly. One example of demand-based pricing is known as *variable pricing*. In variable pricing, the actual price of the product fluctuates based upon demand during a specified period of time. If demand is high, the price goes up. If demand is low, the price goes down. This is how most airlines operate. You may think that variable pricing would be difficult to apply to a theatre, but there are actually a number of theatres worldwide that offer their plays through variable pricing. The upside to variable pricing is that it allows the company to maximize profit. The downside is that it requires constant attention, and prices cannot be advertised in a static form, such as print.

Competition-based pricing refers to a pricing method where the company evaluates and sets its own prices higher, lower, or equal to the competition. Airlines also use some form of competition-based pricing when they consider a starting point for certain routes also flown by their competition. For theatres, in order to consider competition-based pricing, the first step is to determine if the competition is only other theatres, or if it includes other art forms, other entertainments, or all places where discretionary income can be spent, and within what geographic area.

There are also a number of other types of pricing schemes that can be used, and as noted with the airline industry, more than one strategy can be employed. When pricing a theatre it is important to consider consumer perceptions as well. Consumers tend to believe that low price also implies low quality, and high price implies high quality. While that may not always be the case, considering a price that is reflective of the quality of the overall experience is important.[12]

Market analysis

For most theatres, the best analysis to be done is to gather information about the cost to produce the plays, find out who the competition is and what they charge, and then to ask people how likely they would be to buy plays at different price points. A theatre that has been in existence for a while could also include historical data about how many tickets were sold at different prices in the past. The problem for a theatre is that with all this research, the core part of the product changes every time, so a comparison is impossible to make accurately. It becomes incumbent upon the marketer to understand the audience and potential audience well enough to know what types of plays are considered similar to one another. And even with all this data, the pricing decision is still based on hunches.

Conjoint analysis and MaxDiff

There are statistical tools that can be used to determine consumer desire based on each of the different pieces that go into making the product. Maximum difference scaling, or *MaxDiff*, is a process where the marketer asks consumers to evaluate those factors most important to them and those factors least important to them, and then evaluates the aggregate result.[13] For example, in a MaxDiff study, the marketer may ask the consumer to rank each of the following for their preference on a scale, perhaps 1 to 7: low ticket price, liquor at the concessions stand, comfortable seating, and comedic value of the offering. The statistical results from the data collected can help the marketer understand which features to promote, emphasize, and work most to improve. In a *conjoint analysis* study, the consumer is shown a list of several options, made up of different variables of features, and is asked to select their preference from the list. For example, a consumer might be asked which of these four combinations they prefer: (1) low ticket price, comfortable seating, comedy; (2) high price, liquor at the concession stand, comedy; (3) moderate price, liquor at the concession stand, drama; (4) moderate price, comfortable seating, drama. The process is repeated, with different options, until enough data can be collected to analyze, statistically, which feature at which level is most desirous, which is next most desirous at which level, and so on. Conjoint analysis studies take longer for the consumer to respond to, especially depending on the number of features being examined, but they do allow marketers to get a much clearer picture about how best to bundle a product.

Place

The third P in the marketing mix is *place*, which refers to the way in which your product is distributed to consumers. Danny Newman actually considered distribution channels in his sales campaign outline, because he considered many different locations where the sale could be made. While he emphasized his belief in the importance of the sales brochure, remember those coffee parties he advocated? They would be considered a distribution channel. For theatre, distribution channels are different than they tend to be in retail. In retail, typically one company makes a product, and then sells it wholesale to a distributor who makes arrangements with stores to sell it to the public. The distributor has access to the locations where the public might buy the product, and often handles the promotion. This model allows the company that makes the product to focus on its expertise of making the product. In theatre, the problem with this model is that the place where the product is created, the theatre itself, is also the place where the product must be consumed. There are touring productions that operate very much like the retail model described above, but they are certainly not the majority of theatre offerings worldwide. Ticket brokers and ticket outlets are also a form of distribution channel, as are online purchase options. As you can imagine, not much innovation has occurred in the distribution of theatre, due in part to the fact that the play is often only physically available at the location it is produced. But that same problem has not stopped fast food restaurant chains from establishing their own form of distribution channels. Perhaps someone in theatre management will develop a new distribution model in the future.

Promotion

The fourth P in the marketing mix is *promotion*, which refers to the function of communicating information to marketplace consumers about a product offering and features in a way that moves them to purchase. In addition, the promotional process can be used to create awareness about a product or company, stimulate interest, increase demand, or demonstrate how the product or company is different from the competition. To be effective, a marketer needs to know who the potential customers are, and how best to communicate information about the product offering. In a theatre, if the marketer understands the audience and what their preferences are, then it is possible to develop promotional materials that speak to those preferences. Sometimes different promotional materials are required for different potential audience members. Subscribers may be using the same dry cleaner, and may be less price sensitive, but single ticket buyers may be more interested in value pricing. You can see how knowing the difference may assist the marketer.

While the four P's make up the core of the marketing mix, and it is important to understand them, there are three additional P's that are sometimes used, especially in services industries, including theatre. When used together they are referred to as the *7 P's*.

The fifth P stands for *people*, and refers not only to the people outside the company who are buyers or likely buyers, but also to those within the company. As mentioned, knowing the consumers in the marketplace, what they are like, and if there are enough of them interested in the product to support an ongoing business is important. But equally as important is having a staff that truly believes in the product, and can help promote it in the marketplace. These employees will probably perform better, and they will also likely be more open to feedback from the community.

The sixth P is *processes*, which refers to all the processes a company uses to get the product or service from their original inputs all the way to the consumer. In theatre this might mean the processes used to advertise auditions, all the way through ticket sales, rehearsal processes, and ushering procedures for clearing the house at the end of the performance. While most of those things are typically overseen by someone other than marketing, it is actually a function of marketing to ensure that they are all working most effectively to be able to provide the best value for the consumer.

The last P is *physical evidence*, and refers to some sort of evidence that the good or service was received, and how the marketplace has perceived it. Consumer perceptions are very important to the marketing manager, and perception is part of branding. Very strong brands, such as Coca-Cola for example, are known for what they provide to the market, and how good a company they are. This perception, in turn, helps further promote the company.

Questions to research for class discussion:

Search the Internet and find answers for these questions before you read any further. Be prepared to discuss them in class.

9.8   What are the four C's in marketing? Describe them.
9.9   How are the four C's different from the four P's? How are they related?
9.10 What are the seven functions of marketing? How do you find they fit with the P's and C's?

Creating value

As a matter of function, marketing is a process that creates value for both the company and the consumer. It does this by connecting the two and serving as the bridge between them. For the company, the marketer creates value by building the company brand, and strengthening the relationship with customers by bringing the voice of consumers into the company. This is done through market research. For the consumer, the marketer creates value by developing a *value proposition*, which describes what the product is, who the target customer is, and why the product is best among the competition. These items are laid out in a *positioning statement*. For a theatre company, a positioning statement might look like this:

Shangri-La Repertory Theatre will provide millennials with the edgiest classic theatre in all of Southampton, because we are run by edgy millennials who understand the desires of their generation.

The statement says who the company is (Shangri-La Repertory), who its target is (Millennials), what makes its product stand out (edgiest classic theatre), what its marketplace is (all of Southampton), and why it is the best (because we are run by edgy millennials). The big question then becomes, how does a company do this?

In the creation of a product, there is market research to determine where something is missing in the marketplace. New products and services are introduced when a need is identified. The market study is followed by brainstorming and research and development to create a prototype. That is then produced in small quantities and tested. Often it is taken to the market to determine consumer reaction. When the tests all prove positive, market research informs financial projections for cost to produce, and how many will sell and at what price point. Then the product is promoted.

In theatre, that process is a little bit different, because we are often working from a pre-existing script, and we are creating art. In the above scenario, the company follows a *market-driven strategy*, which means the consumers can describe what it is they need and want, and the company then goes about creating it.[14] But what about new products, which are more like the creation of a piece of theatre, where the consumers cannot know they want something until they have seen it in action? That process is a *market-driving strategy*, where the company is developing a new product to introduce to the marketplace. In our technologically driven world, these types of products are being created all the time. And while the process is creative in nature, it is important for the company to continue to focus on consumer needs, rather than behaving as if they are smarter or better than the consumer. Even when operating using a market-driving strategy, marketers regularly test products. Perhaps you have heard of *beta testing*, where a small group of users are asked to evaluate a new product? In many ways this is similar to the preview audience, which is asked to respond to a new play. In a market-driving strategy, the marketer may not be able to determine empirically what new product would satisfy consumer demand, but the market can still inform about what types of things might change how they feel. In theatre, the marketer can gauge the mood of the marketplace. In times of war, patriotism might be desired. In times of depression, themes of love and happiness might be how to satisfy an audience. At times of civil unrest, still other themes might be of greater interest to the audience. Knowing this, the theatre marketer is armed with the necessary information to bring the voice of the audience into the company.

Branding and brand equity

Cattle ranchers used to brand their cattle by searing a unique mark into the hide of each animal to identify its owner. The idea of *branding* is now used in marketing to refer to how a company is identified in the public space. You may think about brands as being the Nike swoosh, the ribbon under the red and white Coca-Cola name, or the way retailer Harrods spells its name, but these are actually *brand elements*. They are simply imagery that helps to make the brand recognizable. The company brand is actually made up of all the ways that the world perceives the company, and it can be created by how the company sets out to be perceived. *Brand equity* consists of all those things that either add to, or detract from, the value of the company.[15] If a theatre company provides excellent quality productions, this contributes to the brand equity. But if the customer service is poor, this detracts from the brand equity. The *logo*, which is an image used to represent and identify the company, may bring about positive or negative feelings depending on the brand equity. Marketers and public relations professionals work to constantly improve the brand, not only by improving what is going on inside the company, but also by attempting to control what goes on outside the company, because the brand can be influenced not only by the great work being done, but also by the stories being told about the company. Even if a theatre produces an exceptional work, if the stories being told in the marketplace are negative, they will have a negative effect on the brand equity.

Sustaining value and developing audiences

Just creating value is not enough for a company. The company must also sustain that value over time, to ensure that the company brand continues to strengthen, and that consumers continue to buy and buy again and again.[16] In theatre, we sometimes refer to one aspect of the marketing function as audience development. *Audience development* is a process of ensuring strong relationships with the audience and its members, as well as developing new audiences. Consider a theatre that is putting on a production of *Cyrano de Bergerac*. The audience development professional may want to not only engage with first-time single ticket buyers to ensure that they appreciated the experience, but also for purposes of nurturing a relationship that will encourage their repeat attendance. With the repeat attenders, the audience development professional may wish to engage in an effort to encourage a subscription purchase. With repeat subscribers the audience development professional may then pass the subscriber to the fund development professional to encourage the customer to provide additional financial support to the company. The process is referred to as *development* because the staff

Build your theatre milestone 9: design your marketing plan

For this milestone you are going to research and write a marketing plan for your theatre. You will want to start with an overall strategy, which you will describe in your positioning statement. Then you will want to explain how your company will address all of the seven P's. Be sure to include any research you have done about the community you are serving, and also what your plans are to do more research. If the community you serve has 50,000 people, you would want to make a realistic guess about how many people may actually attend. You may want to include a statement such as, "In our market of 50,000, where we are the only live theatre, we anticipate 15% purchasing tickets (7,500), and of those 15%, we anticipate half of them purchasing a second ticket in the same season (3,750) representing total annual sales of 11,250." This tells your reader that while you are mostly operating off of hunches, they are not unreasonable hunches. If that statement is preceded by data indicating that 15% of respondents from a community survey have indicated a desire to attend live theatre at least once annually, and 7.5% indicated a desire to attend live theatre at least twice annually, your statement would be even more believable. The more actual research you can include, the more accurate your marketing plan will be.

You will also want to include what tactics you plan to use to execute your strategy, how much each will cost, and what return you expect to see. For example, perhaps one tactic is to encourage church groups to attend. You may discuss the creation and distribution of flyers in Sunday programs, the costs associated with that, and how many tickets you anticipate selling as a result of the distribution of those flyers. If your strategy is to encourage edgy millennials to attend, your tactics might be more appropriate if they are geared around places edgy millennials are known to congregate. If your strategy is to increase your ticket sales by 15,000, your marketing plan should demonstrate through which place each of those 15,000 will be secured. If you expect 40 tickets to be sold to people who click on a Facebook link, discuss the cost of the link, who it will be targeted to, and the anticipated sales numbers. Finally, be sure you include a discussion of your math. If you anticipate 15,000 sales, include the anticipated revenue from them. "Based on the chronological breakdown of the community described earlier, as well as our specific targets of senior centers, we anticipate 50% of our sales (7,500 tickets) will be at the senior price of XX for a total income of XXX. Because our secondary target is families, we anticipate half of the remaining tickets to be sold at the full adult price of XX and half sold at the child discount price of XX for a total income of XXX."

There is no one "right way" to create this marketing plan, so you can be creative. The goal is to be as accurate and exhaustive about how you will implement the marketing mix. You may want to search the Internet for a template to follow, but be sure that you use your own words and cite the template you use, and give credit to the person, people, organization, or website deserving of the credit.

members are developing relationships with the audience members to better provide for the needs and wants of those consumers.

The audience development professional, however, may also reach out to local schools, where students are studying *Cyrano de Bergerac*, and encourage them to attend as part of an educational outreach. Sometimes audience development departments include education directors, who work to provide resources and materials that can enhance the educational opportunities that theatre provides. Audience development professionals may also work to develop relationships with individuals, or groups of individuals, who might otherwise be underserved by theatre, such as individuals with disabilities that might make theatre attendance seem challenging, or social groups that may not have regular exposure to theatre. In these cases, the function of audience development is about lowering barriers that preclude people from attending, so that a new audience can be introduced to the theatre.

Case study

Patrick's focus on marketing meant that he understood not only how to promote his theatre, and the importance of the promotion, but also that his function was to bring the voice of the audience into the company. To do this, he had to conduct a lot of research to be able to understand who the audience was, where they came from, what sorts of things they liked and did not like, and what other people were out there like them. When he started his job, the company had done no research, but even with his small budget and staff, Patrick was determined to find out who it was he was representing. He studied box office data, as well as demographic data about the community, and crunched a lot of numbers. He attended meetings in the community, and talked to other arts organizations. He distributed surveys to audience members, and he conducted a couple of focus groups to try to better understand his community's theatregoers. He also went to the local shopping center and stopped people to ask them questions about their interests, what they felt about theatre, and what they knew about his theatre. In total, Patrick spent over a year collecting all this information, and though he felt he had only scratched the surface, he knew that if he did not act on it, the passing of time would make it become outdated and worthless. So Patrick asked Frank if he could call the executive staff together so he could discuss his findings. While Frank did not understand why this information could not simply be sent out in an email, Patrick was insistent. He knew that if he could discuss the data and his findings, he might be able to start a conversation about letting the audience and their thoughts into all aspects of the company. After all, this was a company, and that meant that the audience was a vital part of the process.

At the meeting, Patrick presented his findings, explained in detail what they meant, and started to educate his colleagues on the marketing mix. There was some concern that Patrick was trying to "take over" the entire theatre, but Patrick stayed calm. He described it this way:

> They had a hard time with most of it because in some sense, everyone felt a lit-tle threatened. The only feedback they ever got was applause, online reviews, and the occasional complaint. I was presenting them with actual research that demonstrated who was out in our community that had an interest in theatre, what those people did, why they did or did not attend our theatre, and what we could do to persuade them to give us a try … or actually, to get many of them to try us again, because over the years we had turned many people off. The biggest complaints I heard were that the people in the community could not possibly know what good theatre was until they came in, and if they left and did not like it, then they must be ignorant, because we presented good theatre. I tried to shift the focus away from the plays, because while that is the core product, and the main reason people came or did not come, it was not the only reason. Eventually, there was no keeping them off the topic of plays. I had planned for this to occur, and I knew I needed to take one of three approaches. I could be very clear that without considering the mindset of our audience, we would have no marketing function, the trajectory for ticket sales would not change, and we should accept that our primary function had no relation to the audience; we should write that into our mission. Second, I could suggest that we take time to step away and reflect on what value we got from the audience, effectively ending the meeting but asking everyone to come to a later meeting ready to bring their own individual ideas to the table about what we get from the audience. My goal for this would be to shift the thinking from the perspective of what we provide, and instead focus on the other side of the exchange with the audience. I could even bring in some key members of my focus groups for this approach. Thirdly, I could go into the details of what shifting more towards an audience-centric theatre meant. For example, I was not advocating that we change the type of plays we produced, but I was suggesting that of the thousands of play titles that fit our mission, we should narrow the list down to the several hundred that would also fit the desires of our audience.

Patrick knew that with each of these approaches there was substantial risk. What are the pros and cons you see with each approach? Are there other ways Patrick could choose to handle the situation? What do you believe to be the best approach for Patrick, and what are the desired results? What do you believe will be the *likely* results of the approach you recommend, and how could Patrick be prepared to handle any negative consequences?

Personal exploration

Your friends and family all have a perception of who you are as a person. Those closest to you probably have the most accurate perception, and those who are not as close may have a different perception. But what is true for all those people (who you can think of as different niche markets) is that you can make changes to you as a product, which may alter their perception of you. Discuss at least two of those different people (e.g. best friends and professors) and how you wish to be perceived by them. Then address the things you do to cause them to perceive you the way they do, and what things you do differently for each group. For example, perhaps you want your friends to see you as the lively, funny, life of the party, so you are very talkative and tell lots of jokes around them. But you want your professors to see you as a contemplative, deep thinker, so you speak little in class, nod a lot, and only ask the occasional question. Finally, discuss whether you believe you are achieving the perception you wish others to have of you. You may even want them to tell you how they perceive you, and see if you are getting what you want. HINT: We often are not getting others to perceive us the way we think they are.

Notes

1 Bernstein, Joanne Scheff, *Arts Marketing Insights: The Dynamics of Building and Retaining Performing Arts Audiences*, John Wiley & Sons, 2011.
2 Hill, Elizabeth, Terry O'Sullivan, and Catherine O'Sullivan, *Creative Arts Marketing*, Routledge, 2012.
3 Johnson, Mark S., and Ellen Garbarino, "Customers of performing arts organisations: Are subscribers different from nonsubscribers?," *International Journal of Nonprofit and Voluntary Sector Marketing* 6, no. 1 (2001): 61–77.
4 Kotler, Philip, and Joanne Scheff, *Standing Room Only: Strategies for Marketing The Performing Arts*, Harvard Business Press, 1997.
5 Walker-Kuhne, Donna, *Invitation to The Party: Building Bridges to the Arts, Culture and Community*, Theatre Communications Grou, 2005.
6 Swanson, Scott R., and J. Charlene Davis, "Arts patronage: A social identity perspective," *Journal of Marketing Theory and Practice* 14, no. 2 (2006): 125–138.
7 Ibid.
8 McDonald, Malcom, "5 Strategic marketing planning," *The Marketing Book* (p. 86), 2016.
9 Hall, Emma, et al., "Increasing loyalty in the arts by bundling consumer benefits," *Arts and the Market* 6, no. 2 (2016): 141–165.
10 Tsai, Chin-Fa, "The relationships among theatrical components, experiential value, relationship quality, and relationship marketing outcomes," *Asia Pacific Journal of Tourism Research* 20, no. 8 (2015): 897–919.
11 Vogel, Harold L., *Entertainment Industry Economics: A Guide for Financial Analysis*, Cambridge University Press, 2014.
12 Reinelt, Janelle, et al., *Critical Mass: Theatre Spectatorship and Value Attribution*, 2014.
13 Miller, Thomas, W., *Modeling Techniques in Predictive Analytics: Business Problems and Solutions with R* (p. 250), 2013.
14 Colbert, François, and Yannik St-James, "Research in arts marketing: Evolution and future directions," *Psychology & Marketing* 31, no. 8 (2014): 566–575.
15 Baumgarth, Carsten, ""This theatre is a part of me" contrasting brand attitude and brand attachment as drivers of audience behaviour," *Arts Marketing: An International Journal* 4, no. 1/2 (2014): 87–100.
16 Ibid.

CHAPTER 10

Creating promotional materials

The challenges Patrick faced in his position were not that unusual from those faced by many people hired into marketing positions. Most laypeople see only the promotional function of marketing, as that is the only one of the four P's visible to consumers on a daily basis. In fact, we are constantly inundated with promotion, from logos on products, to ads on the Internet, television and radio commercials, posters, flyers, banners, billboards, and on and on. Advertising is everywhere. For Patrick, as for most marketers, that fact, in and of itself, posed a great challenge. For a theatre company to stand out, it must go to great lengths to devise promotional materials that capture attention in an extremely crowded marketplace.

Chapter objectives

After reading this chapter, you should be able to explain best practices for creating promotional materials in theatre, discuss the difference between well-written and poorly written promotional copy, explain the uses of fonts and colors in promotion, and demonstrate how to create an effective press kit.

Creating promotional materials

Creating promotional materials can be a very creative process, and sometimes the designer feels their creation is an act of artistic expression, which, in fact, it may be. While it is certainly to one's advantage to have an artist creating materials that are designed to evoke some sort of response, the promotional materials must be evaluated not on their artistic aesthetic, but on their ability to serve the objective they are designed for. Sometimes this means changing a beautiful picture to one that is more likely to evoke a purchase. Beautiful layouts might be a smorgasbord for the senses, but difficult for the logical brain to follow and process. Promotional materials typically need to be designed with function taking precedence over form.[1] This is not to say, however, that there is a right or wrong way to design promotional materials. In fact, much of what you will read in this chapter is simply good advice derived from years of trial and error by marketers.

Before venturing into the creation of promotional materials, the marketing manager develops a strategy from which those materials will be created. This strategy ties directly into the marketing plan, and serves one or more specific goals of that plan. The promotional strategy might be to support other promotional material. For example, a billboard may have only an image and a play title, and nothing else, but it will reinforce an email bearing the same image and play title and that email will include a call to action. In that case, the strategy for the billboard is to reinforce the message in the email. The *call to action* is the instruction the marketer gives to the potential customer to tell them what the marketer wants them to do.[2] Danny Newman heavily promoted his call to action of "Subscribe Now!" which also happened to be the title of his book.[3] He maintained that these exact words, or ones similar to them, were mandatory for the marketer to include in the subscription brochure. Newman felt strongly that the person reading the brochure needed to know exactly what they were expected to do. Most promotional materials have a strategy to speak to a particular audience or type of person, with the desired result of primarily moving them to make a purchase. However, most promotional materials have a secondary objective of providing positive information about a product or service, as a means of supporting other promotional materials, like the billboard supports the email mentioned above. And all promotional materials have some impact on brand equity for the company creating and disseminating them.

Understanding the market

In Chapter 9, we discussed the importance of understanding the marketplace and who the potential audience member may be. You can see why this is important when developing a strategy for marketing materials. If a brochure is being designed with the purpose of creating new theatregoers, the message conveyed in that brochure will be specifically created to introduce them to the facets of theatre which they would likely enjoy, and why those things are going to be pleasurable and good in their eyes. A brochure designed to get theatregoers to attend a specific theatre that they have never attended before would have a very different message, discussing the unique features of that particular theatre over others. And a brochure designed to encourage all theatregoers in the marketplace to purchase a season subscription would have a different message yet again. Or to think of it a different way, if there is a popular artist releasing a new album of music that you believe will have universal appeal, and you would like everyone in your life to listen to it, convincing your peers will require one approach, convincing your parents may require a completely different approach, convincing the senior citizens in your life may require a message that is totally different, and your colleagues at work may need to be told in a quite different way about this new music. Understanding who is being communicated with and where and how they prefer to communicate will help to inform what strategy should be used, and consequently, which types of media might be most effective in reaching those people.[4] While everyone in a community might see a billboard or poster, a play with themes most relevant to a specific group might best be promoted in advertisements in magazines frequently read by that group. If the strategy were to encourage attendance amongst the local LGBTQ community because the play's themes speak most closely to issues that community deals with, promoting in a local LGBTQ publication about those issues would make more sense than placing ads in a national Jewish newspaper. While there may be some interest from readers of the Jewish newspaper, the message about local LGBTQ issues would likely be relevant for a much smaller group of readers.

Creating a message and communicating it

To create and communicate an effective message you first develop a strategy that defines what you are trying to accomplish, who the message is for, what you want them to do after receiving your promotional material, and what are the primary and secondary benefits for them.[5] It is also important to know how you would like recipients of the promotional material to perceive your theatre. If you want people to see your theatre as extraordinarily professional and first-class, distributing black-and-white copied flyers may not create that perception. However, if you want to be perceived as resourceful, frugal, and scrappy, those flyers might do the trick.

Armed with all this information, you can begin to craft your promotional message. That message will likely include both visual imagery and text (also known as "copy"). We will discuss imagery for the theatre below. For text, there are some important considerations. First, remember that less is more. People are very busy, and if they are faced with large blocks of text in a promotional piece, they are unlikely to read it. Try to keep paragraphs down to a couple of sentences, and be careful to eliminate every unneeded word. When describing a play, focus on the reasons your potential audience member would enjoy the play and relate to it. The goal is to consider your audience and write as if you are sending them a personal invitation. If you present *Hamlet*, you would not want to say this:

> Young Hamlet is left to mourn his father's death, is placed in a struggle with love, and fails to find peace in the classic Shakespearean tragedy.

That description certainly does tell your market a bit about the play, but it does so using negative words, or words that may scare away customers. Would you want to pay good money to watch a character mourn, struggle, and fail? And it is possible much of your market will have a negative impression of the words "classic Shakespearean tragedy." You are probably thinking that the implication here is to oversell the play instead. You may have seen a play promotion that said the play was "hilarious," or "riveting," or some other grandiose notion, and you realized those words were more hype than reality. But how about this for *Hamlet*:

> Join a young prince unraveling a murderous plot as he demands revenge and discovers he can trust none of the quirky characters he meets, in a detective story that has fascinated theatre audiences for centuries.

In this description, the subject is actually not Hamlet, it is the reader. We have left the words out, but the sentence could effectively begin, "You should join a young prince." This description allows the reader to see themselves as part of the audience, and speaks to them directly. The verbs "unravel," "demand," and "discover" in this description are active. Not only are they *active verbs*, meaning they are the things Hamlet is actually doing, as opposed to things that have been done to Hamlet, such as "left to mourn," or "is placed," but they are interesting actions. One could "follow a murder plot," but it far more intriguing to "unravel a murderous plot." We often say people "seek" revenge, but to "demand" revenge is much more dramatic. Note also that instead of referring to the play as a classic Shakespearean tragedy, we have referred to it as "a detective story that has fascinated theatre audiences for centuries." In fact, this serves two purposes. First, it makes it clear that this is a play. So often, theatre promotions gain no traction because the recipient of the promotion cannot tell that the thing being produced is a stage play. Second, it sends the message that this work is something that others have enjoyed for a very long time (or it would not be continuously produced). Note also that the description does not mention who is directing or starring in the production. The function of the description is to describe the play in a meaningful way to a potential audience member. Unless the director or stars have recognizable names that will have meaning to the potential audience member, they are simply wasted words. Contractual obligations will probably require inclusion of the playwright's name every time the title of the play is used, though in the case of *Hamlet*, that play is in the *public domain*, meaning it now legally belongs to everyone, so there are no contractual obligations with anyone.

Questions to research for class discussion:

Search the Internet and find answers for these questions before you read any further. Be prepared to discuss them in class.

10.1 What are three examples of poorly written promotional texts that you can find? Why are they poorly written?

10.2 What are three examples of well-written promotional texts that you can find? Why are they well-written?

10.3 Find three different examples of descriptions of the same play from different theatres. Compare and contrast them.

Different platforms, different words

There are so many different ways to disseminate a message, and the same words may not always work for each of them. Our description of Hamlet, above, might be great for a brochure, which is small, has limited space, and needs to get to the pertinent information quickly or risk losing the reader. But for a billboard, which is typically only glanced at, there are too many words for the recipient to read. For a website, that description may be enough to draw the reader in, but when they arrive at the page, they may want to "read more," as so many website buttons encourage. But the word choice may also vary depending on the type of user. Advertisements on hip and trendy websites may be less effective if they are verbose or traditional, but word choice in an announcement on a classical music station might be more appropriate if it emphasizes humanistic or scholastic features.

Telling a story

One of the big tricks to writing play descriptions has to do with the telling of the story. Keeping our descriptions brief, one of two unfortunate things can sometimes happen: we either truncate the plot into narrative so thin that it really tells us nothing, or we forget to describe for the reader what the play is about altogether. But think about this: Have you ever seen a preview or advertisement for a movie or play and thought to yourself, "I have no idea what that is actually about?" It usually means some very wise marketer tested the plot synopsis on people in the marketplace and discovered that it was something they were not interested in. As a result, the promotion avoids saying anything about the plot. Sometimes that works, but it is deceptive, and the people who buy tickets are likely to be disappointed.

In promotional writing, we want to be sure we are honestly describing the features that make our product unique and of value to the consumer. The problem is our product, the play, may be something entirely new to the potential audience member, so we also need to describe it to them. Everyone knows what toothpaste is, so the toothpaste manufacturer does not have to explain the benefits of brushing one's teeth, and can instead focus on why their toothpaste is better and more unique than others. Certainly, people know what plays are, so we may not have to explain that, but we often cannot simply focus on why our production of *Coriolanus* is unique. If people do not know what the play is about, they may be hesitant to make a ticket purchase. If a theatre describes their production of Coriolanus as, "a masterpiece brought up to date by setting it in Baghdad during the Iraq war, with the characters each portraying members of different religious sects," it certainly is covering unique features, but for someone who knows nothing about Coriolanus, those features have no meaning. So briefly encapsulating the plot is important. The key word is "briefly." Most plays have an *inciting incident*, which is the thing that occurs that causes the story's problem. In *Hamlet*, it would be when Hamlet sees his father's ghost and learns that the cause of death was murder. When writing a play description, the inciting incident is often a good thing to include in your description; hence, our description above includes murder. Next, ask yourself what type of a story the play is. Is it a love story? Is it a detective story? Is it a rags-to-riches story? An adventure? A tale of overcoming all odds? Those are all important in describing the play. You do not need to detail the entire plot. People understand how plays work, and sometimes they would rather not have the entire plot explained to them beforehand, as that takes away part of the pleasure of watching the plot unfold. However, they want to have some sense of which direction they will be heading. Providing enough detail to interest them is important.

Conveying an experience, not a play

The key to successfully describing a play (or a theatre company) is to convey an experience.[6] The consumer is not interested in being told about the play, or about the company. Instead, they want to know what the experience will be like; how it will make them feel. The audience member spends money in the theatre because attendance causes thoughts and emotions. These are the features we offer that provide value to the audience, and these are the things we want to explain. But like any good writing, it is better to show them than to tell them. What this means is that rather than explaining exactly what we expect they will feel, we describe the actions that cause the feeling. Joining a character as he "unravels a murderous plot" implies certain emotions may be evoked, and is how you show your reader. But if your description says, "you'll be riveted by this tale," you are telling them. If you guide your reader toward the conclusion you want them to make, they are more likely to respond to your call to action than if you tell them the conclusion you expect them to come to. Rather than telling your audience a play is "fast-paced," explain that the characters "run around with wild abandon." Instead of advising that a play is "laugh-out-loud funny," mention that "mistaken identity, men in dresses, and embarrassing secrets all come tumbling out." Let the reader decide how that will make them feel.

Colors, typeface, visuals

Deciding on color for promotional material is more than simply choosing what you feel might be prettiest or most pleasing to the eye. There is a lot of psychology that goes into which colors to use and why, and part of that has to do with research on how the brain responds to specific colors.[7] But because color preference has to do with background, experiences, and what exposures different people have had to different colors, there really is no great science about color. In Asia, red means good luck, and is the color used to indicate a rise in the stock markets. In North America, red means danger, and indicates a drop in the stock markets. However, there are some universally accepted notions that exist today. Red is the color of blood, and it is one of the most easily seen colors, so it suggests a sense of urgency. Though pink, which is a hue of red, is a color most closely associated with girls and women. It is soft, and often used to denote love and romance. When developing a message for a play, consider how you want your reader to feel about the message and choose colors that are appropriate. But most importantly, keep your colors limited to a few complementary colors. Some color photographs will include a full spectrum of color, but even with photographs, try to use those that are largely in keeping with your color scheme.

Questions to research for class discussion:

Search the Internet and find answers for these questions before you read any further. Be prepared to discuss them in class.

10.4 What are the psychological properties of color?
10.5 Which colors do men prefer more? Which colors do women prefer more?
10.6 What do different colors mean?

When laying out a promotional piece, there are some tips you can follow to make it more readable. The first is, select two fonts, and only two fonts to use in your piece. One will be a headline font and one will be the font for your copy. Headline fonts work best when they are *sans serif*, which means they do not have *serifs*, which are the little curlicues you see at the end of the lines of the letter. For the copy, you will want to use a serif font. Serif fonts are easier to read as the eye moves easier from one letter to the next and one word to the next by following the serifs. Times New Roman is a typical serif font, and Arial is a typical sans serif font. You will also want to use only three type sizes, which are called *point sizes*. While you may be inclined to use a very small point, particularly in printed material, 12-point is about as small as you should go for copy. It needs to be readable for everyone. The headline size is generally twice the size of the copy, so in our example that would be 24-point. And the sub-head size is somewhere in-between, such as 18-point. Using script fonts, or those that are particularly intricate, simply makes your piece more difficult to read, even if it does make it look prettier. Headlines work best when they are done with both upper and lower case letters; and when using emphases, such as bold, italics, all capitals, or underlines, use them judiciously or they will lose their impact.

Visual imagery adds impact to your promotional piece, but just like the text, it tells a story. Consider who your target audience is, and what imagery might be most effective in communicating your message to them.[8] If your research tells you that 75% of the ticket-buying decision-makers in your audience are women, then you may want imagery that is going to be more appealing to women. Photographs should be representative of the story, and they should be attractive and appealing.

Sometimes in theatre promotion, we use word art. *Word art* is a way of taking text and manipulating the color, size, and style to turn it into artwork. In the case of word art, the visual impact can be just as powerful as a photograph. Word art also provides an opportunity to get creative with fonts, as the suggestions that you limit font selection to two and that you limit font size to three can be ignored when creating word art. Word art is particularly useful when you do not have, or cannot get, photographs that are appropriate for the story you are trying to tell. But if you use word art for one play in a brochure that is promoting a whole season, be consistent. Use word art for all the plays.

Questions to research for class discussion:

Search the Internet and find answers for these questions before you read any further. Be prepared to discuss them in class.

10.7 Do different typefaces affect people differently?
10.8 What is white space, and why should you use it?
10.9 What is the best way to lay out a brochure?

How humans react

Even before we can understand words, we start learning from what we see. Human beings are designed to gather information through visuals. In today's society we are inundated with visuals, and it seems that everyone is trying to get our attention with visuals. Human beings react best to visuals that are clean, simple, and easy. We also gather more information from a visual that is active.[9] And while some promotional materials may not allow us to include video, just as active verbs are more appealing, so are active photographs. A photograph of an actor sitting in a chair will have far less impact than a photograph of actors screaming at each other. Humans also respond to faces. Expressive faces tell stories, and allow our brains to interpret what is going on behind the expressions.

Who responds to what?

Different societies and cultures have different responses to different stimuli, as noted in the discussion about the color red. You may have found some distinct differences between the genders regarding responses to colors. Without conducting experiments on the citizens in your theatregoing community, it will be virtually impossible to determine what the best options are for visuals for your particular audience. So smart marketers are always keeping an eye on trends. Where are people going most frequently and how do those places promote themselves? What are the features people are drawn toward? And, of course, there is always the option of conducting surveys to determine preferences. But most importantly, when developing promotional materials, test them before spending large amounts of money on them. Get multiple opinions from real, potential recipients and use the feedback to alter materials. Print a small batch and see what sort of response you get, or pay for only a limited run of Facebook ads and see if they work the way you expect. If not, you can make alterations with little investment. Consider a theatre company that decided to invest all its money in a full-page ad in all the local newspapers promoting the musical *Annie*. To reach the people they thought would be most interested, they ran those advertisements in the Sunday comic strips, which were printed in full color. And their advertisement featured a picture of little orphan Annie and a huge headline that read "She's Coming Back." The fine print below gave a phone number for the theatre and instructions on how to order tickets. This ad appeared in several hundred thousand newspapers and cost a small fortune, but sold less than 100 tickets. In under a year the company was out of business. The company's strategy may have been a good one, and they followed all the rules, but they did not run a test. If they had done so, they would have discovered that people reading the comic strips saw the headline, assumed the comic strip *Little Orphan Annie* was coming back to the newspaper, and then turned the page.

The brochure

Danny Newman spends a great deal of time in his book talking about the importance of the brochure, because it is the central sales instrument in his subscription promotion strategy. Of course, when Danny Newman devised his plan, using the postal service was a primary way to deliver information. Now, the Internet has usurped most of that function. Nevertheless, brochures can be useful to promote a play or a season, particularly if other tools that are disseminated in the marketplace support them. There are a few important things to consider when designing a brochure.[10] First, the brochure, like every other promotional tool, should have a clear function, a planned distribution, and an expected result. Cost is sometimes a factor in designing a brochure, and a brief communication with the person responsible for printing it could help determine the most appropriate size. Many brochures are designed with a standard letter-sized piece of paper folded into thirds, and these are often seen in racks or stands. If that is how you anticipate using a brochure, be careful to ensure that the top one-third of the front cover is eye-catching, as that is the only part that will be visible in the rack.

Newman suggests there are some things you should not do when designing a brochure. Having too many folds – or cute or interesting folds, he suggests – just gets in the way.[11] Creating a booklet can be distracting and complex and damage a potential sale. Order forms should be placed in a way that they can be torn off easily, and they should be easy to follow, simple, and clear. Finally, the brochure should not be designed to have multiple functions, such as being able to fold out to make a poster.

Season themes

Some theatre companies promote their entire season by producing plays that fit within a specific theme. Others simply promote the season's slate of plays, and do not attempt to tie them together. There appears to be no data to suggest that one way produces greater results than the other. For every theatre that has polled the marketplace and found a likelihood of increased sales when using themes, there is probably a company that has found a likelihood of decreased sales when a theme is used. This sort of theme is typically an artistic choice, and not a marketing one, and it is a feature that probably has little value to the consumer. However, marketers do concern themselves with promotional themes. Some prefer to find a fluid theme amongst the plays in a season, and then to capitalize on that theme as they go about devising

Think critically: promoting a season theme

There are two ways to approach this class discussion. First, you can choose sides. Divide the class into two, by whatever means you choose, and debate the argument outlined below. Second, you can have an open discussion, each adding upon others' thoughts, and let the discussion uncover all the important details of all sides of the debate. Keep in mind that regardless of which approach you take, we want to be sure we dig deep into all sides of this important issue, in order to more effectively understand all positions.

CLASS DISCUSSION: When an artistic group of people spend countless hours discussing and debating different plays to include in a season, and are focused on ensuring that all the plays fit into a particular theme, it is incumbent on the company to then promote that theme heavily, ensuring that the marketplace is aware of the theme. The theme has been chosen for a purpose: to shed light on an important topic, issue, or life situation that affects us all. Theatre is a place where we can expand our thinking as well as simply be entertained, and the inclusion of themes allows our audience to know that we are not just making entertainment, but we are creating art that explores the human condition. The theme is part of the art, and demonstrates that we are not simply cranking out plays, but concerning ourselves with the artistry as a whole. On the other hand, promotion is about communicating a message to the consumer that describes the benefits to them of taking action and buying a ticket. If they might be turned off by hearing about our theme and they are thinking it is going to preach to them throughout a season, then it is not adding value for the audience, but taking value away. We do not have to promote every artistic choice we make. Sometimes, those artistic choices are better left for the audience to experience as they see them unfold. Promotional pieces are for persuading people to buy tickets, not for making our artistic decisions sound good, so the only things included in the promotion should be those things that will encourage the sale. What is the better way to proceed when promoting a season with a theme?

their promotional strategies. This would then, in turn, help guide selection of colors, fonts, visuals, and even words. Announcing the theme in a promotional piece may be worthwhile and it may not, but having a thematic approach to a promotional strategy can serve a marketer well.

Website and social media design

There are so many places on the Internet where a theatre company can promote itself, and each has a different manner in and method by which it can be used. Having a strategy is key to effectively using any and all of them.[12] It is also important to test them, and to measure responses. If you are planning to close a sale through any social media, you will want to be able to provide a link to a sale page, and track where the click-through came from. There are a number of pieces of software, from very expensive to free or almost free, that can help you coordinate your social media efforts; ensure you are staying on track with distribution and messaging; track who sees what message, and where, and how; and that can also let you know if your target market followed your call to action. The real trick to online promotion is not creating great promotional material and putting it out there; the trick is driving people to it and getting them to act. There are some important factors to consider when writing copy for social media, because social media tends to be more informal than traditional promotional avenues. Anything put out on social media is there forever, so it is important to be careful not to write anything that may cause problems in the future. On the other hand, anything placed into social media has a very short shelf life. People will see it and move on very quickly, so it is a good place to try out different messages, if you are not sure what message is going to garner the greatest response. Social media requires the writer to be friendly and outgoing. People expect that communicating via social media is communicating with a person, not a corporation, so they want to feel as if they are interacting in a personal way. Even though keeping things short and simple is still important, on social media, being humorous without offending is a good way to be casual and personal. Finally, social media requires some different, non-traditional conventions when it comes to rules for appropriate communication. Some media use hashtags, others use likes, and still others use mentions, or names. If a particular social media is being used as a promotional tool, its particular norms, conventions, and etiquette regarding communication must also be followed.[13]

So many theatres invest in creating a fantastic website, but never consider what that website is for and how they are going to get people to it. Once someone gets to your website, it needs to be easy to navigate.[14] It has been said that one of the most complex websites in the world is also one of the easiest to navigate: Craigslist. It isn't pretty, but it works exceptionally well.

Questions to research for class discussion:

Search the Internet and find answers for these questions before you read any further. Be prepared to discuss them in class.

10.10   What are the steps for planning a website? Describe each of them.
10.11   What are the ways you can drive traffic to your website?
10.12   How do social media sites differ as marketing platforms?
10.13   What are the pros and cons of making a mobile app for a business?

Traditional press releases and radio ads

Press releases can be useful in promoting a theatre production, or even an entire season.[15] Writing them can be tricky, because their function is to do the work that a newspaper editor might otherwise have to do. The well-written press release can be an article of interest to readers of the newspaper. But editors receive hundreds of releases every week and sort through them, printing only the best, most interesting, and most well-written releases. There are a number of Internet sources explaining how to format a press release, and because they are so often distributed electronically now, it is wise to check how each editor you distribute to would like to receive the information. Some prefer the release as an attachment while some prefer the release in the body of an email. Some editors would rather the release and associated photographs arrive in the same email, while others prefer separate emails. Most importantly, when writing a press release, keep in mind that it should read as if an impartial journalist wrote it. Press releases should not be written in the first person. And statements like, "Valhalla theatre is proud to present *Hamlet*," are clearly advertisements. Editors do not want to have to make vast changes, but they are loath to print free advertisements. Instead, consider, "Valhalla Theatre Artistic Director William S. Speare noted on Wednesday that his current production of *Hamlet* is one the company is extremely proud to present." This latter statement is a reporting of a fact, the former, if written by a journalist, would be a speculation about how a company feels.

The press kit

Press kits are folders given to newspaper journalists who attend a play with the intention of writing about it and publishing a review. Inside the folder can be any information the theatre company chooses, but at a bare minimum they typically contain a copy of the program, a press release, and production photographs on some form of electronic media. Press kits can also include copies of advertisements, additional dramaturgical information about the play, transcripts of interviews with actors, designers, or directors, or even a page of comments that can be quoted. The key to a good press kit is that it is free from errors, and provides good quality information without being full of fluff.

Photographs

We know that photographs should show activity as opposed to sedentary figures. How active depends on what is being depicted. The photographs are designed to show someone what they can expect to see when they arrive at the theatre. Photographs depicting a moment in a play should show the characters engaged in activity. If the photographs are taken outside under a tree, the person seeing that photograph will quickly figure that this is not a real photograph representing what they will see. If there is no set ready on which to take photographs, staging an active scene in front of a black wall with a few props will appear to the consumer as realistic, even if it is not the actual set and props they will see once they come to attend. With rare exception, photos should have no more than about two or three people in them. Group photographs are busy, difficult to see, and typically do not give the consumer a clear message of what is going on. Likewise, photos with only one person in them should be active enough that they do not appear like a portrait. Costumes are often the key to good promotional photographs in theatre. Even if they have to be pinned on for the photo shoot, the costuming is what will make a photograph stand out and appear unique from other photographs.

Build your theatre milestone 10: promotional materials

For this milestone, you are going to create two different promotional materials. They can be Facebook ads, websites, brochures, flyers, posters, a billboard, coffee mugs, geo-targeted Snapchat ads, radio announcements, press releases, or anything else you can dream up. For each, you will start by writing a message strategy that defines what you are trying to accomplish, who the message is for, what you want them to do after receiving your promotional materials, what the primary and secondary benefits are for them, and how you would like recipients of the promotional material to perceive your theatre. One of your promotional materials should be designed with a call to action, and one should be a supporting piece that will reinforce the first. Next, you should spend some time discussing where and how these pieces tie directly into your marketing plan, where they will be disseminated, in what volume, and what the expected return will be. Finally, you should discuss your design choices in light of the people you are trying to reach. What colors have you chosen, and why? What fonts have you chosen, and why? How will your design capture their attention, get them to follow what you want them to know, and ultimately convince them of the value of your offering so that they act upon it? Lastly, you will also include the actual designs. These do not have to be perfect graphic designs. Sometimes, theatre managers simply provide the information above to a graphics designer, and let the designer do the rest. In this case, you will at least be drawing up a layout, providing necessary text, and providing samples of the types of images you would use. If you want to be creative, and have the talent, feel free to make fully executable promotional materials. HINT: Some of the companies that sell stock images online allow you to download their images with a watermark on them for the purpose of including them in a layout to decide if they are the right images.

Case study

Frank was ready to announce a new season, and he called Patrick into his office to share the final decision. He laid out all the play titles, and Patrick was pleased. He had been doing both focus groups and surveys to test market reaction to different plays, and the ones Frank was listing were all plays that had tested well. This was going to make Patrick's job much easier. And then Frank said, "and this year, we are going to have a theme."

Patrick thought that was interesting, as the company had never done themed seasons before. As he quickly thought about each title, he realized what the theme would probably be, as Frank said it. "The theme is social injustice. And we need to promote that heavily in everything we do. This season we are the theatre company that is going to address social injustice." Patrick took a brief pause, and then responded.

"Frank, it might be better if we didn't really push the theme of social injustice, just because we don't want anyone to feel like we are lecturing to them."

Frank was not pleased with the response, and he and Patrick had a rather lengthy discussion about it, after which Patrick returned to his office and called his team together. Patrick explained what he said to the team:

I told them that Frank had decided on this theme of social injustice and wanted us to promote it heavily, because he wanted to be a theatre with a theme. At one point Frank even announced that he didn't care if it was social injustice or fire trucks or tiddlywinks, he wanted us promoting a theme. I asked everyone to start clearing their schedules because we were going to have to spend the next few days focusing on research to determine what might happen if we focused on social injustice. We would use a stock of old gift cards a board member had donated to us as incentive to get people at the shopping mall to participate in focus groups. We wouldn't be able to keep them more than half an hour, but that would give us enough time to figure out exactly what we would want to put into surveys, which we would also distribute and collect at the mall. This would give us an idea about how the regular person in the market felt. We would also do focus groups and surveys with our subscribers and single ticket buyers so we could see if the responses were different. It was going to be a lot to do in a very short timeframe. But that wasn't all. We also had to start going through those scripts with a fine-toothed comb, looking for anything in them that might be considered thematic. They all had some relevant social issue, but that wasn't the only reason those plays existed. Telling people about a social issue is a lesson. These were works of art and needed us to understand them on a deeper level than just what they were about. I was certain that what Frank was really after was sharing the importance of our work. He just didn't understand that screaming the importance of our work at the marketplace through the promotion of a theme might not be the best way to go.

Patrick's team did do the work as defined and what they discovered surprised them. Subscribers liked the idea of a theme, though they mostly said it would not affect their buying decision. Single ticket buyers essentially felt the theme was unimportant, but they would consider it in their buying decisions, and they reacted negatively to the idea of a theme of social injustice. The regular public overwhelmingly had no interest in attending plays that were themed around social injustice, and felt that lessons belong in classrooms, not in the theatre. The most interesting thing, though, was that in all three groups, about 10% said they would be extremely interested in the educational opportunities associated with a season of plays that dealt with social injustice, and they would pay a 50% premium for having that educational experience. On the other side, about 20% of single-ticket buyers would not buy tickets if the theme was social injustice, and 50% of the general public said the same thing. Patrick thought about it like this:

> Part of our mission is to expand and grow our audience, which to me meant we were getting both a larger audience and a more diverse audience. But part of our mission was also to educate and enlighten the audience. I could see that an argument for promoting a theme of social injustice might fall on both sides. If we got fewer people, but they paid more for the theme, financially we might be fine, but we would be shrinking our audience. On the other hand, if we didn't promote the educational theme, weren't we denying what we are actually trying to do? It didn't seem right to have a theme and then hide it. But I wasn't sure we needed to push it either. To me, the right solution was to know we had a theme, work on the theme from an artistic standpoint, work on the educational features in a way that made them an added benefit that a smaller group could purchase for a premium, but not disrupt our regular sales patterns. But Frank was so determined that the promotional materials should have a theme. And the obvious one was social injustice. But no matter what I did, seeing that there were people willing to pay extra because of the theme was going to bolster Frank's position. And in the long run, if we started developing an audience around themes and how they educate, well, maybe that was okay. But I'm not sure how that was expanding our audience, particularly because the issues of social injustice were all fairly one-sided in these plays. But that was a whole other dilemma.

When it came to digging deep into the plays, Patrick's team made some interesting discoveries. The first was, that while they all dealt with some social injustice, that was a very general way to tie them together. It was like saying they all had the word "happy" in them, so the theme should be happiness. But all the plays had three things that made them very similar. First, they all had a story of gentle, tender love. Either it was budding love, or renewed love, or secret love, but they all had it. None of it was fiery or passionate. They were personal, touching love stories. Second, each of the plays had at least one, and sometimes many, pivotal scenes that occurred outdoors at night. And in each of those scenes, the moon was a prominent feature. Third, the central character in each play had to make some sort of self-sacrifice to save another person. And in all of the plays, these three things seemed far more closely aligned than the idea of social injustice. Patrick's mind started turning, because when he looked at these things, he began developing promotional strategies that incorporated these thematic elements. He thought he might be able to convince Frank to let him change the theme. But what he really wanted to do was to convince Frank that these thematic elements should be carefully intertwined into promotional materials, without ever stating them directly. Was Patrick's idea the best one for the company, or should they follow Frank's plan, or perhaps some other plan? In light of the parts of the mission Patrick shared, is there a better way to proceed? What would be Patrick's best course of action? What would you do?

Personal exploration

For this personal exploration, you are going to create a press kit about some important activity that is taking place in your life. You will want to search how to format a press release, and then you will write one, being sure you are including all the important details in your release. Your press kit should also include a promotional photograph to go along with your press release, as well as any additional information that could be useful to the reader of the press kit.

Notes

1 Johnson, Janet H., Ken Culp III, and Jennifer Bridge, *Delivering Your Marketing Message: Planning Productive Promotions*, 2016.
2 Farney, Ryan M., "The Influence Exposure Has on Consumer Behavior," Senior thesis, Claremont McKenna College, 2016.
3 Newman, Danny, *Subscribe Now!: Building Arts Audiences through Dynamic Subscription Promotion,* Theatre Communications Group, 1977.
4 Marquardt, Adam J., Lynn R. Kahle, Dennis P. O'Connell, and John Godek, "LOV measures: Using the list of values to measure symbolic brand equity (An Abstract)," In *Creating Marketing Magic and Innovative Future Marketing Trends*, pp. 283–284. M. Stieler (ed.), Springer, Cham, 2017.
5 Alas, Ruth, Annukka Jyrämä, and Sami Kajalo, "Building brand loyalty for an arts organization: Does responsibility matter?," In *International OFEL Conference on Governance, Management and Entrepreneurship* (p. 590). Centar za istrazivanje i razvoj upravljanja doo, 2016.
6 Megson, Chris, and Janelle Reinelt, "Performance, experience, transformation: What do spectators value in theatre?," *Journal of Contemporary Drama in English* 4, no. 1 (2016): 227–242.
7 Garg, Manuraaj, Digvijay Agarwal, and Suprav Acharya, "A study on sensory advertising and impact on consumer behaviour," *PARIPEX-Indian Journal of Research* 5, no. 2 (2016).
8 Bajaj, Aditi, "Effect of visual brand imagery on consumer brand perceptions and self-brand connections," PhD dissertation, Georgia Institute of Technology, 2016.

9 Schroeder, Charles E., Donald A. Wilson, Thomas Radman, Helen Scharfman, and Peter Lakatos, "Dynamics of active sensing and perceptual selection," *Current Opinion in Neurobiology* 20, no. 2 (2010): 172–176.

10 Kotler, Philip, and Joanne Scheff, *Standing Room Only: Strategies for Marketing the Performing Arts,* Harvard Business Press, 1997.

11 Newman, *Subscribe Now!: Building Arts Audiences through Dynamic Subscription Promotion,* 1977.

12 Hadley, Bree J., *Theatre, Social Media, and Meaning Making*, Palgrave Macmillan, 2017.

13 Barefoot, Darren, and Julie Szabo, *Friends with Benefits: A Social Media Marketing Handbook,* No Starch Press, 2010.

14 Kolb, Bonita M., *Marketing for Cultural Organisations: New Strategies for Attracting Audiences to Classical Music, Dance, Museums, Theatre & Opera,* Cengage Learning EMEA, 2005.

15 Fraser, Iain, "The marketing of theatre," In *Arts Marketing* (p. 42), F. Kerrigan, P. Fraser, and M. Ozbilgin (eds.), Routledge, 2004.

CHAPTER 11

Fundraising

Patrick had participated actively in the securing of a grant to fund positions in his department, but this was not his only exposure to the fundraising department. He met daily with the Director of Development to discuss patrons who had been interacting with the box office staff or marketing staff. He regularly watched attendance patterns to see who was attending more frequently, and he made sure that someone would reach out to see if these patrons would like to become subscribers. As they did so, Patrick shared this data with the development department and discussed if he felt they were patrons who were enjoying their connection to the company so much that they might want to be more financially supportive in the future. Patrick also shared the patron's sales history. He knew that as he developed the audience, part of his job was to help these patrons enjoy their connection with the company to the fullest extent possible. Patrick also recognized the importance of promotional material on fund development. Every piece of information he disseminated to the public would have some effect on the company's brand, and Patrick was always watching out to make sure that he was representing the company as extremely professional, wonderfully managed, exceptionally frugal, and always looking for support to become an even better member of the community.

> ## Chapter objectives
>
> After reading this chapter, you should be able to demonstrate how to draft a fundraising plan and a letter of inquiry, explain the different types of funding sources available, describe a gift range chart, and differentiate some of the terms used in fundraising.

Fundraising

The terms "fundraising," "development," and "advancement" are sometimes used interchangeably, however they are not synonymous. *Fundraising* is the process of soliciting financial support. For commercial theatre, that typically means seeking investment capital, and for noncommercial theatre it often means soliciting donations. *Development* is the process of developing relationships. Sometimes it is referred to as *fund development*, meaning specifically that it is the process of developing financial support. Also, sometimes the term "development" is used to refer to the process of developing an entire organization. In theatre marketing it is used as part of the term "audience development." In fundraising, it would be more appropriate if it were referred to as *donor development*, though perhaps some find that distasteful (we will see it is not) so it has been reduced to simply "development."[1] In noncommercial theatre this would be the process where a representative of the company is getting to know the needs and wants of a patron on a one-to-one basis, and helping to align those desires with something the theatre has to offer. In the strictest sense, development is different than fundraising, though the end goal is for the patron to appreciate the connection to the degree that they choose to provide additional needed financial support to the company.[2] *Advancement* is the process of managing relationships, typically between the organization and donors, in an effort to increase the donors' knowledge of the organization, and to strengthen that relationship. Sometimes this process is also referred to as *stewardship*. The terms can all be a bit confusing, as the differences between them are subtle, and so many organizations use them interchangeably. While it is important to understand the distinctions, for purposes of simplicity, throughout this chapter unless otherwise noted we will use the term "development" to refer to the entire process of developing relationships that are managed and ultimately lead to continuing donated financial support.

The board and executives

To add to the confusion, the main function of a board is to steer the long-term direction and strategy of an organization and to protect its assets. Sometimes, driving an organization forward over the long term is also referred to as "advancement," and protecting an organization's assets is called "stewardship." You can see why people find the terms to be confusing.

But the board of a theatre, as part of their function, has some responsibility for ensuring the necessary financial support is in place to secure a future. Many theatres have a board that sets a policy for itself called *give or get*, which implies that each board member will be responsible for either personally giving, or soliciting from others, a minimum amount of contributions each year. While it is important that a theatre can show other potential donors that every member of the board is participating in the financial success of a theatre, setting a policy such as give or get can have unexpected consequences, and needs to be written in consideration of all the value that board members bring. A good rule of thumb is that the board should be roughly divided into thirds, with one-third making the theatre their priority in terms of donation, one-third making the theatre among their top priorities, and one-third perhaps not donating as much in terms of direct financial support, but providing services such as legal, marketing, or accounting, which are of value to the theatre. Sometimes theatres will simply state that they expect board members to make an annual gift appropriate to their giving capacity, but as you can imagine, this is impossible to monitor and therefore simply a suggestion. What is important for board members is their constant devotion to bringing new people to the theatre, either as ticket buyers, subscribers, or donors. Having board members solicit donations can be tricky, as the process of fundraising requires an ability for just the right person to ask at just the right time, of the right potential donor, the right amount, for the right specific cause. Getting everything right takes a lot of planning, and board members rarely have the time or expertise to ensure that everything is correct. This is not to suggest that board members should not be involved in the process. Sometimes board members know and introduce to the company a friend who is the right potential donor, and the board member may be able to provide information about that potential donor, such as the right amount to ask for, or which particular aspect of the company said donor may have an interest in supporting. From there, a staff member, usually a director of development, gets to know the potential donor, helps to find what parts of the company might interest them most – such as the education program, or costumes, or student matinees – and also starts to learn who they trust and value that is associated with the organization. When the staff member determines it is the right time to ask for financial support, they may do it themselves if they feel they are the right person, or they may ask the board member who introduced the potential donor, or the theatre's executive, to come along. One of them will make a case for why financial support is required for the aspect of the company the potential donor is interested in, and then express the amount of money required, based on the amount of money they feel is right for this potential donor. It may sound like a process designed to squeeze cash from someone, but in fact the money is a byproduct of a job well done. The job is to develop a relationship between the potential donor and the theatre. People donate when they are getting something out of it. That may be a sense of personal satisfaction, an opportunity to be recognized, gratitude, a chance to help others, and so on. The development director's job is to make sure the potential donor has an opportunity to get what they would like. If they do their job well, the money will follow.

The fundraising plan and pyramid

Before embarking on the fundraising process, it is important to have a plan. There are many different ways to create a fundraising plan and even more topics that can be included in the plan. While there is no perfect way to make a plan, because every theatre is slightly different, there are some elements that should always be included in a fundraising plan. One of those things is a needs statement. The *needs statement* is a statement that discusses the programs that are operated by the company to fulfill the company mission, and also discusses what financial needs must be met in order to operate each program effectively. A second item that should be included in the fundraising plan is an objectives statement for each program. The *objectives statement* describes how the company will operate each program, and should include all the elements in the acronym SMART: specific, measurable, achievable, results, and timely. A good objectives statement talks specifically about how the company will operate the program, how it will measure its effectiveness, if it will be realistically achievable, states what results are expected, and provides a timeline for completion.[3] Each element of the SMART acronym does not necessarily need to be listed in that order, but the objectives statement should include all aspects of SMART.

A third item every good fundraising plan includes is what specific tactics will be used to generate support. Tactics might include special events, curtain speech appeals, donation envelopes in programs, grants, annual appeals, and many other activities. For each tactic, the plan should discuss who is responsible for working on executing the tactic, what their timeline is, and what the expected results of the tactic will be.

Fundraising plans also sometimes include a gift range chart, which uses percentages to list how many donations will be required in a list of giving ranges, and how many potential prospects in each range are typically required in order to achieve the necessary amount of donations in each range.[4] Different gift range charts may use slightly different percentages based on which industries they have drawn their data from. For example, a development officer may determine the total amount needed to complete the fundraising activity or campaign amount, and anticipate that one big donor will likely contribute 10% of the total amount. To secure that 10%, the development officer will usually require four or five prospects who are capable of making a gift of the size required, and who have an interest in the company. A second gift might typically be anticipated at about three-quarters the size of the lead, or largest gift, coming from a prospect pool of four potential donors capable of making a gift that size. The gift range chart is a list of how many gifts will be required at what size in order to complete the campaign, and also how many prospects at each level will be required in order to find the appropriate number of donors.

An additional element that is often included in a fundraising plan is a list of potential donors, sorted by their anticipated capacity to give. As you can imagine, that sort of information can be quite sensitive, so it should not be shared outside of the theatre, and should be kept locked up.

Questions to research for class discussion:

Search the Internet and find answers for these questions before you read any further. Be prepared to discuss them in class.

11.1 List and describe three additional elements that can go into a fundraising plan.

11.2 Find two different gift range calculators online and describe how they differ. Why do you think that is? How consequential are the differences?

11.3 What is donor prospect research?

11.4 What are the key elements in donor prospect research?

Stewardship

Being a good steward of an organization's assets is an important part of the fundraising process. It involves carefully managing the gifts donated to the organization, recognizing the generosity of donors, investing the funds wisely, accounting for them appropriately, and much more.[5] But at the heart of stewardship is the genuine expression of gratitude for those who have stepped forward to recognize, honor, and support the work of the organization toward achieving its mission. While stewardship can easily become mechanical by sending out form letters as a means of saying thank you or offering different levels of tributes for different levels of giving, nothing is more important than always looking for special, unique, repeated, and honest ways of saying thanks to each and every contributor. Donors are contributing to a theatre because they believe in the company's mission, and understand that they are bettering society by supporting that mission. Part of the fundamental tenants of stewardship are that those donors have a right to have their funds used for the purpose they have given them, to be informed of the mission and functioning of the organization to which they give, and to be honored with gratitude for their contribution. Donors should also be able to trust that the organization is operating honestly and accurately in all its dealings.

Types of giving

There are many different ways that people or other organizations may choose to give to a theatre, and the list can be almost unlimited. Of course, for a commercial theatre, money given is done so as an investment, with the hope of seeing a return on that investment. For noncommercial theatre, gifts may be given *in kind*, meaning that they are the gift of a good or service which is of value, or they can be financial, such as cash, or a stock, bond, or other easily convertible instrument. But more than the type of gift, there are many ways in which a theatre can seek donations, and while theatres often employ many of these avenues, the list is certainly not limited to only these.

Annual fund

The *annual fund* or *annual campaign*, as the name implies, is a fundraising activity that is done every year, and typically only once a year, though many theatres conduct more than one appeal every year. The annual fund is the foundation upon which most development rests, because it is often the entry point of a donor, who can then be recognized; and from that recognition a relationship can be developed. In the annual fund, the theatre develops a goal and gift range chart, and sets forth to reach that goal through some sort of appeal. While the most successful appeals tend to result from face-to-face meetings, those require a great deal of time. Personal solicitations typically prove to be the most successful, and if there is insufficient time for a face-to-face interaction, personal phone calls or letters from someone who knows the potential donor are sometimes the next best thing. But most theatres operate an annual fund appeal by distributing impersonal letters to every person who has attended the theatre and purchased a ticket. As we discussed in Chapter 8, one of the functions of the ticketing process is to capture contact information for people buying tickets for the purpose of asking them for a contribution. Even though annual appeal letters may be impersonal, these are often met with success. To distribute a mailed appeal for donations, the theatre has to have a mailing list, and a list of attendees will be more likely to demonstrate support.

Many theatres typically include their annual fund appeal along with their subscription renewal forms, to save on postage and distribution costs. While this may seem effective on the surface, it is likely that giving levels will be reduced when patrons are being asked to make two large financial transactions simultaneously, one as a ticket purchase, and one as a donation. There is no right or wrong time to make the appeal, but it is important to weigh the factors involved in each unique situation. Some theatres prefer to make the annual appeal with the subscription renewal, noting for subscribers the percentage of income required through donations just to keep the theatre running. Many believe that subscribers are willing to add a donation so they feel they are contributing their fair share of the total amount required to operate the theatre.

Some theatres choose not to make both an annual appeal and a subscription renewal at the same time, though they may include a line for "added donation" on an order form. Instead, they typically have a different time of year when they find requests for donations are more successful. Some choose the holiday time, as people are in the spirit of giving, and for many, there are positive tax consequences for giving; reminding them of those consequences may convince them to give before the year ends.

Still other theatres do their annual appeal around or at one particular production, using the performance as a way to remind patrons of how important the theatre's contribution is to the community. While still not the standard, some theatres choose one, or sometimes more, productions to take the stage at the end of the performance, announce the appeal and what the money will be used for, and ask patrons to contribute something on their way out of the theatre. While this can generate a good deal of money, it has the distinct disadvantage of not allowing the company to capture the names of those who are making contributions, making personal thank yous and follow-up contact impossible.

Part of the function of the annual appeal is to allow the theatre to know who is making a contribution, so it can begin to develop relationships with those people. While securing the gift is certainly an important part of the appeal, being able to renew that gift year after year is equally important, as this is how the company builds and develops a list of donors. The annual appeal also serves the purpose of getting patrons into the habit of giving, and allows the theatre to continuously expand its list of donors, as well as to communicate a continuing message about the importance of the theatre's mission.

Think critically: the curtain speech appeal

There are two ways to approach this class discussion. First, you can choose sides. Divide the class into two, by whatever means you choose, and debate the argument outlined below. Second, you can have an open discussion, each adding upon others' thoughts, and let the discussion uncover all the important details of all sides of the debate. Keep in mind that regardless of which approach you take, we want to be sure we dig deep into all sides of this important issue, in order to more effectively understand all positions.

CLASS DISCUSSION: Having the lead actor of a production take the stage at the end of the curtain call and appeal directly to every member of the audience after a performance is an important way to solicit funds. Patrons have just witnessed the reason the theatre company exists, they should be in good spirits for having experienced great theatre, and they are being asked by the person who just provided the art in the preceding hours. Capturing patrons at this moment is essential, and it also allows them to feel intimately connected with the theatre, as this sort of appeal provides the rare opportunity for the patrons to hear from an actor out of character. When that actor describes a very real need, it resonates in ways that no form letter, no matter how appealing it may be, can do. Additionally, by making an appeal in this way, patrons can choose to make their donation anonymously, tossing nothing or large amounts into the proverbial hat as they exit the theatre. And many theatregoers are accustomed to this style of contribution, as it mimics the way many places of religious worship seek contributions.

However, many artists find the whole idea of soliciting contributions at the end of a play offensive. It cheapens the art, and leaves patrons walking out feeling like they have been harassed. Actors should remain in character when they are in costume and on the stage, and their function is to act, not to do fundraising. In fact, the stage should be for art, not solicitations or announcements. And by doing these solicitations, the theatre may be driving regular patrons away, who would rather not be pressured at the theatre to contribute. Even once a year doing this sort of request is too much, but if they end up raising some money, next year won't the thinking go that doing these two times a year could raise twice as much money? And the year after, perhaps every performance will be used as a tool for begging for cash. When attending the theatre, patrons should be allowed to just attend the theatre. Fundraising is supposed to be done outside of the theatre as a way to support the art; it should not become a part of the art.

Do either of these arguments make more sense than the other? Why?

Endowments

One way to ensure that a theatre company can have a long and sustained future is by building a strong endowment fund. An *endowment fund* is an account established with money that is invested, allowing the organization to use the dividends and interest generated from the investment, usually without ever withdrawing the initial money. An endowment fund, because it provides a continuous stream of income, can help an organization get through more difficult times. Building an endowment fund that generates enough interest to keep the organization stable takes some serious planning and a lot of time. Many universities have established endowment funds that generate millions every year. Typically, when a donor contributes to an endowment fund, they do so with the understanding that their principal contribution will never be withdrawn, and it is incumbent upon the theatre to never do so. Should the theatre close, the original principal amount that was contributed would be returned to the donor or their heirs. Sometimes, donors direct their contribution to be used in an endowment for a certain period of time, after which it may be used at the discretion of the organization, or in a manner in which the donor has directed in advance. This is sometimes referred to as a *term endowment*, since the original principal investment remains in the endowment fund for a limited term.

Some theatres, during very prosperous years, will take excess revenue and place it into an endowment fund, which they can then take advantage of in years that are leaner. These *quasi-endowments* are distinct in that the organization has chosen to not dip into the principal, though they are under no obligation to leave it untouched, and could withdraw it at any time.

Planned gifts

Planned gifts are those that are designated by a donor to be given to the organization at a future time. While that seems like a simple concept, planned giving is actually quite complex to organize and control. While some planned gifts may be simple outright gifts left in a will, others can be a complicated arrangement involving multiple parties, various investment instruments, trustees controlling retirement monies, and so forth. One type of planned gift, for example, is the "deferred gift"; the money is actually transferred to the organization, which may take advantage of some tax laws, but it may not be used by the organization until a specified time. As you can imagine, having an accountant involved with your theatre can be quite beneficial if you are thinking of encouraging donors to consider planned giving.

Questions to research for class discussion:

Search the Internet and find answers for these questions before you read any further. Be prepared to discuss them in class.

11.5 What are the types of planned giving and how does each work?
11.6 What are some important issues involved in the taxation of major gifts?
11.7 What are the pros and cons of planned giving?

A case of a planned endowment:

Richard Stover was a college professor who served at the same school most of his adult life. He eventually became a dean there, and then vice-president and provost before retiring. He was greatly admired and respected, and he served the college with honesty, integrity, and a true concern for students, staff, and faculty.

And though college employees are notoriously underpaid, Stover was careful with his money, and through the years, and with a nice retirement program provided by the college, he saved quite a bit of money for him and his wife Shirley to live on in his golden years. In addition to the plentiful nest egg amassed through his work at the college, Stover also inherited a large amount of money from his father, who had collected a great deal of random artwork that eventually became worth a small fortune. Stover's father had intended for that art to provide a retirement for his son, but since Richard did not need the money, he wanted to do something worthwhile with it, though he also wanted to leave a retirement cushion for his two sons as well. So he met with the planned giving office at the college, and explained that he would happily leave some of the money in his will to the college, if it could be used in a way that would recognize his father. The planned giving officer asked why the entire amount of money could not be left to the college, as the full amount would allow for the construction of a new and badly needed building, and Stover explained that it was for his sons. The officer then explained there was a solution that would satisfy all these needs, and here is what was done: Stover transferred all of his assets to the college. The entire amount was placed in a term endowment. It was then used as collateral to take out a loan in order to finance the new building. Interest from the endowment would be used to pay off the loan by the time Stover's two sons each reached retirement age. At that time, they would each get 50% of the interest on the endowment for the rest of their lives. Once they each passed away, the entire endowment reverted to the college to be used as it saw fit. The plan managed to satisfy the needs of the college, the needs of Stover's sons, and Stover's desire to recognize his father, as the new building was named the Stover Building.

Major giving

Major giving refers to gifts of substantial size that are typically acquired after a long period of developing a relationship with the donor.[6] While much of the work that development officers do is task oriented, such as sending out letters in an annual appeal, researching prospects, and updating databases, the personal interactions with potential major gift donors are what really connect an organization to an individual. Development officers meet with these potential donors to listen to their needs, desires, and wants, and to help find ways where some of them can be satisfied by the organization. They also continue a dialogue about the life and functioning of the theatre, sharing stories and information about the operation that the general public may not be aware of. The development officer is working to allow the donor to have some level of ownership in the theatre.[7] Some consider the process to be loathsome, because they view it as a means of manipulating people to get them to contribute money. The best development officers, however, consider their function to be more of a service to the donor than to the theatre. They feel that the theatre generates the things that will satisfy some of the donor's needs, wants, and desires, and they provide those things with an attitude of sincere goodwill and nothing else. Satisfied donors make contributions because they are treated with care and concern and because their needs, wants, and desires are being met. Savvy development officers make those connections and hope that a gift will follow; they do not make them specifically so a contribution can be acquired.

Capital campaigns

A *capital campaign* is a one-time fundraising campaign, sometimes run over several years, with a goal that will allow for the acquisition of a tangible capital asset such as a building, building renovation, or major new equipment.[8] Unlike an endowment campaign or an annual appeal, both of which have goals that, if unmet, will likely not have major ramifications, if the goal of a capital campaign is not met, none of the money raised can be used. Because this is the case, it is important that the theatre is careful to determine exactly what the cost of the capital asset will be at the time of the expected goal completion, and even then, it is wise to enlarge the goal to account for unexpected changes in the final cost. Capital campaign goals, however, cannot simply be determined by actual cost. They must also be determined based on a real understanding of historic donor activity, and an honest evaluation of what is achievable.[9] Even then, there is no science in making such predictions, so a capital campaign goal must be one agreed to by staff and board, with no broad dissention on whether the goal is too big or not big enough. Once a preliminary goal is set, the theatre then sets different benchmarks along the way. Sometimes these are to do construction in phases, and as the money for each phase is reached, the construction for that phase can begin. Setting benchmarks helps keep the campaign on track. One benchmark that is typically set is when to end the "silent phase." The theatre will typically set out by trying to quietly find some major contributors toward the goal. This period of time is referred to as the *silent phase*, and it not only allows the theatre to determine if the goal seems doable, but also allows for the public phase of the campaign to kick off with great fanfare, as a major portion of the goal will have already been achieved at that point.[10] People can be hesitant to donate when they are not certain the goal can be achieved, but if large gifts have already been made, they are more comfortable with giving, because they feel they are part of a winning campaign. One of the challenges with a capital campaign is that it must be conducted in a way that it does not siphon away contributions from the annual appeal, and that can be challenging, as the same donors often contribute to both campaigns. But it would be pointless to raise capital for a future expenditure if it is done at the expense of annual operating funds that keep the theatre going.

Special events

Special events, sometimes called *fundraisers*, are gatherings where people are charged a price above and beyond the cost of putting on the gathering in order to raise funds. Special events can range in size from very small – such as a coffee house poetry slam – to huge galas with celebrity talent, and everything in between. They can be parties, races, sporting events, award dinners, lectures, or even special play performances. Sometimes these events include additional fundraising pieces, like a live or silent auction of goods or services that have been donated to the theatre for the expressed purpose of raising money. While fundraisers sound like a fantastic way to raise a lot of money, more often than not they are better at creating fun than creating funds, and consequently are sometimes labeled as *funraisers*. Special events require an exorbitant amount of time, and for a theatre that usually means countless volunteer hours. Special events also require some level of financial commitment by those volunteers, as well as a great deal of promotion to their friends and colleagues to ensure a satisfactory turnout. Well-planned fundraisers are designed with a very clear strategy, a well-written plan which includes a marketing plan, and clearly defined goals that can be measured. Large fundraisers can take months to plan and prepare, require very detailed timelines and calendars, and specific budgets that detail every anticipated expense and every expected piece of income. When making such plans it often becomes apparent that in terms of return for invested time, fundraisers are typically the poorest performing of all fundraising tactics. However, even a small financial return is beneficial, and special events provide an array of benefits, including expanding a theatre's network, developing a working volunteer base, and drawing public attention to the theatre.

Grant writing

An additional way to raise money is by writing grants. Grants are formal gifts of money from a foundation or governmental agency that are designated for a specific purpose. Many foundations have specific areas that they are interested in supporting, and there are a number of online resources for finding those that will support the arts. But theatres are not limited to arts grants. Theatres that run educational programs may find granting agencies that support them.[11] Of course it may sound as simple as writing a letter and asking for money, but the process is actually more complex and requires great attention to detail.[12] Different granting agencies have different requirements for what needs to go into your grant application, and there is typically a lot of competition for grants. But there are some standard tips for ensuring you have a shot at getting that money. First, read up on the granting agency you are going to submit an application to. Find out what specific things they are interested in, and what sorts of applications they have funded in the past. Be sure you are asking for an amount of money that is approximately the same as the amount they typically provide. When you have done your homework, get in touch with a program officer, who is the person at the granting agency who will do the initial screening of your application. Do not simply pick up the phone and call them. You could quickly turn someone off if they do not wish to receive phone calls. Inquire via post or email if they would be willing to answer some questions, and if so, what would be their preferred method of contact. When you contact them, briefly explain what you are thinking of applying for, and see if the project you are proposing would be of any interest to them. You will also want their advice on what could make it a stronger proposal, and where they see it fitting into their mission. Remember that this contact is going to be the person who rejects your proposal outright, or takes it to someone else looking to get it funded. If the program officer likes you, they are far more likely to be supportive of your proposal as it moves further up the chain of command at the agency. Some program officers even make the decisions themselves on whether to fund or not.

Once you have this communication, you may be required to send a letter of inquiry. Many agencies require this before an actual proposal is submitted. The letter of inquiry should briefly describe the project or program, and should demonstrate that you understand the agency and how the program fits into their mission. You may also want to reference your theatre's mission, and highlight its contribution to the community. The letter of inquiry may also want to mention board members or other people affiliated with your company whom the program officer may know or recognize. Be sure to include how you can be contacted.

If the agency asks you to submit a full proposal, they will have specific requirements for what needs to go in it. At a bare minimum, you will include a detailed description of the project or program you are proposing, and explain how it fits with your company's mission, vision, and values. You will also want to address any similar programs you have done, and how your company handled those. The proposal will address what needs the program fills, and for whom the program is being created. The proposal will cover who is going to be running the program, what their expertise is, and how it will be run. Finally, and perhaps most importantly, you will want to detail what the expected outcomes of the program are, how you will evaluate those, and what will demonstrate that the program has been successful. This last part is extremely important, as funding agencies do not wish to simply send a check and be done. They are investing in something for the community, and they want to know that their investment has provided a return as expected. Most granting agencies will expect periodic reports and updates as well as a final report after the program is completed, detailing how the program was evaluated and what the results were.

Questions to research for class discussion:

Search the Internet and find answers for these questions before you read any further. Be prepared to discuss them in class.

11.8 How do crowdfunding programs work? Briefly describe three different crowdfunding programs.

11.9 What grants are available for your theatre?

11.10 What other elements might you need to prepare to put into a grant application?

Types of givers

As you have seen, there are various categories of givers. We have broken them down into major gifts, regular contributors, foundations, and government agencies. Actually, however, those are all distinct and very specific, based on their respective capacities to give. When it comes to broader "types" of givers, everyone is either public or private.

Public funding sources

Public-funded sources are those that have been established through some sort of governmental policy or legislation. That legislation often controls how the resources are provided, and it is a very rigid control with little wiggle room. Public agencies – such as cities, counties, and other governmental bodies – are focused on doing things for the greater good of the communities they represent, so they look for opportunities that will impact the greatest number of people. While they can be extremely bureaucratic, require lengthy and detailed application procedures, and complex processes for complying with reporting (often because those documents will become publicly available), they also typically have larger amounts of money to grant. One other distinct advantage to public sources is that they often have staff available to provide assistance in preparing the best application.

Private funding sources

Private funding sources include everyone else, from individual donors, to foundations, to crowdfunding sites. If your theatre is trying something new and different, private sources tend to be more interested. As we have seen, private sources can make gifts that vary in size from small to large, and in many cases they are not bureaucratic at all. Grants from private sources, however, typically are smaller than from public sources. Also, while private sources tend to be more discretionary about how and where they provide gifts, this also means they are far more discretionary about not doing so as well, and the applicant has very little control over the decision.

Build your theatre milestone 11: fundraising plan

When starting a theatre, finding the money to start can be the toughest challenge. Banks will not loan to a business without a history of success. Most foundations and granting agencies are hesitant to provide support to a company with no track record. And even private philanthropists and donors do not want to give to an organization when they are not certain of what the company's contribution to the community will actually look like. And without yet having a mailing list of theatre lovers, it would be almost impossible to solicit funds in an annual appeal. Some local governments will provide start-up loans or grants when they see a need for a theatre in their community. Others may provide a building, city services, or other support. And support like that can go a long way toward bringing additional donors on board. For this milestone, develop a fundraising plan, including how you intend to get your first contribution. As part of this plan, include two letters, the first, an appeal for a gift, whether that is a letter you will write to your friends and family asking for money, something you intend to post on a crowdfunding site, or a letter to city government asking for their support. Be sure to include in this letter exactly what it is you are seeking, and exactly what the donor can expect in return. The second letter should be your letter of thanks. Be sure that both of these letters sound personal as opposed to formal, and that they tell a story rather than simply listing facts.

Case study

Patrick had been doing a great job of improving his company's audience development, and part of that was the result of the additional staff he had that was funded by a grant. One of them was specifically hired to do marketing research, and that data was incredibly helpful. The granting agency had provided the researcher as part of the proposal for marketing, and they wanted to see results from their investment, which Patrick provided on a quarterly basis. But the development department, which had helped secure the assistance, was somewhat jealous. They saw this research being done in audience development, and felt that if they had some research assistance, they would be able to greatly improve upon their fundraising. So the director of development approached Patrick about sharing the research assistant. Patrick was reluctant for two reasons. First, he felt that the researcher was working full-time conducting marketing research, and by sharing her, half of that work would cease to be done. Second, the grant was for an audience development researcher, and the foundation that provided the money expected to see it used as they meant it to be. The director of development heard Patrick's concerns, but offered the following counter-arguments: First, while the audience development research was intense at the beginning, now that research programs were in place, and a foundation of data had been collected, the heavy work had been done, so the assistant would be required less. Second, technically, research in the fundraising side could focus on developing relationships with audience members, so it could ethically be still called audience development research.

Patrick was not thrilled with the idea, but knew that Frank would be supportive of it, so that was not going to be a way to stop it. Some of Patrick's real concerns had to do with reporting. He would have to detail the work being done by the assistant, as well as what the expected results were of that work, and what the real results of that work were. He questioned how he could justify fundraising research, and how he would word it so that it sounded like it was audience development. But more importantly, should he? On the other side of the dilemma, if Patrick refused, or if he said anything to the funding agency, he ran the risk of losing the researcher funding altogether, as well as the funding for two other staff members. Patrick had to be very careful as to how he handled this situation. What could he have done to make sure this worked in everyone's best interest? Who should he have spoken to, and what should he say? What options did Patrick have?

Personal exploration

Think of a project that you have been interested in working on. Draft a letter of inquiry to a friend or relative who could afford to fund your project, detailing the project. In this letter you will want to describe the project briefly, explain how it fits in with your goals for yourself and your life, and also explain how the project will fit with the recipient's goals for you and for life in general. You will want to mention specifically who your project will serve, and how it will serve them.

Notes

1 Charles, Cleopatra, and Mirae Kim, "Do donors care about results? An analysis of nonprofit arts and cultural organizations," *Public Performance & Management Review* 39, no. 4 (2016): 864-884.

2 Ibid.
3 Pilkington, Ann, *Communicating Projects: An End-to-end Guide to Planning, Implementing and Evaluating Effective Communication,* Routledge, 2016.
4 Klein, Kim, "Getting major gifts: The basics," Retrieved January 18, 2017 http://www.ncdsv.org/images/Getting%20Major%20Gifts_The%20Basics.pdf
5 Schorn, Theodore, "Management as stewardship: A path to improved performance," In *117th Metalcasting Congress.* Afsinc, 2013.
6 Waters, Richard D., "The current landscape of fundraising practice," *The Routledge Companion to Philanthropy*, Tobias Jung, Susan D. Phillips, and Jenny Harrow (eds.) (p. 423), Routledge, 2016.
7 Ibid.
8 Kihlstedt, Andrea, *Capital Campaigns: Strategies that Work,* Jones & Bartlett Learning, 2005.
9 Ibid.
10 Walker, Julia Ingraham, "Get back on track with changes in campaign structure," *Jump-Starting the Stalled Fundraising Campaign* (pp. 73–93), John Wiley & Sons, 2009.
11 Russell, Amy Leigh, ""I'll Huff, and I'll Puff, and I'll Blow your house down": Building the resiliency of education departments in nonprofit theatre organizations," *The Journal of Arts Management, Law, and Society* 45, no. 1 (2015): 22–32.
12 DeVereaux, Constance, "Fund-raising and grant-writing basics for arts managers," *The Arts Management Handbook: New Directions for Students and Practitioners*, Meg Brindle and Constance DeVereaux (eds.) (p. 290), M. E. Sharpe, 2015.

CHAPTER 12

Leadership

By now you have probably recognized that many of the issues Patrick faced were not caused by mistakes people made in doing their work. Instead, they were typically situations that arose due to poor leadership. No one appeared to be a poor leader, or not trying to do the right thing, but somehow, their choices had unintended consequences, or results that should have been considered before choices were made. And while it may seem like all these situations could not happen to one person, that is only because you are reading about them all in a very short time frame. These sorts of problems occur in theatres all the time, and if any one person were to be documenting them, you might find a similar string of case studies. Generally, they are all rooted somewhere in the leadership process.

Chapter objectives

After reading this chapter, you should be able to describe the difference between management and leadership, explain which roles in theatre exert more leadership, evaluate the importance of risk in the business of theatre, describe different personality styles and explore how they interact, discuss your own leadership style, and explain the relationship between leadership and innovation.

Leadership

We know that the four functions of management are planning, organizing, leading, and controlling.[1] By that definition, leading, or leadership, is actually one of the functions of management, suggesting that every leader is technically a manager.

The terms can be a bit confusing, and for many, it is often easier to think of leadership as a process rather than the work a leader does. Leadership and the study of it have existed for centuries. But it was not until the mid-twentieth century that the field of leadership became an academic area of inquiry at universities.[2] Leadership is more than just another way of saying management. Instead, *leadership*, and its continuously developing definition, has to do with how one guides people and organizations of people. But because the academic field is so new, the definition seems to be regularly refined. Leadership studies are really more interdisciplinary in nature than simply being a part of the study of business, though business schools are often where leadership departments are found.[3] But the academic study of leadership can also be found in disciplines such as psychology, sociology, education, and the arts.[4] Because leadership has to do with behavior, it makes sense that you might find it in the social sciences, but because it also has to do with behavior in organizations, it also makes sense that it would be linked to organizational studies, which are typically found in business schools. We study leadership in the arts because some of the situations theatre managers face are unique to theatre, such as those we have seen Patrick face.

Transformational versus transactional

In 1978, James MacGregor Burns published a book called *Leadership*, which discussed the nature of leadership, and defined it as either transactional or transformational.[5] While Burns did not coin the terms, in his book he expanded upon them to the degree that it became foundational in the study of leadership. Burns was a man who studied and wrote about US presidents, and his work also took him into the study of government, public policy, and leadership. Burns saw *transactional leadership* as being a give and take between leaders and followers.[6] Followers received leaders' rewards or punishments for their work in a transaction that got the work done either effectively and efficiently or not. *Transformational leadership* is a style that allows for mutual respect and understanding between leader and follower that causes both to have greater motivation. Transformational leaders inspire followers to want to work more efficiently and effectively toward a shared vision of where the organization is going. Transformational leadership has to do with promoting change for the future, while transactional leadership, sometimes called *managerial leadership*, is more about keeping things moving effectively.

McGregor's theory

Before Burns, in the 1960s, Douglas McGregor developed a theory about how managers worked, and it has become known as Theory X and Theory Y. This theory focuses very clearly on how leaders and followers behave in a workplace setting, and is seminal in the study of leadership. McGregor postulated that Theory X managers believe their employees are lazier than management, are less intelligent, or are only working for the purpose of earning an income.[7] As a result, Theory X managers are very hands-on, reward good work, and punish bad work, and supervise very closely. Theory Y managers believe their employees are self-motivated, hard working, and find satisfaction in the work they do. Theory Y managers supervise less tightly, and are more likely to develop meaningful relationships with their employees. While you may think that Theory Y sounds much more pleasant, particularly in the arts, there are certain times, situations, and people who perform better under Theory X than Theory Y. But what Burns was really trying to explain was that employees are not simply cogs in a big machine, they are people who have different motivations. Understanding what motivates people is an important part of leadership. Though, as we will see, those things that affect our own beliefs may alter how we think of others. Knowing what drives our own personalities is as important as knowing what motivates others. As it turns out, effective leadership can be situational. Think about final tech week on a production, when things are not going well and time is running out. Often, in those times, a Theory X managerial approach is helpful in order to get things where they need to be for the play to open on time.

Questions to research for class discussion:

Search the Internet and find answers for these questions before you read any further. Be prepared to discuss them in class.

12.1 What are some different theories of leadership and how do they differ?
12.2 How is management different from leadership? Can one person be both a manager and a leader? Should they be?
12.3 Which positions in theatre would you say are more leadership positions, which are more management positions, and why?
12.4 What is the difference between authority and leadership? Must they be formal, or can they be informal?

Risk

One of the hallmarks of leadership is the element of risk. We think of *risk* as exposure to something that can be dangerous. But buried in that definition is a sense of the unknown. Visiting your grandma seems unlikely to be a risky venture because you have probably done it many times and never had any adverse effects. This does not guarantee that nothing dangerous might occur, but the risk of going to grandma's house is extremely minimal. If a man on the street pulls a gun on you and tells you to hand over your money, you have many options, but we know that the least risky option would be to do as you are instructed. You might also try to talk him out of asking for your money, you might run away, you might try to attack him, or you might scream, for example. What the results of any of these actions will be are unknown, but we are all told that in a situation like this, you should simply comply; that choice seems the least risky.

In leadership, there is a constant weighing of choices to determine which may have the most positive outcome, or the least chance of negative consequences, because leadership is about guiding people and organizations into the future, and the future is unknown. A play's director opting to do something risky in the play does so based upon their experience and intuition, and perhaps other inputs such as knowledge of previous audience response, hoping that the payoff will be an astounded audience. However, if the choice fails to deliver, the result may be terrible box office sales. In this example, you can probably see why marketers like to do research and even why commercial producers like to have focus groups to respond to how they feel about the art. Commercial producers have lots of money at stake, so they need to minimize risk, and focus groups provide data to help them make informed decisions. But this is not to suggest that in theatre we should always look to minimize risk as much as possible. In fact, sometimes choices are risky because there is simply no way to know what will happen since the choice may be to attempt something entirely new; when those choices pay off, they usually pay off quite well. Perhaps you have heard the phrase, "the bigger the risk, the greater the reward." In the creation of art there is always some element of risk. The best leaders have enough experience to know when to make risky decisions and how much risk to take, but they also know that they should only risk as much as they can afford to lose.

Great leaders take risks. They do their best to minimize those risks, but they take them all the same. They gather information, advice, input, data, and the like, they weigh it against their own experiences and best judgment, often they use a bit of intuition, and then they make a decision, hoping the result will be rewarding. Managers are less often in a position to take risks. Leadership defines where an organization is going, and managers execute the strategy to get the organization there. But regardless of who is taking the risk, if the decision fails, wise leaders know to examine what occurred and why, so they can learn from the failure and use that information the next time they have to take a risk.

Informal networks

While the organizational chart demonstrates the formal chain of communication within an organization, there is also a structure referred to as the *informal network*, which is the series of relationships employees develop on their own, within an organization, to accomplish their work.[8] As it turns out, just because one is supposed to ask a certain person for advice, guidance, or instruction, employees typically find ways around the formal structure in order to get things done quickly. Actors are supposed to ask their director when they have questions about how their character should be interacting, but very often they ask each other to streamline the process. The same thing is true on the business side of a theatre. Informal networks consist of three different facets.[9] The first is the trust network. The *trust network* is a network of connections between people representing whom they trust to share private or political information, and whom people would expect to protect or support them in a crisis. The *advice network* represents the connections people make in order to get guidance and solve technical or task problems. For an actor, this might be the person they go to for guidance on how to do a specific accent. The third component of informal networks is the *communication network*, which is the series of connections people make in an organization with which they speak on a regular basis about matters related to the organization.

Understanding how your organization is operating on an informal basis can be very important. If you have ever been a part of a play production that just does not seem to be coming together appropriately, you have probably been a part of a process where informal networks were hindering the work. So how do you find out what informal networks exist? Typically, organizations will ask employees to take a secret survey asking whom they go to when they have a problem, whom they trust to keep their concerns about work issues confidential, and whom they communicate with on a daily basis. The results are then plotted on a map, which will demonstrate where major connections in the communications are occurring. Often, only a few people are central to the informal network, and have been granted a great deal of informal authority from their colleagues.

One last note about informal networks: you may think that you know how they are operating without doing a survey, but it is very rare that anyone can know that information beyond their own small social circle. Typically, formal leaders are surprised to find that the people they should be relying on to make the organization most effective and efficient are not the ones who have the formal authority.

Work styles

Carl Jung was a Swiss psychologist who studied with Sigmund Freud, and developed a number of different models for understanding why and how people behaved. One of his models considered four functions that humans use to experience the world. The fours functions are thought, emotion, senses, and intuition.[10] In the early part of the twentieth century, Katharine Cook Briggs and Isabel Briggs Myers built on Jung's four functions to develop the *Myers-Briggs Type Indicator (MBTI)*, which is a questionnaire designed to determine where a person falls on a spectrum for each of the four functions.[11] The MBTI helps to give us a sense of what type of personality we have so we can understand our interactions with the world and with others. There are a number of different tests and analyses that can be done to help people understand how they interact with the world and with others, but the MBTI is the foundation for most of them. It provides useful information to know about yourself, but also useful information to know about others that can aid in communicating and relating to them in the way they need in order to be most effective. If a person is a very logical, data-driven, linear thinker, they may approach memorizing dialogue and developing a character quite differently from one who is very emotional, supportive, and nurturing. And those two might not jive well with a third person who is detail-oriented, organized, and produces well-planned-out work, or a fourth person who is big-picture oriented, and always coming up with new ways to do things. Even if a leader does not know the results of a personality test, astute observation can tell a person much about the personalities of people they are working with, and this can inform how best to work with them so that they have the environment and interactions most conducive to their success.[12]

Questions to research for class discussion:

Search the Internet and find answers for these questions before you read any further. Be prepared to discuss them in class.

12.5 Are leaders appointed, or do they emerge?

12.6 Can leadership be shared among several individuals? Why or why not? Cite examples.

12.7 Do leaders cultivate creativity? Is that an important part of leadership? Why or why not?

12.8 What are the principles of effectuation? Do they matter in arts leadership?

Adaptive leadership

At the John F. Kennedy School of Government at Harvard University, Ronald Heifetz has been studying and writing about leadership for years, and he is the founder, with Marty Linsky, of the idea of adaptive leadership. *Adaptive leadership* is the idea that a leader can help an organization adapt to change by diagnosing a situation or organization, and making gradual alterations that challenge the way things have been operating.[13] Notice the word *diagnose* in that sentence? Heifetz is actually a trained psychiatrist and a cello player, yet he is an expert on leadership. The fact that his background in the arts may have helped him develop this school of thought surely caught your attention. Heifetz actually used his experience in music as part of his study, because he recognized the importance of practice, and believed that one could also practice leadership, in the same iterative fashion as one practices the cello. The ideas behind adaptive leadership suggest that, just as a doctor diagnoses a problem, a leader must diagnose a situation and put together a plan to address it. In his book *Leadership on the Line*, Heifetz uses the example of a doctor who must tell a dying patient the diagnosis, but must do so in a way that the patient is able to handle the information and act appropriately. Simply blurting out the bad news all at once might cause the patient to run screaming from the room and look for another opinion. But if the doctor explains the situation with a course of action and possibilities for treatment, the patient is more likely to pay attention.[14] The doctor can then bring the patient in line with thinking for how to plan for the future, including getting affairs in order, just in case, as well as how to proceed medically and what the chances for success may be.

Heifetz explains the theory of adaptive leadership with a metaphor about a dance floor, full of people all doing their own dances, much like an organization is full of people who are all part of the same process, but each doing their own thing. From the dance floor, one can only see the few people surrounding oneself, and there is little chance of making any adjustments that will have a lasting effect on the whole.[15] However, by getting off the dance floor and onto the balcony, one can see the whole picture and diagnose where adjustments can be made that will have lasting effects. The analogy of getting on the balcony also is a reminder that by being in the middle of things, we feel invested in what is going on, but by stepping out of that action, we allow ourselves to see things from a larger perspective without feeling like we have an individually vested interest in the activity.

Communication

Leadership communication is considered by many to be the key to inspiring and motivating people. While there are leaders less skilled in communication, the greatest leaders tend to be quite good at communication. They remain focused on the future and are able to articulate clearly and passionately. Strong leaders also recognize that we may all interpret words differently, and they work to ensure that their choice of words represents exactly what they intend. Consider US President Bill Clinton. During his presidency he stated under oath regarding an alleged sexual relationship that, "there's nothing going on between us." When it was revealed that there had been sexual activity, and Clinton was questioned about lying, he stated, "It depends upon what the meaning of the word 'is' is." Clinton contended that what he meant when he said there is nothing going on was that at that present point in time there was no relationship. He pointed out that if one defined "is" as meaning "is and never has been" that was different. Perhaps it was just clever lawyering, or a way to get around the truth, but in fact, Clinton clearly understood that the unclear use of even a single word could cause vastly different results.

Think critically: a leader's ethical dilemma

There are two ways to approach this class discussion. First, you can choose sides. Divide the class into two, by whatever means you choose, and debate the argument outlined below. Second, you can have an open discussion, each adding upon others' thoughts, and let the discussion uncover all the important details of all sides of the debate. Keep in mind that regardless of which approach you take, we want to be sure we dig deep into all sides of this important issue, in order to more effectively understand all positions.

CLASS DISCUSSION: A coworker has been saying some rather unflattering things about your boss, and saying them to several people, you included. Some of what this coworker says is based on truth, and some of it is based on an exaggerated portrayal of the situation. But the basis of what is being said is true, though not necessarily important for getting work done. Your boss has gotten wind that something is being said by someone and comes to you demanding that you tell him what you know. If you wish to be an honest, ethical person you may wish to tell your boss what is being said, by whom, and to whom it has been told. The information has been causing more and more of a divide in the office, and by telling your boss what is going on, you could effectively stop that divide from widening. You also recognize that while the information has its basis in fact, it is being inflated, and thus it is, in some sense, just gossip. Even bringing it up may give more credence to it than it deserves. Besides, the information has no credible impact on the company or the work. And tattle telling would only put you on the outs with your fellow employees. Nevertheless, you are known as a trustworthy, stand-up person who does the right thing, and the right thing in this case is to answer the question your boss has posed, right? You certainly do not wish to deceive anyone. And when asked directly, you are known for providing direct answers. Certainly your coworkers will appreciate that you have been true to this behavior, even if it gets them into trouble with the boss. What is the best way to proceed and why?

Great leaders spend a good deal of time planning out exactly what they intend to communicate, they know what goals they wish to achieve from their communication, and they anticipate the responses and feelings of those who will receive the communication. Think about the doctor in Heifetz's example. To be effective, the doctor has to consider how the patient will feel when he receives the message. Leaders are also very cognizant of the messages they send and receive; they listen with intent, carefully consider what the message is, and they use it, even if it is criticism, to grow.

One other thing about leadership communication has to do with the level of directness. Great leaders are not afraid of having difficult conversations. They address issues with a calm, logical understanding. Difficult conversations occur because people are passionate about the topic. For example, if a scenic designer feels strongly that a set should look like the underground tunnels of a sewer and the director disagrees, there is going to be a difficult conversation. The wise leader approaches those conversations by attempting to set their passions aside, with a focus on hearing why the other person feels the way they do. The director might sit the designer down and ask for the details behind why the sewer idea was so strong, how it would impact the rest of the production, and why it was the best choice for the set. With that knowledge it becomes much easier to find a solution that is workable for everyone.

Relationships

To inspire and motivate others to work toward a common goal, leaders must develop relationships. And while it is not necessary to be friends with those one leads, if followers are not friendly, then they are unfriendly or at best, indifferent, and neither of those alternatives seems conducive toward working together.[16] But relationships for leaders include not only relationships with followers, but also relationships with peers, colleagues, with authority, and even with their own word. The best leaders build trusting, open, and honest relationships in all their dealings. One newer school of thought on leadership is called *authentic leadership*, which is defined as leadership based on honest, trusting, and ethical relationships. The idea behind authentic leadership is that an authentic leader is open and honest, clear, behaves in an ethical manner, constantly assesses their strengths and weaknesses and self-corrects, invites opposing opinions for self-education as well as to inform decisions, and makes decisions that are true to their beliefs.[17] Rather than being focused on profits, authentic leaders tend to be focused on improving people and processes as a means for greater success. The best artistic directors are often authentic leaders, true to their beliefs, open to new ideas, and focused on improving a theatre by developing the best people and the best productions.

Questions to research for class discussion:

Search the Internet and find answers for these questions before you read any further. Be prepared to discuss them in class.

12.9 What is pragmatic leadership? When can it be successful in arts organizations (if at all)? Why or why not?

12.10 What makes something innovative? Does it require special leadership?

12.11 What drives innovation? Why and how?

12.12 Does leadership matter in innovation?

12.13 How does one measure the success of innovation?

The four pillars

In the book *Leading the Creative Mind,* Anthony S. Lake talks about how leadership in the rehearsal room and leadership in business have important parallels. In that book, he compares business practices to four pillars used by directors: keeping pressure on, encouraging, containing anxiety, and lowering defenses. While there are many aspects to leadership, these four do draw some nice metaphors from theatre.

If you take some time to consider the job of a theatre director, you will quickly come to realize that it seems like an inordinately difficult task. They must take a whole collection of egos, talents, and personalities, and coordinate those over a very short period of time into a fully realized production. Even when there are no obstacles or challenges to surprise them along the way, the process seems like it should be almost impossible to achieve. But the four pillars are recognizable things that directors do that are perfectly applicable to leading any creative team, even if that team is doing marketing or fundraising.

Keep the pressure on

Ronald Heifetz uses the metaphor of the pressure cooker, which is a kitchen pot that cooks food very quickly by closing in a locked seal and raising the pressure inside the pot. Sitting on top of the sealed pot is a small regulator that allows just a small amount of steam out; enough so the pot never explodes.[18] In this environment, food can cook very quickly. Theatre directors, and leaders of all creative people, function as that little regulator. They make sure that the pressure inside the pot never gets so high that the pot explodes.

In the instance of a pressure cooker, if the heat is not hot enough, nothing ever gets cooked. Theatre directors keep the pressure on, which is essentially keeping the heat high enough. Things are always just a little tense, because there is a sense of urgency to what is being created. There is an opening night, and the director is the one who tells the production if they are making sufficient progress to be able to achieve completion by opening night. But actors, for example, sometimes put so much of their emotion into their work that they can become overwrought and weighed down by the challenge of finding their character. In those instances, the director might crack a joke and then tell them they are heading in the right direction, getting where they need to go. This lets off some of the pressure.

In the business sector, sometimes urgency is lacking. There may be goals for a new project or program, but if that urgency is not there, and that sense of pressure does not exist, the project or program never "cooks."

Encouragement

We know that people who are optimistic in life typically have better outcomes. For example, they tend to live longer. Optimism is a powerful force. We are not all rosy and optimistic, but in the business environment, optimism, when it is within the constraints of reality, can spread and help achieve success. You can imagine what happens when pessimism spreads. Things get slowed down, there is little interest in results, and projects can fail. Good directors work to maintain a positive experience for their casts and design team. They remain positive and try to spread that optimism. Even directors who are not themselves passionate optimists still spread an optimistic zeal for the production. Actors can get bogged down in tragic characters, and good directors help them disengage from those negative emotions so they can remain positive about the production. Businesspeople do the same. They consider outside influences on team members, and help the team members separate those negative feelings from the positive future the work of the team will bring.

Containing anxiety

Sometimes we hear people refer to "control" in a pejorative way. You may have heard about someone being referred to as controlling. But control can actually be a positive force, and it is one of the four basic tenets of management. Control is what we use to maintain stability, or to at least give the sense of stability. Think of a ship's captain. The ship may be rocking, but as long as we trust the captain has everything under control, we feel safe.

Anxiety comes from a fear of the unknown. And change means heading into the unknown. So with change comes anxiety. Good directors recognize that there will always be anxiety about the production, at least until opening night, and they maintain, and share, their sense of control over the production to contain anxiety. If you have ever worked with a director who did not exert a sense of control over the production, you understand the challenges and discomfort that exist when it is lacking. This is true for any business leader. Demonstrating a strong sense of control, particularly in times of change, contains anxiety.

Lowering defenses

Creative people bring their egos with them when they show up to work, and they use those egos to help themselves be creative. That is probably true for all people, but creative people are especially reliant upon their egos. That means that the creative person is putting a lot of themselves, their personality, their taste, their preferences, their ideas, their individual choices, into their work. Yet projects, programs, and change all require collaboration, which is an iterative process, where each day, sometime each hour, small, incremental adjustments are being made.

Think about a play. Every day there is a rehearsal where things are improved upon and fine-tuned and honed. Actors make choices, and some are kept while others are discarded. So how does a director get actors to lower their defenses enough to not take personally the instruction to discard certain choices they have made? Well, it comes with a personal connection. This does not mean the director has to be best friends with each cast member, but great directors get to know their actors well enough on a personal level that they can guide the actors through direction that might bruise their egos.

Great business leaders do the same thing. They know how to approach each individual, they constantly guide toward a mutually beneficial future, and they are consistent and trustworthy in that behavior.

Leading change

Through all of this discussion on leadership, you may have noticed a consistent thread about change. We have already recognized that leadership is about moving an organization toward its vision, and in order to get there, the organization has to consistently change, and do things differently. If there is no need to change, then the organization would already be where it set out to be. And even then, it would be time to devise a new vision of the future.

In the 1940s Kurt Lewin developed a model for how businesses addressed change. Known as the *Lewin Change Management Model*, it basically considers change like you would a block of ice. If the ice is in the shape of a cube, and you want it in the shape of a sphere, you have to unfreeze it, change the shape, perhaps by putting it in a different container, and then refreeze it. Lewin saw organizations requiring similar treatment.[19]

In the unfreeze phase, leaders communicate the need for change. They explain why things are not working in the best way possible and they begin to address how change could improve that. The goal is to break down the status quo. People are put off balance a little bit, and in some ways this is where the pressure cooker is being turned on and heated up. It is a preparatory step to change, and can be the longest, most difficult part of the process, but Lewin, and many others, see this as essential for change to be effective.

The second part of the process is change. This is where people start to accept the new ideas or concepts and incorporate them into their work lives. They begin to embrace the new future and the new way of thinking, and they actually participate in the change. It is a process that does not happen overnight, and there is not a distinct line between when unfreeze ends and change begins. Just like an ice cube that melts slowly, unfreeze happens slowly. And as the water appears it is moved into the new container. Change is that new container. Some people are slower than others to come around to change. This is natural. But it is important that the change process helps people to come to an understanding of the value and importance of change.

In the refreeze phase, things start to stabilize. There are no longer changes being made to job descriptions and personnel. The organization settles in on the new way of doing things. For a theatre production, this is opening night.

John Kotter at Harvard University defined an eight-step process that incorporates some of Lewin's thinking, and also contributed to Lake's four pillars that compare business and theatre.[20] You'll probably see how they all have some commonalities, and all have slightly different ways of emphasizing the same things.

In Kotter's model the first step is developing a sense of urgency. Kotter notes the essential nature of seeing what is going on outside the organization, and communicating the imperative for change.[21] He sees this as a chance to discuss issues that could become crises if opportunities are not addressed and taken. In the theatre, this might be the establishment of a play to produce and an opening night. His second step is forming a powerful coalition of people who have the authority to affect change, and who have the insight to develop a vision of where the organization can go. This could be the director gathering with the production team. In his third step, the team develops the vision, and they also develop a broad strategy for how to execute that vision. This is exactly what the production team does as they meet and prepare for the production. In the next step, the team communicates the vision throughout the organization. Imagine when designers share their designs with technical personnel, or directors meet with the cast for the first time to share the vision.

In step five, the team empowers everyone to act on the vision. They do this by allowing some room to explore and create, they remove obstacles that might make executing the vision difficult, and they change the way things always have been if those things are not conducive to the vision. Directors give actors the chance to explore their characters on their own, finding what works best for them in the new vision. In step six, leaders reward small wins, and plan for short-term changes. This could mean all sorts of things, but first and foremost it means recognizing and rewarding the efforts of those working for change. Directors give positive feedback to actors as they make strides toward the production vision. And directors also make plans for technical rehearsals, dress rehearsals, and other benchmarks in the rehearsal process that will lead to opening night. In Kotter's seventh step, leaders consolidate improvements, and make room for further change. They do this by – having demonstrated their competence and earned credibility as to where they were taking the organization – bringing on new staff who can further implement change, and essentially give new life to the overall change process. Directors may sometimes replace actors who are not making sufficient progress, they tighten their focus into smaller details, and they begin to focus on the final incorporation of all the elements of the play. In Kotter's eighth step the leader finalizes the change, and ensures that there are processes in place to allow it continue. In theatre, this would be, essentially, opening night, where the production is finished, and the director makes plans for how to replace actors as they choose to leave the production if its run is long enough to sustain replacements.

There are many ways to look at leading change, and they all have some similar traits. But at the core of all of them is that there must be understanding by leadership that change is a process, it involves human challenges that must be addressed, and knowing what the phases are that the change processes go through can be extremely helpful in facilitating that change.

Initiative and innovation

Initiative and innovation are two hallmarks of leadership, and they are important in the creation of theatre. That includes both in the business office and in the artistic office. *Initiative* is the process of taking action before others do. We consider it of great value when employees take initiative, because they are stepping forward and getting something done without being instructed to do so. Initiative is also required for innovation, as someone has to take the first step. But *innovation* is more about developing something new. Typically, innovation requires inputs from different perspectives. Someone takes a first step by putting two or more things together that have never been put together before. For a theatre production, this often means getting different perspectives from different people in order to innovate. Innovation is a hallmark of leadership because it is part of moving forward into the unknown, creating change, and improving an organization. Just like innovation is important in the creation of a piece of theatre, it is just as important in the business office, where processes, relationships, and plans can always be improved upon in our rapidly changing world.

Politics and the creative process

One final note about leadership: sometimes it involves dealing with politics. In this sense, *politics* is about forming alliances, exercising power, expressing opinions, and governing processes. When a process is creative, politics are likely to emerge. The notion of innovation depends on the fact that something developing is actually unknown until it is created. This means there is a great deal of room for influencing the development of the unknown. For the person in the leadership position, whether that is the executive director, the artistic director, or someone with informal authority, it is important to monitor the politics and constantly work to ensure that they are not impeding the creative process. There are thousands of tricks for watching out for political obstacles and helping to counteract them. A quick Internet search will provide plenty of resources.

Build your theatre milestone 12: leadership

In this week's milestone you are going to discuss your leadership style and why it is appropriate to your theatre as well as the leadership styles you expect to have in charge of various aspects of your theatre. Start by discussing what technical expertise each person brings to the company, and why they are or will be suited to the position they will be assuming. Be sure to include education and experience, as well as any activities each person has been engaged in that will demonstrate the type of person they are. Finally, discuss the type of leadership anticipated from each person, how they build relationships and communicate, and what their unique vision will be for the area they are going to oversee.

Case study

Patrick had been doing well in his job, and had made a decent amount of progress in improving the marketing functions of his theatre. That improvement, in turn, was leading to increased sales. But Frank was not satisfied. He wanted to see full houses at all costs. Patrick described it like this:

Frank was always after me to make sure the house was full. He was absolutely convinced that if every seat in the house were full, people would see that and clamor to get tickets in advance for the next production. He was also certain that if people saw a full house, they would know that the production had to be exceptional, and that is why people would love the theatre. And there was definitely some truth in it. Danny Newman talked about it in his book. People who saw a 'sold out' sign would be more inclined to purchase early for the next one. So in that sense, every sold-out house was also a marketing tactic for the next production. And full houses do make an impression on the audience. So Frank was not simply coming out of the blue. The problem was, he wanted me to fill the house at any cost, including finding strategic ways to give away tickets, if that is what it took, to make sure every seat was filled. He was pressing me more and more to offer all sorts of special discounts, and that flew in the face of everything the data was telling me. People were not too concerned about the cost of our tickets. We simply had not had enough time to effectively communicate the vast bundle of attributes that created value in our product.

The problem seemed like a fairly straightforward one for Patrick, as he could continue to explain to Frank what the data was showing, and how the long-term progress was more important than jeopardizing it in the short-term. He could also balance Frank's desires with doing quality marketing work, offering some discounts, providing complimentary tickets to strategic groups, and trying to keep the house very full while continuing with his marketing plan. The problem was, the theatre's board was really pressing Patrick to increase revenue. In order to do that in the short-term, Patrick would have to advocate raising prices, which ran counter to the idea of offering discounts.

The board was being less than subtle that their expectation of me was to increase revenue. In order to do that, we had to be strategic about pricing. Offering discounts for using coupons, buying early, or being part of specific groups meant that, essentially, everyone could get a ticket at a lower price, and there was nothing to demonstrate that people weren't willing to pay full price. But why would they when they got discounts? Also, since I was giving away a lot of tickets, people were coming to expect to be able to get in free at least on occasion. They were starting to develop a pattern. All these theatre lovers expected tickets for cheap or free. It was great for developing a theatre-going habit, and it was great for filling seats, but it was not going to increase revenue in the long run. Increasing revenue meant doing strategic marketing, and the discounts needed to be minimal and very carefully extended. And we needed to stop doing all the comps. But it would take a few years before we would see full houses again. Revenue growth would be slow, but it would happen, and eventually, we would be in great shape. But if we had to choose between Frank and the board, we were going to be forever stuck in limbo.

Patrick knew that good leadership meant helping everyone on a course toward the future that included slow, incremental change, and bringing them all together. But it seemed daunting given the opposing opinions, and the fact that neither position was really a good one for improving the company in the future. How do you think Patrick should proceed?

Personal exploration

Search online for a free personality quiz and take it. Then, discuss the results with a friend and see if there are areas they agree or do not agree with. Write up the results of the quiz as well as your discussion with your friend, and explain what facets seem correct about you, what facets seem incorrect, and why. Were there things that you learned about your personality that you were not aware of? Are there facets that you would like to change?

Notes

1 Kerzner, Harold, *Project Management: A Systems Approach to Planning, Scheduling, and Controlling,* John Wiley & Sons, 2013.

2 Khurana, Rakesh, *From Higher Aims to Hired Hands: The Social Transformation of American Business Schools and the Unfulfilled Promise of Management as a Profession,* Princeton University Press, 2010.

3 Rhine, A.S., "Leadership in the theatre: A study of the views of practitioners on effective and ineffective styles," *The International Journal of the Arts in Society* 4, no. 2 (2009): 387–398.

4 Brungardt, Curtis L., Lawrence V. Gould, Rock Moore, and Joe Potts, "The emergence of leadership studies: Linking the traditional outcomes of liberal education with leadership development," *Journal of Leadership Studies* 4, no. 3 (1998): 53–67.

5 Burns, J. M., *Leadership/James MacGregor Burns,* Harper & Rowe, 1978.

6 Ibid.

7 McGregor, Douglas, *The Human Side of Enterprise,* McGraw-Hill, 1960.

8 Rank, Olaf N., "Formal structures and informal networks: Structural analysis in organizations," *Scandinavian Journal of Management* 24, no. 2 (2008): 145–161.

9 Ibid.

10 Jung, Carl Gustav, *The Structure and Dynamics of the Psyche,* Routledge, 2014.

11 Myers, Isabel Briggs, Introduction to Type*, CPP, 1976.

12 Ibid.

13 Heifetz, Ronald, Alexander Grashow, and Marty Linsky, *The Practice of Adaptive Leadership,* Harvard Business School Publishing, Boston, 2009.

14 Heifetz, Ronald A., and Marty Linsky, *Leadership on the Line,* 2002.

15 Ibid.

16 Sparrowe, Raymond T., Budi W. Soetjipto, and Maria L. Kraimer, "Do leaders' influence tactics relate to members' helping behavior? It depends on the quality of the relationship," *Academy of Management Journal* 49, no. 6 (2006): 1194–1208.

17 Leroy, Hannes, Frederik Anseel, William L. Gardner, and Luc Sels, "Authentic leadership, authentic followership, basic need satisfaction, and work role performance: A cross-level study," *Journal of Management* 41, no. 6 (2015): 1677–1697.

18 Heifetz and Linsky, *Leadership on the Line*, 2002.

19 Levasseur, Robert E., "People skills: change management tools – Lewin's change model," *Interfaces* 31, no. 4 (2001): 71–73.

20 Kotter, John P., *Leading Change,* Harvard Business Press, 1996.

21 Ibid.

CHAPTER 13

Boards, governance, executive staff, and volunteers

As we saw in Chapter 12, Patrick had been involved in a political challenge. His board and his boss seemed to disagree on how Patrick should be doing his job, and for the long term, Patrick knew they were both wrong. It became incumbent on Patrick to exercise a certain amount of leadership in helping them all come together on a vision for the future that might require altering how they felt about the present. The situation was political, it required strong leadership skills, and it placed Patrick in the middle of a typical conundrum: roles and responsibilities of the board and the executive were blurred when it came to governance.

Chapter objectives

After reading this chapter, you should be able to explain how a governing board should operate, describe ways to put together a board, explain the roles of executives and board members, debate the challenges regarding difficult board members, explain the importance of volunteers in theatre, and demonstrate how to write leadership descriptions.

Boards, governance, and volunteers

Commercial productions typically do not have a board or volunteers, but in not-for-profit theatre, these roles are very important. Because the structure of a business often requires a governing body such as a board, and because so many theatres operate with a board that governs their work, it is important to understand how boards operate when they are most efficient, and what mistakes are usually occurring when they are not operating efficiently. Boards are sometimes referred to as a *board of governors*, a *board of trustees*, a *board of directors*, or perhaps other names, and board members may be referred to as *directors, trustees,* or *governors.* Throughout this chapter those names may be used interchangeably, though we will mostly refer to them as board members. This chapter proceeds on the assumption that a board has the fiduciary and strategic duty to move the theatre forward in a successful fashion, protecting its assets and guiding its long-term growth. The chapter also addresses the role of the executive(s) of a theatre, who are hired and supervised by the board. Lastly, the chapter looks at the roles of volunteers in the theatre, how they are supervised, and how their positions may be confusing when combined with other functions in the theatre. While we are talking about both jobs and functions, this chapter deals more with the nature of the relationship between boards, executives, and volunteers, and less about how to create and staff those jobs.

Board recruiting and retention

Because the milestones in this book are structured with the notion that a new theatre is being created, understanding where to find potential board members will be important, especially when considering a governance structure that requires a board. But equally as important as finding board members is ensuring that they have the tools necessary to do the work they are being asked to do, and making certain they are satisfied and remaining active on the board for as long as their terms and the by-laws allow.[1]

How to find board members

Before figuring out where to find board members, it is vitally important to determine what work the board members will be expected to do. It is at this very first step that so many organizations make mistakes. Remember that the functions boards perform are usually limited to guiding the organization's mission, vision, and values, and not actually implementing any of them. The staff handles the implementation part. The board determines the long-term strategy for the theatre, which is the plan for achieving the organizational vision. Boards also hire, supervise, and sometimes terminate the chief executive(s), and they monitor the progress of the theatre toward achieving its goals. But boards are not responsible for the day-to-day management of the theatre, and board members do not make operational decisions. In a theatre, sometimes season selection is considered a valid part of the board's responsibility, because it may be tied to long-term vision, but just as likely is the possibility that the board is simply informed of the season that the staff have selected to present. The key here is to determine if season selection is actually part of long-term strategic planning, or if it is an element of executing that plan. If it is the latter, then determining the season is not the function of the board. So while it might be useful to have theatre people on a theatre board, it is not necessary that board members be versed in how to operate a theatre, as their function is not operational in nature.

One point of confusion that often occurs is rooted in the fact that theatre board members are typically volunteering for their board position.[2] But regardless of the fact that they are not paid for their service as a board member, it is a position of great responsibility. As we will see later in this chapter, volunteers in a theatre may wear many different hats, and it is important that they understand the distinctions between the jobs they are volunteering to do, and the differences in authority.

Because the board has a strategic and fiduciary duty, this is where to begin. A theatre may wish to have board members who bring expertise in areas that will be useful to the theatre, such as legal, accounting, marketing, or fundraising, but any volunteer work a board member does in an area other than strategic long-term thinking for the theatre is work that is being done on a volunteer basis, separate and distinct from the work being done as a board member. As a board member, one may be required to supervise the executive, but as a volunteer, the executive is then doing the supervising. When the lines get blurred, problems can occur, particularly when board members are also volunteering to do staff work, because they bring their operational experiences with them into the boardroom, and they bring their board oversight into the operation. As you can imagine, maintaining a good set of relationships and a smooth operational structure can prove to be challenging. That is why knowing what work needs to be done is vital, and drawing up clear descriptions and reporting structures is essential.

Board members are recruited primarily for their strategic oversight of the theatre. When they are recruited, they deserve to be given a detailed job description, which explains exactly what their duties will be. If they are going to be asked to provide additional volunteer work, such as legal or accounting, they should be given an additional job description for that work, explaining what will be required there as well. And it should be made clear how the two positions report on the organizational chart, and that they are distinct positions, even though they may be occupied by the same person.[3] Likewise, if as a board member individuals will be expected to make a donation, their function as a donor to the theatre is separate and distinct, and should have its own set of instructions. By clarifying in advance how each different position participates in the organization, theatres help both board members and themselves keep everything operating smoothly.

More often than not, board members are found through personal contact. When starting a theatre, it is not unusual for friends or family members to serve on the board, helping to get the theatre going and guiding its growth. As boards expand, or replacement board members are required, it is often the person who works most closely with donors who knows people who have demonstrated a real passion for the theatre, and who might make excellent board members. And while those people may be donors, when they step into the position of board member, it is a new and distinct function from their participation as a donor.

Still other organizations find people in the general public who have a penchant for volunteering. There are websites in most countries that help link boards with potential members. For example, Trustee Finder in the United Kingdom, Volunteer Match in the United States, and Seek Volunteer in Australia all help connect organizations in need of board members with potential board volunteers.

How to ensure board members know what to do

In Chapter 6 we talked about conducting a job analysis to inform how to write a job description. That same process can be used to assess board positions and help board members know exactly what it is they should be doing. But there is much that process may leave out. In Chapter 2 we explored strategic planning and some of the elements that go into the strategic plan. While such a plan may or may not be created by a board, the board would definitely vote on it. Board members may not know how to conduct strategic planning, or what goes into a strategic plan, but they will need to understand why the plan is important, and how to determine what is appropriate and executable for a theatre's long-term vision. Board members may not be experts at financial planning, but they need to know and understand where the money is coming from, how much needs to be raised each year, and what programs that money is funding. Remember that a main duty of a board member is fiduciary in nature.[4] While board members may not be fascinated by the details of the budget, it is important that they understand when they sign on to a board that they will be responsible for knowing and understanding the major points of that budget. Board members may also be more effective if they are periodically updated on the state of theatre generally, as well as the state of entertainment and art options in the local community.

Questions to research for class discussion:

Search the Internet and find answers for these questions before you read any further. Be prepared to discuss them in class.

13.1 What are some additional ideas for putting together a board that are not discussed in the chapter?

13.2 What is the difference between directors and advisors?

13.3 What is an independent board? Is that important in theatre? Why or why not?

13.4 How do you evaluate a board?

13.5 What are the top nonprofit board governance mistakes?

Executive staff

Throughout this chapter we have referred to the executive staff as chief executive(s), because in theatre, often the board assumes responsibility for hiring both an executive director and an artistic director, who are jointly the chief or main executives of the theatre. While they may both have different areas of expertise, and supervise different parts of the theatre, if they are both hired and supervised directly by the board, they are both chief executives. Typically, the board may advise the executives on the hiring and evaluation of additional staff, but the board typically has no direct authority to hire or supervise anyone other than the chief executives.[5]

Roles

Though an artistic director and an executive director may have different areas of oversight, if they are both hired by the board and are both chief executives, then they have certain roles under the supervision of the board. Primarily, executives are hired to supervise and execute the long-term strategy for the theatre, as determined by the board, and to do so in an effective and efficient manner.[6] The executives are also required to execute their roles within the boundaries of the policies that the board has established. Those policies are often derived from the organization's values.

Executive role

While there is no standard set of duties for the executives in relation to how they work with the board, there are typically a number of expectations that need to be met, and they often fall to the executives. First, theatre executives have to support the board, help keep it organized and efficient, and provide the board with information necessary for it to execute its strategic and fiduciary functions. This is an area that can prove to be challenging because in some sense, the executives may feel they are directing the board even though the board has the supervisory position with the executives.[7] The executives also serve as a bridge between the board and the staff, and often have to assist the board in devising and executing an evaluation of the executives themselves. You can see why this has the potential to lead to confusion about reporting structures.

Executives also, of course, have responsibility for overseeing and supervising the programs and operational functions of the theatre. Additionally, executives oversee the operation of facilities, including maintenance and development, and they are responsible for devising the annual budget and preparing it and presenting it to the board for approval. While the board approves the budget, the executives oversee the execution of the budget, meaning the generation of income and the process of making expenditures. The executives also must oversee the organization in a way that ensures all laws are followed, and no risks are taken that could jeopardize the theatre. Executives are also usually responsible for interfacing with the community, participating in appropriate community groups and functions, and serving as the face of the theatre; and executives are usually very involved in the fundraising function of a theatre, whether that is seeking investors for a commercial theatre, or interfacing with donors to a nonprofit theatre.

Board roles

As we mentioned, having clear job descriptions for board members can go a long way toward ensuring that the board functions properly. Board members are not in their role simply to be fundraisers or to do the work of the staff or the executives. They have important responsibilities for governing the theatre and ensuring its long-term success. That is why the board oversees the executives, and monitors them to ensure the executives are successfully fulfilling the organization's mission. Board members guide the executive staff, but they do not manage the theatre themselves. They may provide advice, guidance, or mentoring to the executives, but they do not execute strategy. Part of the board members' aforementioned fiduciary duties involve not only overseeing and approving the annual budget, but also planning for long-term financial success, and ensuring that what is happening today financially can be built on in the future. This might include planning for facilities, repair, maintenance, or other large future needs. In some sense, board members are responsible for evaluating organizational risk, and making decisions that will help minimize it. To that end, board members develop organizational policies that come from the organization's mission, vision, and values, and set in place the strategic plan for long-range development.[8] Typically, boards also must approve large financial transactions. A board that functions well does not rely on the executives or staff members to guide or direct the board or its meetings, but instead develops its own agenda for the long term, calling upon the executives, staff, and outside consultants when needed to inform its decision making. The functions of a nonprofit board work best when the board operates independently of the executives, because unlike the commercial board, which has a duty to ensure the largest return for investors, the nonprofit board is focused on mission fulfillment. When the relationship between boards and executives is too familiar, board members may feel less obligated to scrutinize the theatre and work to develop decisions that will maximize long-range success, and instead defer decision making to the executives.

As mentioned earlier, it is not unusual for a theatre to seek out donors to join its board. This is not to suggest that a function of the board should be fundraising. Instead, it is to suggest that amongst the pool of donors, there are likely people who have great interest in the theatre, and who have the time and the expertise to help shape the theatre's strategy. They may not know how to develop a theatre's strategic plan, but they have experience in developing organizations, and understand the fundamentals of governance. Board members who are only interested in having their name on the letterhead are better served if a separate *board of donors* or *board of advisors* exists, to which they can lend their support. It is not unheard of to have very large boards like this, which function in support of the organization without making strategic decisions.[9] Instead, they may be convened on a regular basis to hear information about the theatre, to meet and hear about people working in the theatre, to be told about challenges the theatre faces, and to be given an opportunity to assist in meeting those challenges. The boards may have their own policies and procedures for how they will govern themselves, and they may have members who also serve on the board of directors, but these advisory boards have no decision-making authority for the company.

Leading the board and being led

To effectively lead a theatre, one person must be the designated official authority to handle that role. This person is actually not the executive but, in fact, is usually the chairperson of the board. Their responsibility is to coordinate the efforts of the board, and often to work closely with the executive to ensure that strategy is being effectively implemented, and necessary information is being provided to the board. The chairperson and the executive need to build a strong relationship for the model to work most effectively. While the two people do not have to be friends, they need to have mutual trust for one another, because they will be relying on each other for information and will likely be setting the agenda for the organization together. That strong relationship is typically rooted in a shared understanding of the theatre's mission and vision, and a joint passion for that mission and vision. This goes beyond simply knowing what the mission and vision are. Instead, the chairperson and executive should discuss what the mission and vision mean to them to ensure that they are both interpreting it in the same way.

As we have seen, being clear on what the roles are for each position is essential, and while formal job descriptions will help to clarify responsibilities, the chairperson and executive should discuss exactly what they expect from one another, as well as what they provide to each other.[10] Additionally, they should agree on how they each serve the organization and its constituents within the context of the theatre's mission and vision. Once they have agreement, the board chair will typically seek input from the entire board on the nature of the working relationship, and ask it to expand on how the executive and the entire board will interact. While these decisions are not made without consulting the executive, it is important that the board is guided to understand that defining the nature of the relationship, and setting expectations for how the executive and board will interact, are decisions that belong in the hands of the board and not dictated by the executive.

Further, the chair and the executive should work together to develop a relationship that regularly steers the board toward examining strategic issues and making strategic decisions, and that guides them away from operational discussions.[11] One way to do this is to develop a *consent agenda* for board meetings, which is a collection of operational action items requiring approval by the board that are routine and not in need of scrutiny. If an item in the consent agenda is of concern to any board member, they can remove it from the consent agenda and ask for further elaboration. Items typically included in the consent agenda include routine staff hiring and separations, notifications of smaller purchases, and minor budget adjustments.

Sometimes the theatre staff are needed to help develop the board agenda and board materials. When this is the case, it is important that the executive not slip into the role of board leadership. Preparation of materials should be done in consultation with the chair, and always with the intention that items on the board's agenda should be focused on strategy or policy, and not administration or management. While the executive and staff may develop a strategic plan, the board should regularly review it, and it should be implemented only upon board scrutiny and approval. If board members stray into matters of administration or management, such as setting salaries for staff, or determining what types of office equipment should be ordered, either the board chair or the executive, or both, should help steer the board back into matters of policy and strategy.

You may wonder how often a board is required to meet if their focus is only on strategy. The answer is that it depends on the people, the organization, and the strategy. But an organization that has developed a very clear strategy, with objectives and benchmarks, might expect a board to meet monthly. During those meetings the board may be updated on where the theatre is on executing its strategy, and it may make decisions to clarify or alter the strategic plan. For the chair and the executive, this means ensuring that the board meeting agenda is designed to align with organizational strategy.

Questions to research for class discussion:

Search the Internet and find answers for these questions before you read any further. Be prepared to discuss them in class.

13.6 What are some good tips for working with nonprofit boards?
13.7 What are the pros and cons of board member term limits?
13.8 How do you stop a board from micromanaging?

Meetings

While boards may choose to operate informally, there is the potential for problems and conflict. As long as everyone is in agreement, and moving along happily, informal discussions work fine. But no group is always going to be in total agreement and, in fact, one of the reasons we have multiple people on a board is to bring to the table a diverse set of opinions that can strengthen a theatre. But with diverse opinions comes occasional disagreement. What if one person is particularly strong willed and forces their opinion on others? What if everyone wants to speak at the same time? What if some feel they are not heard? What if the discussion is going around and around and never getting anywhere? Imagine that a board is dealing with strategy, and in some sense that means making predictions for the future. No one knows exactly what will happen, though there will be plenty of opinions. Consider how government operates. Officials are always attempting to predict what the results of a new law will be.

To alleviate all this potential confusion, organizations, including theatres, need to agree on how they will meet and what the rules of their meetings will be. One of the reasons the board has a chair is because this person has certain responsibilities, which include facilitating effective meetings, and making certain the rules are followed. In most cases, boards operate under the rules of *parliamentary procedure*, which are a collection of rules tested and modified over time in the British parliament. Those rules are documented in a book titled *Robert's Rules of Order*, which enumerates exactly how organizations can deliberate in an appropriate, collegial, and fair manner.[12]

But just following the rules may not always be enough. There are hundreds of tips and tricks for running good meetings, and they are too numerous to mention here. However, there are a few that are extremely important. First, we know that planning ahead and laying out the agenda in advance, in a consultation between the board chair and the executive, is essential. Additionally, supporting materials and the agenda should be provided to board members well in advance so they can come to the meeting prepared and informed. Sending out vast quantities of information can be overwhelming, and is likely unnecessary, but if there is a substantial amount of information, an executive summary sheet of what is in the packet may assist board members in their preparation. The executive summary should only summarize factual information, and should not be written with a bias or slant one way or another. Meetings should be planned with timing in mind. If the meeting is scheduled for two hours, it is important to consider how long each discussion is likely to take, and to not schedule more items than can fit into the time allotment. If some items on the agenda consume more time than anticipated, the chair may choose to move those items to a later agenda when additional time can be scheduled to address them. Theatre board members are often volunteers and have committed to spending a certain amount of time doing the work of the board. It is vitally important that this commitment is respected and board members are not surprised with additional work or additional consumption of their time.

Board agendas need to move in a way that is not exhausting to board members. If there are several difficult, weighty topics to be discussed and debated, it is best to separate them with other items that are lighter and easier. This not only gives board members a chance to relax between topics, but it helps to smoothly shift gears from one topic to the next. These intermissions should include recognition of board members and the work they do. If board members are volunteers, part of their compensation is recognition for a job well done, and board meetings are a good place to provide some of that recognition. Board meetings should also have a few minutes set aside where the board can meet independently of the executive. This is not necessarily to provide an evaluation of the executive's work, but to allow board members to ask questions about strategic implementation without the influence of the executive who is doing the implementation. This moment in a board meeting also empowers the board to understand their role as strategic decision-makers, and provides a level of trust between the board and the executive.

Lastly, every item on the agenda should have an anticipated outcome. We know that the anticipated outcome for the consent agenda will be that it is passed. But what about discussing a new partnership to sell tickets with the symphony? Is the goal simply to discuss it, or is the anticipated outcome that a vote will be taken on whether to implement such a partnership or not? Too often agenda items are discussed, but no action is ever taken on them because there is no plan for what the action should be.

Questions to research for class discussion:

Search the Internet and find answers for these questions before you read any further. Be prepared to discuss them in class.

13.9   What are some dos and don'ts for running board meetings?
13.10 How do you keep a board meeting interesting?
13.11 What committees should a theatre's board have and what do they do?

Effectiveness and dealing with problems

When the planning is done carefully and intentionally, and board members and executives are clear on their roles and responsibilities, more often than not, boards are effective. But sometimes, board members are very passionate about an idea, and they can become a problem if they are not comfortable with accepting a majority opinion in opposition to their idea. This is not to suggest that differences of opinion are any way to identify problem board members, but on occasion, even after careful vetting and lots of discussion, a board member is voted in and turns out to be a poor fit for the board. Sometimes, they simply have a personal, common practice of getting into the details of management and administration, and they refuse to move from that place. Perhaps they have been on the board for a very long time, and do not wish to see things operate differently than they have for many years. Maybe they just want to be the savior, and believe their ideas are the only ones capable of doing the job. Whatever the case may be, problem board members can wreak havoc on a theatre.

Problem board members distract from doing the serious and important strategic work boards need to do to ensure the longevity of the theatre. If the theatre is serving the community, and a board member is distracting from that obligation, then the community is not being served as promised. Problem board members can cause other issues, as well. Recruiting new board members can be extremely difficult as they are often chased away by the prospect of having to work with a problem board member. Existing board members will find they are dissatisfied with their work if a problem board member constantly challenges them, and resignations will increase. If problem board members are not dealt with, they can ultimately chase off executives who would prefer to work in a less problematic environment. All of this is not to say that boards should move quickly to eliminate any member who challenges the status quo. In fact, it is probably best to counsel and mentor a problem board member first in an effort to help them fit in more appropriately. After all, they were probably asked to be on the board for a good reason.

However, in those instances where guidance leads to no behavior change, it can be extremely difficult either having that person on the board or getting them off of the board. In reality, there is either a policy for how board members can be removed, or they must either step down or be voted off, but making sure such a transition is smooth and comfortable is important. Before any action is taken, a senior member of the board, preferably the chair, should sit down with the problem board member, thank them for their service, offer them an honorary position that does not attend board meetings or vote, and present them with other appropriate recognition for their service. But if the board is going to vote a member off, the member should be allowed to resign first. The goal is to keep a friend and supporter of theatre, even if they were not the best fit for the board.

Think critically: challenging board members

There are two ways to approach this class discussion. First, you can choose sides. Divide the class into two, by whatever means you choose, and debate the argument outlined below. Second, you can have an open discussion, each adding upon others' thoughts, and let the discussion uncover all the important details of all sides of the debate. Keep in mind that regardless of which approach you take, we want to be sure we dig deep into all sides of this important issue, in order to more effectively understand all positions.

CLASS DISCUSSION: Boards are put together to oversee strategy and policy. A good board has lots of unique opinions and personalities that can drive strategy and lead to a bigger and better theatre company with each and every passing year. Some board members will be more active and aggressive, and some will be more passive. No one exerts the exact same amount of passion and energy as the next person, so we can expect that one board member will always be the one who is furthest from consensus, always questioning and demanding answers. That is what makes a solid board. So to complain about a board member who has been selected to be on the board, simply because they are more vigilant in doing what they were asked to do, is horribly unfair. When an executive complains about that board member, or that board member is made aware of concerns, it is just inviting trouble. They are going to start scrutinizing the organization even closer, because they will be aware that someone is nervous about their diligence. We may think of some board members as thorns in our side, but in fact, it is those board members who keep a theatre from becoming complacent. On the other hand, if many people are complaining about a board member, and that board member is consistently contrary to the consensus of the rest of the board, they are wasting valuable time, and drawing the board's focus away from its strategic function. Such board members, even if they are sweet, kind, or generous and donate heavily to the theatre, must be removed from the board. The function of the board is to provide strategic direction to the best of its abilities, not to the best of its abilities given that it has one bad apple. Some simple words might be communicated first to try to get the board member to rein in their behavior, but those words should be said with the intention of eliminating the board member if they do not change their behavior immediately. Sure, the board member is probably a volunteer, offering of themselves for the benefit of the theatre and the community, but if they are not fitting in, they need to go. Yes, they may go out in the community and speak poorly of the theatre and its governance, but that is the risk that must be taken. Or must it be? If an opposing opinion is such a problem, perhaps the theatre could simply sideline the board member without removing them from the board.

Volunteers

While it is typically not true for commercial theatre, most theatres rely on volunteers to get the work done and keep the organization running efficiently. Often volunteers are found serving as ushers, or perhaps stuffing envelopes and doing routine tasks in the offices. As we have seen, board members traditionally volunteer for the work they do for the theatre. Theatres also recruit volunteer interns and apprentices who do work at the theatre for the purpose of gaining education and experience.[13] *Volunteers* are people who offer to provide a service or do work freely. But that definition does not necessarily mean there will always be no financial compensation. When we talk about volunteers in the theatre, however, we typically mean unsalaried help. In any case, for purposes of their safety and the security of the theatre, though volunteers may be unpaid, they are still protected under occupational safety and health rules that govern employees.

Who are they? Where do they come from?

Volunteers come from everywhere and every walk of life. As we noted, they can be students looking for an opportunity to learn and gain experience. Often, retired senior citizens choose to do volunteer work as a means for staying active and having something to be responsible for. Business leaders often volunteer to serve on boards as a way to expand their professional circle of contacts. Mothers and fathers volunteer to serve organizations their children are involved with. In short, volunteers are everywhere. The challenge in recruiting volunteers is not in finding where they are hiding, but ensuring that you can provide a good fit for them.

This means, like all management tasks, you have to start with a plan. If the goal is to recruit volunteers it is important to know what goals and objectives need to be met, what work will be required in order to accomplish them, and what training will be required of the people doing the work. And just like any job, a detailed job description for volunteers is important. Being able to explain to a potential volunteer what work you would like done is vitally important. Potential volunteers will be reluctant to sign on unless they know what will be expected of them. That job description may also include details about what sort of training is involved. As part of the plan, it is also important to consider what costs might be incurred by bringing in volunteers to do the work. Will you be feeding them? Will they need specific tools? What will the costs of appropriate recognition be? It sounds simple enough, but without the appropriate plan, volunteers can quickly grow tired, or worse yet, can be counterproductive. Imagine an usher who is poorly trained and is surly to patrons, causing them unhappiness. That amount of damage is difficult to undo.

In addition to the labor they provide free of salary, volunteers also serve in a capacity as a supporter of the theatre. When a volunteer is connected to a theatre, they provide good will about that theatre outside the scope of their volunteer work. Many theatres capitalize on this by constantly recruiting volunteers and nurturing relationships with volunteers. Much like the director of development provides stewardship and continuing gratitude to donors, someone at the theatre may want to be responsible for doing the same with volunteers. If time is money, then volunteers are making a donation that is just as needed as the contribution donors make.

As part of the planning process, it is wise to spend some time thinking about what benefits volunteers will receive for doing each job. While we have said that volunteers are unsalaried, this does not mean they do not gain anything from their service. Perhaps the compensation a volunteer receives is only a kind "thank you" at the end of a volunteer shift, but this intrinsic reward is often enough to keep a volunteer invested. Others like to receive a listing in playbills, public displays of gratitude, free tickets, invitations to recognition dinners, elevation of status, or other rewards. Compensating salaried employees is easy because we know the threshold for the appropriate reward for doing the job. Every volunteer is slightly different, and they all receive some sort of reward for their work, but figuring out how best to reward volunteers can be tricky. What is most important is taking the time to determine a place to start. Once that has occurred, a strong volunteer recruitment program does not simply set out to get a certain number of volunteers to do the work, but continues to recruit volunteers to ensure a constant flow of support for the organization.

Board members

We have noted that often board members are volunteers. Finding them can be a little tricky, as the experience and expertise theatres seek for board members can limit the number of potential board members in a community's volunteer pool. It is not unusual to see active volunteers serving on several boards in a community. Searching through donor lists to see who is already demonstrating support to the theatre is a great place to seek potential board members. Also asking current board members for names of potential new members is a great place to look. Sometimes, local businesses will have an interest in sending an employee to volunteer on a board, simply to keep the business engaged and connected to the community, so speaking to executives at businesses can be a great way to find board members. Chambers of Commerce can sometimes be helpful in connecting potential board members to a local theatre company, and their members participate specifically for the purpose of being engaged with the community. Members of the board provide their wisdom, their experience, and sometimes their expertise. In exchange, they receive the status of being on the board, the good feeling of serving their community, an opportunity to interface with other influencers in the community, and even a resume credit that may help their career in the future.

Interns

Interns are typically students offering their services for low or no cost in exchange for an opportunity to learn how an organization runs and gain experience working in the organization.[14] In theatres, interns are typically given positions within the operational structure, rather than what would be considered periodic work such as ushering, board service, or doing one-time projects such as stuffing envelopes. A theatre company that has done the appropriate planning and training is able to put interns into positions of authority, letting them do the day-to-day work that is required to run the theatre. Many internships are available doing technical work for a theatre, or serving in marketing, fundraising, artistic, or business offices. While a poorly planned internship may leave the volunteer doing menial labor such as filing and making coffee, typically the well-planned internship is structured in a way that provides the appropriate benefits to the intern: recognition, education, and experience.

More theatres are now also looking to colleges and universities not just as a place to recruit interns, but as partners. Academic programs are embracing service learning, which is a way students learn through providing community service. Theatres engaging with universities find students interested in providing all sorts of service as part of their academic pursuits, from developing marketing plans and conducting market research, to providing non-certified financial audits, developing process improvement plans, developing fundraising events, and much more.[15] Faculty are often actively searching for community partners who can provide service learning opportunities, and the savvy theatre manager is always looking for academic partners in every discipline.

Job descriptions

As you have seen, the development of a job description is an important part of the planning process for volunteer management. While that process may not require a job analysis as detailed as one for a salaried position, it probably should. Just like a salaried position, the job description should make clear the expectations of the position, the skills required, the training provided, the reporting structure for the position, and perhaps even the list of benefits provided to the volunteer. In essence, though no salary is being paid, in every other respect the volunteer should be treated exactly like a valued employee. If additional training is required, if discipline is necessary, if coaching, support, or promotions in the volunteer ranks are called for, they should be handled as if the volunteer were a paid staff member. Volunteers are not slave labor, nor are they incompetent. Often they are given the most thankless tasks, and they provide the work for no money. Their time is valuable, and the cost savings are great. Volunteers deserve to be treated respectfully.

Effective volunteer management

One of the challenges with treating volunteers in a manner equal to the paid staff is that volunteers rarely *need* their volunteer position. Paid staff members usually need work in order to earn a living. Volunteers have far less at risk, so it is much easier for them to require flexibility. A theatre may demand that volunteers alert them well in advance if they are going to miss a volunteer shift, but a volunteer who is suddenly invited to lunch with a friend may choose to simply not attend a volunteer shift because the worst ramification they may suffer is not being asked to volunteer anymore. That can be a huge challenge. Imagine if several ushers all decided not to show up to the same performance. It could prove to be a terrible mess. What this suggests is that the communication between staff and ushers must be constant, positive, and respectful. Management should be open to hearing the thoughts and concerns of volunteers, as well as always considering that the work given to volunteers is providing some level of appropriate challenge, and some level of appropriate reward. If ushers must all sit in the lobby during an entire performance they may be less likely to show up than if they are sitting inside the theatre watching the play, for example. Volunteers also need to have a built-in amount of flexibility beyond what management would typically provide to a salaried employee. This can go a long way toward ensuring the volunteer work gets done as required. Finally, management can never lose sight of the importance of demonstrating gratitude to volunteers.

Build your theatre milestone 13: governance descriptions

You have done a job analysis and written job descriptions for the top staff jobs in your theatre. Now it is time to do the same for your board members and volunteers. For this week's milestone you will want to write clear job descriptions for the officers of the board such as chair, secretary, and treasurer, as well as for general board members and volunteers. You will want to include the scope of work expected for each position, keeping in mind that while board members may be asked to be donors, their responsibilities as a donor are distinct and different from their responsibilities as board members. Also be sure to include how board members are expected to interact with staff. You are writing materials that you should be able to present to someone who is considering being on your board. The materials should spell out exactly what is expected of the potential board members, and also what are the responsibilities of the executives and staff who are not within the scope of responsibilities for a board member. Your volunteer job descriptions may be generic to account for many different potential roles (though you will want to briefly list and describe those roles) but they should be clear about what is expected of volunteers, what they receive in return, and how they will be trained and evaluated.

Case study

One of the issues that Patrick faced had to do with pressure from the board to increase revenue. Certainly the board had a fiduciary responsibility to the organization, though Patrick wished they would work through that issue directly with his bosses, rather than letting him know they wanted him to work to increase revenue. It put him in an uncomfortable position in the middle of a strange governance situation. Patrick hoped that Megan, Frank's boss, would mediate the situation and help Patrick to have clear direction, but that did not seem forthcoming. But as Patrick paid periodic visits to board meetings at Megan's request to provide the board with information on his progress, Patrick began to see there was a deeper problem. Many board members had been on the board for a long time, and they had never had to contend with tightening budgets. When the company first started, there was less competition, and sales were robust. Now, while sales were still good, Patrick had to be exceedingly strategic in order to grow the company. At one particular meeting, Megan brought to the attention of the board that their composition was not really a good match for the San Francisco community in general, and there was little new insight being brought for long-term strategy, and this was a new world in which they lived. The discussion went on for a while about how to address these assertions, and the ideas started to come forth that it might be wise to set board term limits, find a way to keep the long-term institutional knowledge of elder board members, and bring in some new, more diverse thinking. And then the board chair turned to Patrick. He recalled the ensuing discussion this way:

I'm always happy to help, and I certainly agreed that the board needed some newer thinking and more diversity to match the community, but I did not want to be in a political mess, and that's where he put me. He right then and there said I was being appointed to chair a task force that was supposed to go recruit new board members who would help guide the theatre into the next decade. I guess I should have been flattered that they respected my opinion that much, but making that appointment was wrong in so many ways. It jumped right over Frank and Megan, it was the board making an administration decision, it asked me to do something outside the scope of my work, and it came with a significant amount of time and effort required. If I wanted to actually do this, I would have to conduct a lot of research. On the other hand, I wasn't sure I wanted to get out of it. I mean, being responsible for bringing in a new board means you are the initial point of contact for those people. That would certainly be good for my career at the company. And I could shape the board in a way that could be focused on how we serve the market. There were plenty of upsides. What I had to figure out at that moment was how I was going to accomplish all these things, trying to keep everyone happy.

What options did Patrick have before him? What challenges or potential challenges did he face, and how could he address them to minimize their impact? What was the right way to proceed in the best interest of the company? What was the right way for Patrick to proceed personally? Was there a right way to proceed in everyone's best interest?

Personal exploration

What type of volunteer are you? Write about the types of things you enjoy, and why you enjoy them, and then search the Internet for volunteer opportunities that might satisfy your needs and desires. Describe what those volunteer opportunities are, what you would gain by volunteering for them, and what they would require of you. What are the obstacles that stop you from volunteering? How could those obstacles be overcome?

Notes

1 Hiland, Mary, "The next level: Understanding effective board development," *Leading and Managing in the Social Sector* (pp. 139–154). Springer International Publishing, 2017.
2 Forenza, Brad, "Sustained community theater participation as civil society involvement," *Nonprofit and Voluntary Sector Quarterly* (2016): doi:1011.77/0899764016660385.
3 Murray, Kevin, "Theater production management guidebook," *The Arts Management Handbook: New Directions for Students and Practitioners* Meg Brindle and Constance DeVereaux (eds.) (p. 38). Routledge, 2011.
4 Hiland, Mary, "The next level: Understanding effective board development." *Leading and Managing in the Social Sector* (pp. 139–154). Springer International Publishing, 2017.
5 Walmsley, Ben, "Arts and cultural management." *Entertainment Management: Towards Best Practice* Moss, Stuart and Ben Walmsley (eds.) (p. 157), CABI Tourism Texts, 2014.
6 Ibid.

7   Murray, Kevin, "Theater production management guidebook." *The Arts Management Handbook: New Directions for Students and Practitioners* (2015): 38.

8   Walmsley, Ben. "Arts and cultural management." *Entertainment Management: Towards Best Practice* Moss, Stuart Walmsley and Ben Walmsley (eds.) (p. 157), CABI Tourism Texts, 2014.

9   Spires, Laura, "Striving for success in times of change: Leadership in nonprofit theatres," PhD dissertation, The Ohio State University, 2015.

10 Brown, Gerry, *The Independent Director: The Non-Executive Director's Guide to Effective Board Presence,* Springer, 2015.

11 Ibid.

12 Weitzel, Al, and Patricia Geist, "Parliamentary procedure in a community group: Communication and vigilant decision making," *Communications Monographs* 65, no. 3 (1998): 244–259.

13 Brindle, Meg, "Careers and internships in arts management," *The Arts Management Handbook: New Directions for Students and Practitioners* (pp. 185–219), Meg Brindle and Constance DeVereaux (eds.) (p. 38). Routledge, 2011.

14 Ibid.

15 Bringle, Robert G., and Julie A. Hatcher, "Implementing service learning in higher education," *The Journal of Higher Education* 67, no. 2 (1996): 221–239.

CHAPTER 14

Theatre advocacy and community engagement

Besides the obvious potential benefits to Patrick and his theatre that leading a board member recruiting task force could provide, Patrick also reaped the long-term benefits of such a job. Putting together and leading a task force of this nature would allow him to reach out into areas of the community that may not yet have been served by his theatre. He could look for potential board members who would have platforms from which they could talk to the community about the importance of theatre in general, as well as help his theatre make direct contact with, and engage, members of the community. While engaging like this may have served his present purposes in marketing to some degree, Patrick knew that the benefits over time of making those deep connections to the community, where the company could advocate for the importance of theatre, would prove fruitful for years.

Chapter objectives

After reading this chapter, you should be able to describe different types of advocacy and explain the value of advocacy, identify important parts of an advocacy plan, including whom to address and how to address them, evaluate the value of hiring a professional advocate, explain community engagement and describe its value, and demonstrate how to write advocacy and engagement statements for a theatre.

Theatre advocacy and community engagement

When we think of advocacy, we think of promoting an idea, thought, program, or product. And really, advocacy is part public relations, because *advocacy* refers to the process of providing publicly visible support for a policy or cause. Legislative lobbying is one form of advocacy. (Though while all lobbying is advocacy, all advocacy is not lobbying.) In theatre, we tend to think that what we are all doing, all the time, regarding the art form is advocating.

We tell everyone we know how great theatre is, and what a wonderful experience they will have when they attend the theatre. This certainly is advocacy, but as we will see, advocacy can be so much more, and when done in a methodical fashion, it can change how a community responds.[1] Think about advocacy groups that lobby your legislators. They do so by supporting their cause in a fashion that is designed to get laws passed for the purpose of long-lasting support. Getting laws passed is also a function of advocacy, and even community theatres can advocate to their local government and get laws passed.

Consider the Ringling Bros. and Barnum & Bailey circus, one of the last traditional circuses, which closed its doors after 146 years of entertaining the world. While the circus had faced a number of difficulties during its last fifteen years, advocates against animal cruelty had targeted the circus and created a huge outpouring of sympathy for the animal performers in the circus. That attention eventually got the circus to remove the elephant act from its performance, and by the time that action was taken, the damage was done. Audiences were rejecting the circus based on the advocates' claims that it was cruel to animals. And even though the circus won a settlement in a very expensive lawsuit against the advocates, noting that the claims were false and damaging to the circus, that was not enough to reverse its decline in audience. In this case, while advocacy did not end up putting an end to an entire industry, because the modern circus still exists, advocacy did manage to essentially put an end to the traditional mega-circus, which some would say marked the end of an art form.

So if that is advocacy, what is community engagement and why is it different? In theatre, *community engagement* is thought of as the process by which a theatre has direct interactions with a community for the purpose of providing benefit to the community.[2] You may be thinking to yourself that this sounds like the mission of theatre, to provide benefit to the community. But the process of engagement means more than simply providing a program and promoting its presence. Instead, engagement is more focused on the direct interaction. Many theatres have educational programs, outreach programs for underserved populations, social benefit programs, and even civic partnerships. All of these types of programs typically require some sort of engagement.

Advocacy

The activity of advocacy is really rooted in a desire to influence opinions, so as to achieve results that will benefit people. That means that in attempting to influence opinions, we are wishing to affect decisions. In the case of the arts, advocates spend a great deal of time educating and informing people about the value of the arts. There are numerous studies indicating that not only does theatre provide entertainment, for example, but it also enriches lives. Theatre provides a host of educational and economic benefits to the community, provides jobs, creates a sense of civic pride, encourages community interactions, supports neighborhood improvement, generates tax revenue, and on and on. But those studies tend to sit on shelves unless theatres advocate for the importance of theatre in our communities. This type of advocacy is *policy advocacy*, where a group or organization is attempting to influence policies that may negatively affect an organization or industry. Policy advocacy is different from something like *system advocacy*, which is typically internal advocacy aimed at changing the structure or system within an organization or industry. For example, when a group of voting members in the Society of West End Theatres wants to change voting rules, and advocate for that change, they are engaging in system advocacy. *Case advocacy* is typically a process of advocacy where a single person is being protected or promoted in order to improve their individual lives. For example, you probably do case advocacy for yourself when you are seeking to borrow money from someone. You attempt to influence their opinion and decisions by educating them about the importance of the outcome you desire and believe is the best outcome: money for you.

Why does it matter?

So why does being an advocate for theatre really matter? It may seem that just having one voice cannot really do much, even if that one voice is just you, or just your theatre, or just the group of your local theatres. You may even feel that participating in a national theatre advocacy group may not be able to change much. The process of change is slow, and we may not see the immediate fruits of that labor. Think about recent social developments in the world, from addressing global warming to LGBT rights. Each issue is at some stage in transforming opinions and associated laws, but those are issues that have had advocates educating people about them for years. We may now begin to see changes in the laws, but the people who started that advocacy may not have even lived to see those changes. If you believe in the transformative power of theatre, then you probably also believe it is something we should be able to provide to everyone. And that requires advocacy. It is advocacy that gets laws passed providing additional governmental support to theatre.[3] It is advocacy that encourages participation in theatre. It is advocacy that ensures that people are educated about theatre. Advocacy is how we ensure that our voices are heard. When there are no advocates for an idea or opinion, the assumption is that no one is in possession of that position or opinion, so there is no need for change. Advocacy is the way we make our voices heard. If you think the state of theatre and public appreciation for it is fine the way it is, maybe you believe there is no reason to advocate for theatre. But if you believe that more people should be more involved in theatre for all the reasons stated above, then perhaps you should consider advocacy. Not only does advocacy make for a better world, but it is also part of the long-term process of increasing the size of our audiences.

Determining what to say

When it comes to advocacy in theatre, there are many issues one could choose to focus on. Perhaps it is the state of theatre as taught in public education. Maybe it is the rising cost of theatre tickets. Perhaps you would like to advocate for more public funding of theatre. Maybe you need to advocate for a local theatre award, or for greater local recognition of theatre in general. You could advocate for the addition of free or inexpensive space for theatre artists to rehearse and perform. The list can go on and on, and sometimes can be overwhelming, but a theatre that takes its role as an advocate seriously will go back to its mission, vision, and values and should be able to determine an issue or two which are most important to it, and in areas where the company would like to see change. Once the specific issues are determined, there is planning to be done. Some theatres, by virtue of their mission, vision, and values are advocacy theatres by their very nature. Consider theatres that are dedicated to advancing causes through the work they do: LGBTQ+ Theatre, deaf theatre, women's theatre, and even children's theatre can be advocacy theatre if their mission is to promote a cause through the art of theatre. But if a theatre does not have a cause written into its mission, and it believes in the importance of advocating for issues related to theatre in the world today, it needs an advocacy plan.

First the theatre will fully research the issue, collecting all the pertinent history and background information. How did the issue arise? What were things like before? If it is a local issue, the theatre will want to know how the community feels about the issue. Even if it is a much larger issue, knowing where the community stands on the issue is important. Issues requiring advocacy divide a community. If you believe things should be different than they are now, some people are being left out of something they would desire. If you believe that theatre artists should have free, local space to rehearse and perform, who is being left out from rehearsing and performing because such space does not exist? Next, it is important to know why people like things the way they are. Maybe some people believe there is adequate rehearsal space. Perhaps some in the community think theatre is a waste of time, or elitist. Perhaps some do not believe precious tax revenue should be wasted on theatre. Whatever the concerns, knowing what your opposition is thinking is important, because it also means you can find out who is influencing those opposing opinions. Then you will have to consider what those people in opposition may require in order to support your ideas. Think of the planning list like this: What is the history? Who is being affected? What is causing the problem? What is the result of the problem? What/who has made it difficult to address? What could solve the problem? Once the planning is done, you should be able to clearly state your objective with the results you expect to achieve. Be sure that the objectives have goals that are measurable. For example, if you want more people in the community to attend theatre, then know that within five years you would like to see 20% greater attendance from local residents.

Questions to research for class discussion:

Search the Internet and find answers for these questions before you read any further. Be prepared to discuss them in class.

14.1 How can you use social media for advocacy?
14.2 What is networking? How would you use networking in advocacy? What theatre advocacy networks already exist that you could participate in?
14.3 What are the pros and cons of hiring a professional advocate?
14.4 What laws restrict nonprofits from doing advocacy, and what, exactly, do they restrict, if anything?

Determining how to say it

Once you know what issue you want to advocate for, you need to figure out exactly what you want to say about it. That may seem obvious, but if you believe more people should be attending theatre in your community, then just saying that may not be enough. You will have to explain *why* more people should be attending, educate about the benefits of greater attendance, and also discuss how to achieve greater attendance.

To clarify a message, it is important to study all the pertinent data and research, and to conduct further studies if necessary, deepening your understanding of what the community feels and believes, and knowing what research is going to support the opposition's opinion. The more educated an advocate is, the better they will be at educating others, encouraging support for the cause, and reshaping how the issue is discussed.[4]

Key communication routes include the media, which may mean being friendly with journalists and personally explaining the details of the issue and educating them on your position, and it may also mean writing detailed and clear press releases that attempt to sway the reader by addressing all the points for and against the issue. Making direct contact with people is also an important part of communicating and educating. This means writing letters, staging public events, speaking to people in positions of power including legislators (even if you are not seeking their decisions to affect your issue) and spreading the message honestly and truthfully via electronic communication means.

Advocating for an issue, regardless of how innocuous you may believe it is, is likely to bring about opposition. Consider a theatre simply seeking the local school district to allow students one day a year to have a field trip to the theatre. It seems like a great idea, right? But there will certainly be plenty of people who will want to argue that doing so takes away from one classroom day, and adds to the chipping away at education. Knowing that the opposition will be trying to stop the change is important, but thinking through *how* they may try and stop the change is equally important.[5] If you believe they will send flyers to every parent of a child in the school district, you may want to do the same. Remember that the opposition is likely to do everything, from deny your research to deceiving people, in order to accomplish stopping the change. Advocates need to remain calm, honest, truthful, and diligent in their pursuit for change.

Think critically: advocating for local change

There are two ways to approach this class discussion. First, you can choose sides. Divide the class into two, by whatever means you choose, and debate the argument outlined below. Second, you can have an open discussion, each adding upon the others' thoughts, and let the discussion uncover all the important details of all sides of the debate. Keep in mind that regardless of which approach you take, we want to be sure we dig deep into all sides of this important issue, in order to more effectively understand all positions.

CLASS DISCUSSION: One of the reasons local community theatre is such a great asset is because it brings community members together. They may be involved in creating the production, or simply in attending, but regardless of how they interact, by doing so, they are strengthening the bonds of community. One local government recently set aside funds to bring in experts from foreign countries to further enrich the community. In the legislation, the funds are set aside for several different types of foreign experts with the thinking that new ideas may develop and diversity can be enriched in the community. The fund will support botanists to come and work with local nurseries, gardening clubs, and arborists; chefs to work with local clubs and restaurants; education experts to work with schools and daycare centers;

and engineers to work with local architects and planners. The government, however, excluded the arts from the list. Some believe that, given the fund's limited resources, it is better to focus on areas that will affect the largest segments of the population; although providing foreign theatre directors, for example, may help theatres, those theatres, in turn, only provide art for a limited number of people. Others see the issue differently. They suggest that by not including theatre in yet another program designed to strengthen the community, the funding is intentionally lessening the impact of theatre by virtue of the fact that it is raising the impact of other areas. Theatre contributes so much, yet is marginalized by being left out of this funding. And this despite the fact that tax revenue is collected to pay for this program, and that revenue is coming from everyone, so it should be used for the greatest good. But won't it be doing the greatest good if it is raising up an under-represented field, rather than slightly lifting a well-represented one, such as the culinary arts? How would you go about advocating for one side or the other? Who would your opposition be? Choose sides and consider how to be the most persuasive.

To whom do you say it?

Most often, advocacy means delivering your message to anyone who will listen, but the best advocacy is targeted at the people who can make the decisions to affect change. If it is a local council, you may know one or more of them and be able to interact directly. But even in that situation, before launching an advocacy campaign, a group will attempt to determine who their allies are. Those allies may be people who share similar interests, or who may share a similar interest. And beyond simply determining who they are, it is important to get them engaged in the advocacy effort. The greater the number of voices, the louder the message will be. Allies may bring different strengths and networks to the table, so it is important to determine roles and responsibilities in advance. Because each person, group, or organization may be better suited to advocating to government, the media, or other community partners.

Questions to research for class discussion:

Search the Internet and find answers for these questions before you read any further. Be prepared to discuss them in class.

14.5 What are the 10 D's of opposition?
14.6 What are the 10 D's of entrepreneurship, and how could they relate to advocacy?
14.7 What are the best ways to write an advocacy press release?
14.8 What skills should you look for when hiring an advocate?

Governmental bodies

We have already discussed the notion of advocating to governmental bodies and legislators, and if it is done with the intent of getting them to make a decision in favor of the issue being advocated for, it is called *lobbying*. And while we see grassroots lobbying occurring when our legislators are bombarded with email, phone calls, petitions, and even yelled at when they are giving public speeches, these may not be the best tactics for gaining change. When approaching a legislator, there is no communication of greater quality than a face-to-face interaction. This may require communicating directly with the legislator's staff first, but a polite and cordial approach, with a very clear objective, is your most likely path to success. The staff has time to spend with constituents, and they are there for the purpose of hearing the thoughts and ideas of those willing to share them. Get to know the staff, and develop a relationship based on being a sensible, considerate, and honest source of information. Typically, when the staff members trust that your behavior is appropriate and your information is accurate, they will assist in getting you time directly with your legislator. When you have the opportunity, continue to look and behave professionally. Legislators are likely to ask questions that suggest they are opposed to your request for change. Provide information, but be willing to listen and not be defensive. This means that you may have to compromise your position to gain action. Remain open to this possibility. Change often occurs incrementally. Make sure you are absolutely clear on what objectives you wish to achieve – you detailed those in your planning – and explain exactly why you are passionate about the issue. Citing your research and data is certainly important, and legislators do like to have that if they are ever questioned about a decision they made, but they tend to be much more interested in personal stories, as personal stories are more compelling and emotional. Finally, be sure to thank everyone, staff as well as legislator, for listening, even if they do not immediately take action. They are likely to sit down together to discuss the ramifications of making a decision for change like you have advocated for, and if you have provided the appropriate information, and they trust and believe you, they are more likely to be swayed to your side of the issue.[6]

Using the media for advocacy

Media is actually plural for *medium* and refers to those forms of communication that are disseminated to the general public such as newspapers, magazines, radio, television, and Internet publishers. *Media advocacy* is the process of using the media to advocate for an issue. Media advocacy can be beneficial, because the media communicate with lots of people at the same time, and that access can very much help to sway public opinion on an issue.

Just like advocating to governments, advocating to the media is best done when you can establish a personal relationship. Getting to know journalists and supplying them with accurate and honest information in a professional manner will go a long way in your favor. Journalists have a duty to seek out opinions on both sides of an issue, so knowing your opposition and what they will have to say is important. When you explore an issue with a journalist, be assured that they will talk to your opposition about their opinion. This means that a journalist who is showing interest in an issue is going to work to make certain they have all the facts. If you are deceptive, or withhold pertinent information, they will find it and likely will not be considerate to your position. Having a relationship with the media requires totally honest and full disclosure, trustworthiness, and accuracy. If you are consistently accurate and trustworthy, then the journalist is likely to consider you a solid source of information on the issue. When a journalist does contact you, respond immediately. And when there are new developments on your issue, alert the media immediately.

So how do you start a discussion with journalists? Typically, the start is by sending a press release and following up with a personal contact. Sometimes, buying paid advertising can get the media's attention, and alert them to the issue you are advocating for, and they will contact you. And while the media rarely responds to a smaller organization's announcement of a press conference, if you are in a larger one and dealing with an important topic, press conferences can be an entrée into the media and can generate attention. Finally, letters to the editor in local papers can have impact, particularly if many members of the community write in advocating the same position. However, understanding your opposition is vitally important when using letters to the editor to draw attention to your issue. The last thing any issue needs is an ongoing battle of opinions in the newspaper. Remember that a main goal of advocacy is to educate, and that is done with fact. Opinion letters may attempt to influence without using fact.

Strategic partnerships

In addition to government and media, there are an almost infinite number of potential partnerships that can be developed to advocate for a position.[7] And in theatre, it is important to identify who those partners may be, and to engage them. If the issue is about getting schoolchildren into theatre matinees on a field trip, partners could include teacher associations, parent groups, youth organizations, child advocates, foster homes, and on and on. Engaging and educating every potential partner can go a long way toward shaping public opinion. And if a theatre company has a position it is advocating for, making certain that everyone working in the theatre is aware of the position is essential. Box office staff and ushers have the most direct contact with the public, and if they are unaware of the position the theatre is taking, those connections are wasted. This is not to suggest that every interaction with a patron should be used to press a position, but if the opportunity presents itself, box office staff and ushers should know how to take advantage of those moments, as long as they are doing so in a way that is in accordance with theatre policy and the law.

Community engagement

In some sense, community engagement is also an activity that is geared toward creating change in a community, but rather than doing so by changing opinions to generate action, it is about a direct interaction with individuals and groups in a community.[8] Theatre companies engage communities in many ways, including through touring productions, providing education programs associated with theatre, doing lectures or demonstrations before or after performances, and supporting underserved groups with direct contact between the theatre and those groups. Engagement in the theatre could mean providing tours of a theatre facility, or sending artists into schools. The process of engagement provides benefit to the theatre as well as to the groups being served. Engaging with community members and groups supports the promotion of the theatre by drawing attention to its good work, and also develops a sense of community associated with theatre.

What is engagement?

We have stated that "engagement" is based on a direct interaction with community members and groups to provide benefit to the community. But more precisely, engagement is a way of creating a symbiotic relationship with a community in which the theatre is embedded. By engaging, the theatre is able to deepen its ties to the community, as well as embed itself. While many theatres develop engagement plans as the result of incremental growth in the community, or through grant funding that launches engagement programs, planning for engagement is the most likely way to ensure success.

Short and long-term benefits

Community engagement allows theatres to change the way communities interact with each other, particularly because theatre itself is interactive to some degree, has a social component, and is rooted in communication. Not only does engagement allow a theatre to serve the community in deep and rich ways, but it allows for connections to be made between the theatre and community members that might not otherwise occur without engagement programs. Community engagement allows theatres to demonstrate to their communities that theatre is not simply entertainment, but an important way to enrich our lives. Further, engagement by a theatre allows a community to see that theatre is an art form for everyone, not just the elite, and it is a way to bring together different people with different backgrounds and ideas. Oftentimes, those shared experiences bring new ideas forth, and theatres can take advantage of such new ideas to explore new art. The relationships that are built through community engagement can help reduce societal tensions and conflict.[9] By engaging the community, new audiences, both in the short term and the long term, are developed, because those who might not otherwise be involved or associated with the theatre are given an opportunity to learn and understand theatre. Engagement programs can also develop new theatre artists, volunteers, or supporters, and they create a new web of connections.

Developing engagement plans

In the engagement plan, the theatre considers whom it seeks to engage, and what outcomes are anticipated by the engagement. In some sense, this is similar to engaging donors in order to connect them to the company, but in the case of community engagement, the goal is not to see more donated money coming in, but to see more people coming in. The plan will also consider who are the people the theatre knows who are the target for engagement; who are the people the theatre does not know who are targeted for engagement; and who are the people the theatre knows and does not know who may be partners in the engagement, including potential funders of the engagement plan. The plan will also demonstrate what strategies and tactics will be used for engagement, and how those will be evaluated against the anticipated goals. Typically, the engagement plan will address what resources will be put into the plan, what partners will be part of the plan, and how resources will be shared. It may also discuss how the plan ties to the organization's mission and vision, and what the benefits to the community will be in both the short term and the long term.

Questions to research for class discussion:

Search the Internet and find answers for these questions before you read any further. Be prepared to discuss them in class.

14.9   What are the most common mistakes made in community engagement?

14.10 What are some important tips for developing a good community engagement strategy?

14.11 What are three financial support grants that exist for arts engagement programs? Describe who provides them and what they support.

Investing in the community

Doing community engagement work requires a commitment to investing in a community, and not just doing the work to reap a benefit for your theatre. There can be a grey area in the middle. Sometimes engagement work is supported by grants, which provide financial benefit to the theatre. Ultimately, the question is what your theatre is truly committed to doing, and this is likely enshrined in a values statement. For a commercial theatre, engagement is typically aimed at improving and increasing sales. It is a financial investment designed to provide a financial return. For the community-based theatre, at the core of the investment is an understanding of what sort of engagement can make an impact on the community, and improve it as a place to live and work. The ultimate goal of engagement is to improve society through action. This means that engagement requires an understanding of what long-term goals are expected (this is typically derived from the vision) and what incremental phases can help to lead you there. Those incremental phases, the programs of engagement, are typically derived from the mission. Effective engagement programs, just like advocacy programs, are supported and participated in by all members of the theatre, at least to some degree.

Build your theatre milestone 14: engagement and advocacy

For this milestone you are going to write statements for your theatre's engagement and advocacy plans. What programs do you have that will require engagement, or what programs do you expect you will eventually develop that may require engagement? Who do you expect to be engaging with, and how will you engage them? What will be the goals of that engagement? Who will be responsible for doing the engagement? How will you support the engagement in your budget? What issues does your theatre feel passionately about that are relevant to the theatre's mission, vision, and values? How do you plan to incorporate advocacy into what your theatre does on a day-to-day basis? What goals do you wish to achieve with advocacy? What research supports your position? Who will be involved with your advocacy and what avenues do you expect they will take to advocate for the issue? With whom will you develop partnerships, and for what purpose? Will you try to get your patrons to be partners? Who will oppose the change and why? How will you counter their opposition? Answer these questions as well as others you believe are pertinent to engagement and advocacy. Be as thorough as possible as you develop these statements, as they will be the foundation for your planning.

Case study

One afternoon, Patrick's colleague in the development department called a meeting with all department heads, Frank, Megan, and the chairman of the board, to discuss a new proposition. The company had a chance to secure a substantial grant to support a program that would provide arts and education activities for students. The money would fund an entire theatre program that was designed to do a multitude of things: allow for theatre classes for children at the theatre, provide for the touring of children's theatre productions into schools and youth group meetings, support artist-in-residence programs in classrooms, and provide free theatre tickets to children and their parents. It was an incredible opportunity to do some immensely important engagement with the community in ways that would serve thousands of children now, as well as serve the theatre by drawing attention to the organization in the present. It would also help develop a love for theatre in children that may pay off in the future. But there were some stipulations. The grantor wanted the money to support girls from underserved populations, and in San Francisco, that meant predominantly African-American girls living below the poverty line. This was certainly a good program, and it was important work that needed to be done. And there were only a couple of theatres in the area with the right staff, and enough assets, to be able to do this sort of engagement successfully. In many ways, it was a golden opportunity to use theatre for something extremely important. And the ongoing funding, promised for a minimum of five years and based on meeting certain benchmarks, ensured that the theatre would be able to really focus on making the programs successful and engaging the target population. But there were certain challenges as well. Patrick had this to say:

> We were all excited by the prospect of being able to do this extremely important work, and to use theatre for such a good cause. It was a chance to really make a difference in San Francisco in a way that would make a huge difference in so many people's lives. But we had some instant fear about accepting the grant and moving forward on a number of fronts. The first was a concern that the target population was not who we were in existence to serve. We were all excited about being able to serve those girls, but it meant restructuring who we were. And we were all a bit concerned that the target was too limited. Why not target boys and girls? Why not target all underserved people? The second big issue was that the size of the grant would overpower what we were presently doing. Once we put those new programs in place, the majority of our operation would be devoted to engagement, and the minority of our operation would be producing great theatre. That was not necessarily a bad thing, because we all were doing theatre to make a difference in people's lives, but to make that decision required some fundamental shifts in what the company was. The third issue was that, financially, it would put us on a

solid footing for five years, and possibly in perpetuity if the work was solid and making an impact, and we were certain that this would be the case. The engagement programs would essentially protect the theatre from market fluctuations that can kill a nonprofit theatre. It might have just been a question of changing our mission or sticking with the current mission, but we had always included in our mission a strong emphasis on engagement with our community, because we always believed that making a difference was the key to what we were doing. So in some sense, this was a way to really shine at doing what our mission guided us to do. But it was going to take our focus away from producing theatre, and that scared all of us. This great opportunity was also an extreme threat to our company. I walked away from that meeting wishing we had never even been told of the grant, because I didn't want to have to be part of the discussion of where it may or may not take us, and if we should accept the money or not.

There were obviously a number of issues that had to be discussed and considered, and in the end a decision had to be made. While the programs funded by the grant were essentially keeping in line with the theatre's mission, and in fact would help the company provide for the community in a much better way than it had been able to previously, the grant would seemingly shift how the theatre had been operating since its inception. And if the company rejected such a large grant, how would donors feel about contributing in the future, given that such immense support was rejected? How much weight should the team give to each of the pros and cons of accepting the grant money? What are the most important issues, and which ones are of lesser importance, and why? Philosophically, is engagement, and likely the advocacy that would follow if the grant were accepted, so important that it should become dominant over the actual production of theatre? Commercial enterprises follow the money in order to grow, and change their missions accordingly, but should a nonprofit theatre? If so, why? If not, why not? What decision would you recommend to the board if you were in Patrick's shoes, and what issues would you use to persuade them to make the choice you advocate?

Personal exploration

Describe an issue that is important to you personally that you could do advocacy for. How would you go about planning and executing an advocacy strategy for the issue? Where would you get research? What research would you do on your own? What sort of change would you like to see occur? Who will be your likely opposition and why will they oppose the change? Who could you develop strategic partnerships with? How would you approach them, and what would you want them to do as part of your advocacy?

Notes

1 Dolan, Jill, "Rehearsing democracy: Advocacy, public intellectuals, and civic engagement in theatre and performance studies," *Theatre Topics* 11, no. 1 (2001): 1–17.
2 Ibid.
3 Gallagher, Kathleen, and David Booth, eds., *How Theatre Educates: Convergences and Counterpoints with Artists, Scholars, and Advocates,* University of Toronto Press, 2015.
4 Gallagher, K., "Emergent conceptions in theatre pedagogy and production," *How Theatre Educates: Convergences and Counterpoints with Artists, Scholars, and Advocates,* Kathleen Gallagher and David Booth (eds.) (pp. 3–13), University of Toronto Press, 2003.
5 Metz, Allison Manville, *Applied Theatre in Schools in the United States: The Triangulation of Education, Art, and Community Practice in Theatre in Education (TIE),* ProQuest, 2008.
6 Dreeszen, Craig, "Intersections: Community arts and education collaborations," *The Journal of Arts Management, Law, and Society* 22, no. 3 (1992): 211–239.
7 Backer, Thomas E., "Partnership as an art form: What works and what doesn't in nonprofit arts partnerships," *John S. and James L. Knight Foundation. Retrieved April* 21 (2002): 2008.
8 Grisolia, José Maria, Ken Willis, Colin Wymer, and Andrew Law, "Social engagement and regional theatre: Patterns of theatre attendance," *Cultural Trends* 19, no. 3 (2010): 225–244.
9 O'Connor, Peter, Briar O'Connor, and Marlane Welsh-Morris, "Making the everyday extraordinary: A theatre in education project to prevent child abuse, neglect and family violence," *Research in Drama Education* 11, no. 2 (2006): 235–245.

CHAPTER 15

Theatre education

In some sense, Patrick knew that the engagement programs they were going to be creating would have aspects focused on theatre education. It was something he felt passionately about, especially since he had degrees in the arts. But he also realized that his expertise was not in education, but in arts marketing, and he did not want an education program to be geared toward marketing, even if it did assist him in his work. He knew that, fundamentally, an education could not be designed to serve two masters. Education was about providing for and helping students to achieve specific goals. And that had to be done in a way that experts had found were the right, best practices.

Chapter objectives

After reading this chapter, you should be able to discuss the different terms used regarding education and theatre, briefly describe the history of theatre in the classroom, explain different educational theatre programs that theatre companies provide, argue the issue of relevance in theatre education, and demonstrate how to develop an education plan.

Theatre education

Where did you find your interest in theatre? It is quite probable that while you may have been introduced to theatre by a parental figure, you really developed an interest from school activities. That may have included taking drama classes and learning how to perform, participating in a school play, seeing a play as part of a school activity, reading a drama in a language class, or being introduced to theatre professionals. Regardless of the way a person is introduced to theatre, such experiences can have a profound and lifelong impact on the quality of their life.

When we use the term "theatre education," several ideas come to mind about what it means, and they are all perfectly valid. *Theatre education* refers to the process of educating students in the art of theatre, of course, but there are other definitions that it might refer to as well. For our purposes, we use theatre education to be a catchall, meaning that not only does it include the process of training and education in the dramatic arts and its associated fields, including theatre management, but we also use it to refer to what is sometimes called educational theatre. *Educational theatre* is a term that is used to explain theatrical productions that are created for the specific purpose of educating the audience on a topic. The term educational theatre is also sometimes used interchangeably with *theatre in education*, which refers to the process of using theatre as an instructional tool to educate students in other disciplines.[1]

For our discussion in this chapter, we will examine a little of each of these notions of theatre education, as well as explore what potential ramifications may occur due to recent reductions in theatre exposure in school. While it is almost impossible to determine what long-term effects will occur if students receive less consistent quality exposure and experiences in theatre, we can certainly speculate with some confidence on likely results, based upon what we know about exposure to the arts as a youth.

History of theatre in schools

Theatre as an academic field of study really did not exist until the late nineteenth century, perhaps owing to the fact that religious and moral objections to theatre varied over the centuries.[2] Theatre as a standard subject in school became much more mainstream in the mid-twentieth century, and after this time there is a good deal written about changing curricula over the years. This is not to suggest that theatre was not taught, but only that its worldwide expansion as a standard subject become more formally recognized in the late 1800s. Theatre management, as an academic pursuit, truly came into existence in the early 1960s when a handful of universities recognized the need for effective management of student productions. But at the time, the field of management was not necessarily regarded as much more than the assignment of tasks for the promotion of plays and the selling of tickets.[3] Today, undergraduate and graduate degrees are offered in many countries and at hundreds of universities with titles such as arts administration, theatre management, arts leadership, production management, stage management, and performing arts management. All of these programs are tied together by virtue of their focus on management training and education, and its core principles that are framed by the four functions of management: planning, organizing, leading, and controlling.[4]

Questions to research for class discussion:

Search the Internet and find answers for these questions before you read any further. Be prepared to discuss them in class.

15.1 What is AAAE? What do they do? Who are their members?

15.2 What is ECATC? What do they do? Who are their members?

15.3 What is the ANCER network? What do they do? Who are their members?

15.4 What are three different degree programs that exist near you that focus on the field of management in the arts? How are they alike? How are they different?

While we explore theatre exposure and experience as a child a little further in the chapter, let us first consider why education and training in theatre is valuable, above and beyond the joy and intellectual stimulation that theatre can bring. One thing students of theatre learn is improvisation, not only in actor training, but also in the technical shops and in management. Because our budgets tend to be meek, students of theatre become adept at improvising. And with improvisation comes a talent for remaining calm in a crisis. Theatre practitioners learn to find solutions and to move forward without letting things collapse. And when it comes to living on a tight budget, many students of theatre master the skill. But learning in the theatre environment also means doing work in project management, and developing a sense of how to coordinate efforts in a way that culminates in a completed and successful project. Project management requires the development of advanced critical thinking skills, as the script, which is the manual, requires interpretation and adaptation in order to come to life. Along the way to project completion, we learn how to solve problems in the management of the project, and to make alterations for the good of the final result. These are skills which can only be discussed in other environments, but they can actually be practiced in theatre. Learning in the theatre also provides an opportunity to work amongst an incredibly diverse collection of personalities, styles, behaviors, cultures, and backgrounds. Theatre has traditionally welcomed anyone, from the fringes to the mainstream, and being able to experience all those perspectives trains us to work under myriad circumstances. People trained in theatre tend to be exceptional team players. They know how to work with others. A theatre education also provides an excellent opportunity to see and experience the practicality of practice. While practicing in any discipline leads to improvement, often that improvement is so tiny and incremental that it is difficult to see as the result of practice. In theatre, we see the improvements on an almost daily basis and develop a true understanding of the value of practice. Students of theatre also learn how to gauge how others will respond to what they say and do. As a leadership trait, this is incredibly valuable, and it pairs well with the courage required to take part in theatre, as the end product may or may not be exceptional, and for all the hard work put into it, a theatre student puts their own ego at risk on opening night. Most importantly, we now live in a creative world, where innovation and creation are highly valued traits. Many of the largest and most profitable companies that are creating new products, services, and delivery methods that have grown as a result of our technological advances are looking for employees who are trained to use their imaginations to consider possibilities that do not yet exist.

Long-term effects of changing theatre education

There has been some research to suggest that the quality and amount of time devoted to theatre in school has been eroding. The research is limited, and the consequences of that decline in arts education have yet to be discovered. While some nations fund more extensive research regarding the trends in the arts than others do, when it comes to global changes in arts education, virtually nothing is known. One study, however, suggests that because education trends in curricula change as a result of world pressures and changing global societies, we can make some inferences.[5] What is relatively clear is that the amount of quality time spent in classrooms on the arts in general has dropped over the last several decades. It is not surprising, since our competitive economies have required continuously greater need for experts in the fields of science, technology, engineering, and mathematics (STEM), particularly in light of globalization, communication changes, and technological advances. However, some hope exists that the drop in arts education could potentially be reversed by the needs of those companies that look for students who have been trained to think creatively.

Strangely, the growth of arts education in the early twentieth century came from an academic belief in educating the masses with a holistic approach that would create a less specialized academic and a more generalized, enlightened society, and in some sense, technology may be pushing us back to specialization.[6] Theatre practitioners have some cause for alarm with the decline in arts education in elementary and secondary schools. A number of studies have been done which correlate exposure to the arts as a youth as a precursor toward arts participation as an adult. What this means, essentially, is that while we may see a decline in actors, designers, directors, and even theatre managers, what is of greater concern is that we will likely see a continuing decline in audience.[7] What researchers have yet to discover is what sort of participation in the arts is the actual precursor to arts attendance as an adult. Does it matter? Perhaps. If we as a society believe in the value of the arts generally, and theatre specifically, as a means for enriching our lives, and educating and entertaining us, then we need to ensure it continues. Given economic pressures to focus student time more specifically on STEM fields, it behooves us to understand what specific involvement as a child will have the greatest impact as an adult. For example, do children who interact with the arts as a result of classroom intervention become more likely to participate in the arts as an adult, or do children exposed to the arts by a parental figure have a greater likelihood of adult attendance? If we knew the answers, we could better serve our communities. And what sort of participation is most relevant and most likely to lead to adult participation? Consider these definitions:

Arts Education: Learning, instruction, and programming based upon the visual and tangible arts. It includes performing arts like dance, music, and theatre, and visual arts like drawing, painting, sculpture, and design works. Arts education is a process where you were taught or trained in one or more art forms as part of a pre-determined curriculum. For example, if your entire class were required to participate in learning how to play the harpsichord, or to read out loud the roles in "Romeo and Juliet," those would be considered some examples of arts education. Arts education might also be learning about the meaning of a painting, or the sounds in a recording of a symphony, but note that in our working definition of arts education, the entire class is participating as part of structured classroom activities.

Arts Engagement: Participating in the arts is a process meant to connect you with the art. Arts engagement is a process where you are given an opportunity to participate in the creation of an art form as a voluntary activity. If you were voluntarily allowed, as part of a smaller group of people, to be in a school play or band, your mother enrolled you in piano lessons or ballet, or you were taken to a sculpting studio, those would all be considered some examples of arts engagement.

Arts Exposure: An opportunity provided to you to experience one or more of the arts. Some examples might include being taken to a play, either as part of your class or by a parental figure, being taken to an art museum, or having someone play a symphony for you.[8]

Developing an action plan

Most theatres interested in growing audience size undertake some sort of marketing plan to accomplish that goal. The wise theatre manager recognizes that while promotion is designed to reach sales goals in the short term, it is education that will lead to increased sales in the long term.[9] Consider the notion of asking audiences as well as non-attenders what plays would be the most likely to draw them into the theatre. It takes little guesswork to speculate that the results would be a list of well-known or popular play titles. The lists might vary from community to community, but one thing is certain: unknown titles will never make it onto the list by virtue of the fact that they are unknown. To change that situation, the clever marketer endeavors to educate the community about certain plays, what they are about and how they may cause the audience to react, so as to elicit greater response, and accordingly, greater sales. But it takes an inordinate amount of money, or a great deal of time, or both, to accomplish this task. Thus, many theatre managers now plan seasons several years in advance, allowing their marketing staffs ample time to engage in the process of educating the community about plays that may be coming to the stage in the future. The less education about the theatre people have to begin with, the greater the educational work to be done later in life.

If children are receiving less and less exposure, education, and engagement with theatre, is there any amount of education that can alter adult participation? No one really knows, but theatres have begun to realize that waiting to find out is not a wise option, and they have started to invest heavily in education programs.

To develop an education program, just like advocacy and engagement, the theatre must develop a plan, and this starts with knowing what end result is hoped for. If the goal is to increase attendance, the education program will need to be in existence for a long period of time, following participation levels of adults who were educated as a child.[10] Such an undertaking would require years of surveying those who participate as children, and what kind of participation they engage in as they age. Sometimes there are multiple goals in an education plan, and for each goal, the theatre enumerates what actions it will take to accomplish that goal. The plan includes a clear timeline for accomplishing the goals, with specific benchmarks assigned along the way to ensure the process is working smoothly. Potential obstacles or problems are considered and evaluated in the plan, and the cost for enacting the plan is also addressed to ensure the appropriate resources will be available. Finally, tasks are assigned in the plan, and it is enacted. On paper the entire plan may sound simple, but education plans can be lengthy, complex, difficult to monitor and evaluate, and even harder to keep running consistently.

Education programs

So what sorts of education programs do theatres create? One of the most prevalent is the student field trip during class hours, where students are brought into the theatre to see a performance. Typically the theatre will charge some vastly discounted fee per child, which goes toward covering the cost of performing. For many children, these exposures may be their only opportunity to experience theatre.[11] And while it seems that a single, simple exposure may not be enough to lead to adult participation in the arts, theatres will often couple the exposure with additional support, including lesson plans for teachers to use in conjunction with play attendance, in-class engagement with players from the performance, or other activities associated with the play.[12] There is a danger in presenting these sorts of performances, as theatres can become reliant on the income generated by bringing large quantities of guaranteed audiences into the theatre, even at a discounted price, and the original goal of education can become secondary to the financial incentive.

Many theatres operate *in-house education programs*, meaning they teach classes in theatre to students. Again, these are typically offered at a cost to the students, and as a result, students with lower socioeconomic standing are left out unless scholarships are provided. Typically, these classes are taught in conjunction with a final presentation by students, oftentimes fully realized productions to which tickets are sold. Again, financial incentive can warp intentions if the theatre is not careful to stay focused on its original goals, monitor its progress toward the goals closely, and ensure that every benchmark is being met.

Theatres also use touring productions as a way for youth to experience theatre, travelling city to city or even neighborhood to neighborhood or school to school, performing programming geared specifically for children. Typically, these tours charge a fee, and sometimes their main function is to sell theatre and not to primarily provide an experience, though the two goals go hand in hand. Some theatre companies are organized specifically for the purpose of touring theatre, and the business model relies on selling entire productions, but not on the marketing and promotion, which is done by the entity purchasing the production. There are a number of productions like this, created for the purpose of being educational theatre, whose intent is to provide an important lesson or message to students. Healthcare organizations sometimes have such touring programs, which are designed to travel into schools and provide both entertainment and an important message during an assembly.

Adult education programs

While the rationale for providing educational programs to youth is clear, especially in light of dwindling experiences in schools, theatres do not limit their educational programming to children.

Questions to research for class discussion:

Search the Internet and find answers for these questions before you read any further. Be prepared to discuss them in class.

15.5 What are theatre education workshops? What sorts of things happen in them?

15.6 What are theatre master classes? How are they organized?

15.7 What other types of educational programs do theatres offer? What do they consist of?

Relevance

Why the topic of relevance in a chapter on education? In fact, why include the topic of relevance in a textbook on theatre management at all? Because *relevance* has to do with things that are closely associated or connected, and considered appropriate. In theatre, we sometimes lose site of the importance of relevance in what we do. But the best productions are those that are relevant. This does not mean that they are necessarily topical, or modern-day, but it means we can find a close and appropriate association to them. Consider the musical *Hamilton*. Audiences find it extremely relevant. And before you think to yourself, "well, that's because it uses hip-hop music, which is current," also consider the idea that it addresses the course of human events from a very historical perspective. The United States is presently a superpower, and that is largely due to the foresight of its founding fathers, including Alexander Hamilton. So the historical relevance, in addition to the musical pastiche, is important to its success. But the rags-to-riches path of Alexander Hamilton also has personal relevance to many, so that adds to the relevance. Further, the musical is intentionally cast with people of races not representative of the characters they play, which adds a cultural dimension that not only demonstrates a change in society, but also denotes that we are all one humanity, and this notion is extremely relevant in society today. For actors, designers, directors, and producers, the opportunity to work on something unique and groundbreaking has also proven relevant. Relevance may well be the driving force behind *Hamilton*.

Our education programs need to be considered in light of their relevance. If we are simply parading children through the theatre to watch a play that may or not be of interest to them, we have taken little time to consider relevance. And it seems unlikely that we will be able to make a lasting impact on a child who finds buying candy at the concessions stand more relevant than our theatrical offering. Likewise, just teaching acting classes because we feel we are experts in the subject does not make them relevant for our students. The word of caution here is that an effective education program has to have relevance; and in order to maintain that relevance we must continually evaluate it.

Financing

There are plenty of ways to finance a new educational program, and on paper, they all sound easily obtainable. But in fact, there are countless schools, clubs,

Think critically: relevance in theatre education

There are two ways to approach this class discussion. First, you can choose sides. Divide the class into two, by whatever means you choose, and debate the argument outlined below. Second, you can have an open discussion, each adding upon the others' thoughts, and let the discussion uncover all the important details of all sides of the debate. Keep in mind that regardless of which approach you take, we want to be sure we dig deep into all sides of this important issue, in order to more effectively understand all positions.

CLASS DISCUSSION: We do not find relevance and create art based upon it. We create art and find relevance in it. Sometimes what we create will resonate with the audience, and sometimes it will not. But choosing a play title that is not of importance to a director, and consequently, not relevant to them, is far more damaging to our work than letting the play be relevant to the director and hoping that it will resonate with the audience as well. On the other hand, if we are not looking for ways in which the play can be relevant, it is highly unlikely we will magically stumble upon them. Planning for relevance is no guarantee we will achieve it, but knowing where we think we are headed gives us a far better chance of getting there.

The same is true for theatre education programs. We need to determine what is relevant to those we wish to educate, and devise plans that incorporate that relevance into tactics that will achieve the expected goals of the education.[13] Otherwise, we have nothing to measure and cannot affect real change. On the other hand, the function of education is to teach. It is lovely if people find relevance in what they are learning, but in order to become a better, more informed, and more engaged society sometimes we have to wander into areas in which we do not find relevance. If relevance is the criteria for how we are educated, won't we be catering to personal choice, rather than providing a well-rounded understanding of the world? How will a student ever be able to discover, explore, and develop a lifelong interest in theatre if we only provide an introduction when they demonstrate how it is relevant to them? They are both valuable points. Is one stronger than the other, or is there a middle ground?

organizations, and people who believe they have something of value to teach, and there are limited resources to fund all those great ideas. Theatres have a slight advantage over many educational programmers in that they can incorporate the selling of tickets to offset some cost of operating an educational program. But getting the program started, devising curriculum with measurable objectives, ensuring that educational goals are being met, understanding cognitive processes of students and their development, encouraging critical thinking growth, and similar challenges, often require a lot of expertise and preparatory time. Individual donors often find educational programs to be a source of pride for them, and they seem more inclined to contribute because of them. Foundations and granting bodies often offer support for educational programs, but these funders traditionally have very stringent guidelines, and they require very detailed reporting that demonstrates success. The wise theatre manager does not see this issue as a challenge, but rather as an opportunity to design the right kind of program.

Strategic partnerships

We know that developing partnerships can be valuable in fundraising, and that is especially true when doing fundraising for theatre education programs. Funders may trust that a theatre practitioner, whether a manager, actor, or designer, has the requisite skills and ability to share with students, but funders want to ensure that the necessary knowledge of the curriculum and ability to teach it also exists. Developing partnerships with teaching experts can prove invaluable when creating an educational theatre program.

Questions to research for class discussion:

Search the Internet and find answers for these questions before you read any further. Be prepared to discuss them in class.

15.8   What grant support exists for education programs in theatre?
15.9   What types of educational programs in theatre seem to have gotten the greatest support, and why?
15.10   What marketing tips will help a new educational program take off?

Theatre in Education

Theatre in Education, or TIE, is an academic field that looks at how to use the tools and practices of theatre to teach other subjects.[14] Some simple examples might be the history teacher who plays the role of a famous character in history, or an actor portraying a sick patient for nursing students. If you consider that students are in fact a form of audience, it makes sense. TIE looks at the audience, their age, and their ability to process information, and interacts with them in ways that encourage the development of ideas through storytelling.[15] TIE allows students to explore concepts, rather than simply providing information about those concepts to them.

Erica McWilliam, an expert on education, has written and spoken extensively about the need to shift our modern-day education paradigm to one that encourages creativity.[16] She notes that while educators have long taught as a "sage on the stage," delivering information from a position of great knowledge, they then shifted to being a "guide on the side," where they pointed students in the direction of information. She posits that we must now shift to being a "meddler in the middle," who encourages more creative thinking and exploration.[17] She uses the story of *Hamlet* to illustrate her point, saying that the sage on the stage would lecture about *Hamlet*, perhaps reading passages, discussing metaphor and symbolism, explaining character and relationships, and detailing plot. The guide on the side might have students read the script in class, or watch a video to learn about the play. But the meddler in the middle tells students a murder most foul has been committed, and asks them to find out who did it and why. As you can see, just because we know theatre does not mean we know how to teach theatre. Teaching requires understanding, knowledge, skills, and talents. The greatest teachers are not always the greatest practitioners. Mozart had a teacher who helped him become great. Olympic athletes do as well. Teaching is a talent.

Student-driven education

One last note about developing an education program for a theatre. An idea that is often used with the best and brightest students is that they are given some guidelines, but then allowed to explore ideas and concepts on their own, synthesizing them and sharing them with others. In theatre education programs, we have a great deal of leeway to develop programs that allow students to explore concepts. Devised theatre is one methodology that allows students to develop ideas and concepts, and then form them into theatre in a collaborative fashion. In some sense, devised theatre is student-driven education, and it also may begin to blur the lines between what is theatre and what is education.[18]

Build your theatre milestone 15: education plan

Develop an education plan for your theatre. Describe your target population(s) and what goals you anticipate achieving with your education plan. What actions will you take to achieve those goals? Will you have more than one program? Describe them. What is your timeline for implementation, and what benchmarks will you set? How will you monitor progress? What resources do you plan to allocate to your education program, and what positions will be assigned to handle which tasks? What long-term benefits do you expect your theatre will see as a result of your education program, and when in the future do you anticipate seeing the fruits of your labor?

Case study

Patrick had been having several conversations with Belinda, his company's Director of Education. The theatre had a robust education program that entailed Belinda creating some papers that discussed weekday morning matinee performances which school groups could attend, and providing the necessary paperwork to attend those matinees. Once she created and duplicated those papers, she gave them to Patrick, who distributed them to all the local schools. Then Belinda simply waited for the phone to ring. And it would ring off the hook. Each year, the theatre did ten of these matinees, serving more than 8,000 students and providing a substantial portion of the theatre's earned income. In recent years, attendance had dipped a tiny bit, but raising the price per student by a small amount offset that. Patrick had suggested that Belinda consider developing some support materials teachers could use in association with the programs.

Look, Belinda was busy enough just coordinating getting all those students in the doors, and I knew she had no expertise in developing lesson plans, but I also knew that our target audience was not actually the students, but the teachers. We needed to provide something of value to the teachers to get them to commit to these weekday matinees. It was a challenge for them to get the funding, arrange the transportation, and make it all happen. In exchange for their effort, they got one day off from teaching, but since they are being held to higher and higher standards for their classes, taking a day off has to be of greater and greater value. I figured if the teachers had some lesson plans, we were doing some of their job for them, as well as enriching the experience of attending the theatre.

Belinda did her best to develop some lesson plans, and she was excited to share them with Patrick. She had done some research online, and felt like what she had created would be a great way to spend classroom time. But Patrick was not sold.

What she created was nice. It was games and word associations and things like that. It was definitely going to fill time. But what I was thinking was that if we could satisfy some of the published standards these teachers had to meet, and we could do so using the play as part of that experience, we were satisfying a lot of goals. But we were going to have to demonstrate how that would be effective for everyone if we had any shot at making our education program truly educational. We needed a qualified education expert to help us craft materials designed to meet those standards that also incorporated attendance at the plays. This meant we were going to have to pay someone for every play we presented. And I knew what the budgets were like. It also meant we would have to measure results, and to do that we had to have specific goals, not only for the students, but also for ourselves. We needed to be able to show that by adding this value to our educational program, we would increase attendance. And that would not be easy. We were close to capacity already, and there was little incentive to add additional performances, as that would put us into weekly overtime with all the union employees.

How should Patrick proceed? Ask yourself what this case is really about and what pieces of information you have to analyze. What are the issues you have to analyze, and what are the facts for each issue? After considering all that, what do you conclude?

Personal exploration

Write an educational plan for yourself going forward from here, both through your graduation and through your life. What goals do you want to achieve? What things should you know in order to get there? What experiences will benefit you the most? You may have to do some research to find these answers. Consider what things you enjoy. Don't just think in terms of jobs or tasks, but in terms of results. For example, if seeing others happy brings you joy, you may want to consider that. If creating inspiration in others is what you like, explore that. Maybe you like to avoid decision-making, and simply like to do what you are told. That is something to explore also.

Notes

1 Wooster, Roger, *Theatre in Education in Britain: Origin, Development and Influence,* Bloomsbury, 2016.
2 Zazzali, Peter, *Acting in the Academy: The History of Professional Actor Training in US Higher Education,* Routledge, 2016.
3 Agofure, Joseph, "Illuminating the gap between drama and pedagogy: an overview of applied drama/theatre and it's educational benefits," *Franklin Business & Law Journal,* no. 3 (2016): 95–114.
4 Kerzner, Harold, *Project Management: A Systems Approach to Planning, Scheduling, and Controlling,* John Wiley & Sons, 2013.
5 Kamens, David H., John W. Meyer, and Aaron Benavot, "Worldwide patterns in academic secondary education curricula," *Comparative Education Review* 40, no. 2 (1996): 116–138.
6 Efland, Arthur, *A History of Art Education: Intellectual and Social Currents in Teaching the Visual Arts,* Teachers College Press, 1990.
7 Rabkin, Nick, and Eric Christopher Hedberg, "Arts education in America: What the declines mean for arts participation, based on the 2008 survey of public participation in the arts, research report# 52," *National Endowment for the Arts* (2011).
8 Rhine, Anthony S., and Patrick J Murnin, *The Effect of Arts in Childhood with Participation as an Adult in the Twenty-first Century,* 2017. Manuscript submitted for publication.
9 Stinson, Madonna, and Bruce Burton, "Keeping the stage alive: The impact of teachers on young people's engagement with theatre," *Youth Theatre Journal* 30, no. 1 (2016): 68–78.

10 Ibid.

11 Duffy, Peter, "Theatre curriculum in the US: A great tasting sandwich on stale bread," *Research in Drama Education: The Journal of Applied Theatre and Performance* 21, no. 1 (2016): 37–41.

12 Fleming, Josephine, Robyn Gibson, Michael Anderson, Andrew J. Martin, and David Sudmalis, "Cultivating imaginative thinking: Teacher strategies used in high-performing arts education classroom," *Cambridge Journal of Education* 46, no. 4 (2016): 435–453.

13 Miller, Ray, "The courage to teach and the courage to lead: Considerations for theatre and dance in higher education," *Theatre Topics* 26, no. 1 (2016): E-1.

14 Ejiofor, Benjamin Asodionye, and Faith Ibarakumo Ken-Aminikpo, "Theatre in education: A technique for effective social studies teaching in junior secondary schools classes," *Journal of Education and Human Development* 5, no. 2 (2016): 155–168.

15 Bell, Charlotte, "Seeing like a classroom: Theatre and performance in education," *Studies in Theatre and Performance* 36, no. 2 (2016): 145–158.

16 McWilliam, Erica, "Unlearning how to teach," *Innovations in Education and Teaching International* 45, no. 3 (2008): 263–269.

17 Ibid.

18 Perry, Mia, "Theatre as a place of learning: The forces and effects of devised theatre processes in education," PhD dissertation, University of British Columbia, 2010.

Suggested additional reading

Chapter 1

Celentano, S. C., & Marshall, K. (1998). *Theatre Management: A Successful Guide to Producing Plays on Commercial and Non-Profit Stages*. Scarecrow Press.

Conte, D. M., & Langley, S. (2007). *Theatre Management: Producing and Managing the Performing Arts*. EntertainmentPro.

Volz, J. (2004). *How to Run a Theatre: A Witty, Practical, and Fun Guide to Arts Management*. Back Stage Books.

Chapter 2

Allison, M., & Kaye, J. (2011). *Strategic Planning for Nonprofit Organizations: A Practical Guide and Workbook*. John Wiley & Sons.

Barry, B. W. (1997). *Strategic Planning Workbook for Nonprofit Organizations*. Amherst H. Wilder Foundation.

Bryson, J. M. (2011). *Strategic Planning for Public and Nonprofit Organizations: A Guide to Strengthening and Sustaining Organizational Achievement* (Vol. 1). John Wiley & Sons.

Lord, G. D., & Markert, K. (2017). *The Manual of Strategic Planning for Cultural Organizations: A Guide for Museums, Performing Arts, Science Centers, Public Gardens, Heritage Sites, Libraries, Archives and Zoos*. Rowman & Littlefield.

Varbanova, L. (2013). *Strategic Management in the Arts*. Routledge.

Chapter 3

Herring, H., & Elton, T. M. (2016). *Leading Congregations and Nonprofits in a Connected World: Platforms, People, and Purpose*. Rowman & Littlefield.

Liteman, M. (2003). *Planning for Succession: A Toolkit for Board Members and Staff of Nonprofit Arts Organizations*. Illinois Arts Alliance.

O'Leary, R., & Bingham, L. B. (Eds.). (2009). *The Collaborative Public Manager: New Ideas for the Twenty-First Century*. Georgetown University Press.

Wolf, T. (2012). *Managing a Nonprofit Organization: Updated Twenty-First-Century Edition*. Simon and Schuster.

Chapter 4

Byrnes, W. J. (2009). *Management and the Arts*. Taylor & Francis.

Donahue, T., & Patterson, J. (2012). *Stage Money: The Business of the Professional Theater*. University of South Carolina Press.

Farber, D. C. (2005). *Producing Theatre: A Comprehensive Legal and Business Guide*. Hal Leonard Corporation.

Grobman, G. M. (2005). *The Nonprofit Handbook Everything You Need to Know to Start and Run Your Nonprofit Organization* (6th Edition). White Hat Communications.

Chapter 5

Daft, R. (2006). *Organization Theory and Design*. Cengage Learning.

Kesler, G., & Kates, A. (2010). *Leading Organization Design: How to Make Organization Design Decisions to Drive the Results You Want*. John Wiley & Sons.

Lawler, E. E., Worley, C. G., & Porras, J. (2006). *Built to Change: How to Achieve Sustained Organizational Effectiveness*. Jossey-Bass.

Tschirhart, M., & Bielefeld, W. (2012). *Managing Nonprofit Organizations*. John Wiley & Sons.

Chapter 6

Fletcher, A., & Irelan, S. R. (2015). *Experiencing Theatre*. Focus.

Hartnett, J. (1996). *OSHA in the Real World: How to Maintain Workplace Safety While Keeping Your Competitive Edge*. Silver Lake Publishing.

Volz, J. (2011). *Working in American Theatre: A Brief History, Career Guide and Resource Book for Over 1000 Theatres*. Bloomsbury Publishing.

Willingham, A. L. (2015). *Twelve Things You Need to Know before You Graduate to Get a Job in Theatre*. CreateSpace Independent.

Chapter 7

Elder, E., Imhof, M., & Ryder, S. L. (1979). *Will it Make a Theatre: A Guide to Finding, Renovating, Financing, Bringing Up-to-Code, The Nontraditional Performance Space*. Art New York.

Hankin, J. A., Seidner, A. G., & Zietlow, J. (1998). *Financial Management for Nonprofit Organizations* (Vol. 109). John Wiley & Sons.

Worth, M. J. (2013). *Nonprofit Management: Principles and Practice*. Sage.

Zietlow, J., Hankin, J. A., & Seidner, A. G. (2011). *Financial Management for Nonprofit Organizations: Policies and Practices*. John Wiley & Sons.

Chapter 8

Kinni, T. (2011). *Be Our Guest: Revised and Updated Edition: Perfecting the Art of Customer Service*. Disney Electronic Content.

Nelson, R. (2010). *How to Start Your Own Theater Company.* Chicago Review Press.

Webb, D. M. (2012). *Running Theaters: Best Practices for Leaders and Managers.* Skyhorse Publishing.

Chapter 9

Andreasen, A. R., Kotler, P., & Parker, D. (2003). *Strategic Marketing for Nonprofit Organizations.* Upper Saddle River: Prentice Hall.

Bernstein, J. S. (2014). *Standing Room Only: Marketing Insights for Engaging Performing Arts Audiences.* Palgrave Macmillan.

Kotler, P., & Armstrong, G. (2010). *Principles of Marketing.* Pearson Education.

Chapter 10

Hill, E., O'Sullivan, T., & O'Sullivan, C. (2012). *Creative Arts Marketing.* Routledge.

Knapp, P. M. (2001). *Designing Corporate Identity: Graphic Design as a Business Strategy.* Rockport Publishers.

Landa, R. (2016). *Advertising by Design: Generating and Designing Creative Ideas Across Media.* John Wiley & Sons.

Newman, D. (1977). *Subscribe Now!: Building Arts Audiences through Dynamic Subscription Promotion.* Theatre Communications Group.

Chapter 11

Ciconte, B. L., & Jacob, J. (2011). *Fundraising Basics: A Complete Guide.* Jones & Bartlett Publishers.

Tempel, E. R. (Ed.). (2010). *Hank Rosso's Achieving Excellence in Fund Raising.* John Wiley & Sons.

Chapter 12

Heifetz, R. A., & Linsky, M. (2002). *Leadership on the Line: Staying Alive through the Dangers of Leading.* Harvard Business Press.

Lake, A. S. (2011). *Leading the Creative Mind.* Common Ground Publishing.

Stein, T. S. (2016). *Leadership in the Performing Arts.* Skyhorse Publishing.

Chapter 13

Chait, R. P., Ryan, W. P., & Taylor, B. E. (2011). *Governance as Leadership: Reframing the Work of Nonprofit Boards.* John Wiley & Sons.

Leblanc, R. (2016). *The Handbook of Board Governance: A Comprehensive Guide for Public, Private, and Not-for-profit Board Members.* John Wiley & Sons.

Rentschler, R. (2014). *Arts Governance: People, Passion, Performance.* Routledge.

Chapter 14

Borwick, D. (2012). *Building Communities, Not Audiences: The Future of the Arts in the United States*. ArtsEngaged.

Borwick, D. (2015). *Engage Now!: A Guide to Making the Arts Indispensable*. ArtsEngaged.

Rosewall, E. (2014). *Arts Management: Uniting Arts and Audiences in the 21st Century*. Oxford University Press.

Simon, N. (2016). *The Art of Relevance*. Museum 2.0.

Chapter 15

Jackson, A. (2007). *Theatre, Education and the Making of Meanings: Art or Instrument?* Manchester University Press.

Jackson, A., & Vine, C. (Eds.). (2013). *Learning through Theatre: The Changing Face of Theatre in Education*. Routledge.

Lazarus, J. (2012). *Signs of Change: New Directions in Theatre Education*. Intellect Books.

Rome, C., & Dillard, Z. (2015). *Real-World Theatre Education: A Teacher's Guide to Growing a Theatre Education Program*. Educational Stages.

Index

Printed by Printforce, the Netherlands